Against Purity

Against Purity confronts the difficulties that white Western feminism has in balancing issues of gender with other forms of difference, such as race, ethnicity and nation. In this pioneering study, Irene Gedalof places recent feminist theory from India in critical conversation with the work of four key Western thinkers – Rosi Braidotti, Judith Butler, Donna Haraway and Luce Irigaray.

This unique volume provides an original and much-needed reading of the work of a range of influential Indian feminists, and shows how their approach can be used to complicate and illuminate white Western feminism. It shows how Indian feminists emphasise many factors in shaping women's identities – sex, gender, race, nation, caste, class and religion. Irene Gedalof argues that feminists today should work 'against purity' to develop more complex models of power, identity and the self, ultimately to redefine 'women' as the subject of feminism.

Against Purity is essential reading for students and researchers in women's studies, postcolonial and cultural studies, sociology and race and ethnicity.

Irene Gedalof is Lecturer in Women's Studies at the University of North London, and an Associate Fellow at the Centre for the Study of Women and Gender, University of Warwick.

Gender, Racism, Ethnicity
Series editors:
Kum-Kum Bhavnani, *University of California at Santa Barbara*
Avtar Brah, *University of London*
Gail Lewis, *The Open University*
Ann Phoenix, *University of London*

Gender, Racism, Ethnicity is a series whose main concern is to promote rigorous feminist analysis of the intersections between gender, racism, ethnicity, class and sexuality within the contexts of imperialism, colonialism and neo-colonialism. Intended to contribute new perspectives to current debates and to introduce fresh analysis, it will provide valuable teaching texts for undergraduates, lecturers and researchers in anthropology, women's studies, cultural studies and sociology.

Other titles in the series:

White Women, Race Matters
Ruth Frankenberg

Fear of the Dark
Lola Young

Gendering Orientalism
Reina Lewis

Cartographies of Diaspora
Avtar Brah

'Other Kinds of Dreams'
Julia Sudbury

Against Purity

Rethinking identity with Indian and Western feminisms

Irene Gedalof

London and New York

First published 1999
by Routledge
11 New Fetter Lane, London EC4P 4EE

Simultaneously published in the USA and Canada
by Routledge
29 West 35th Street, New York, NY 10001

Routledge is an imprint of the Taylor & Francis Group

Typeset in Times by Routledge
Printed and bound in Great Britain by MPG Books Ltd, Bodmin

British Library Cataloguing in Publication Data
A catalogue record for this book is available from the British Library

Library of Congress Cataloging in Publication Data
Gedalof, Irene.
Against purity: rethinking identity with Indian and Western feminisms /
Irene Gedalof.
Include bibliographical references and index.
1. Feminism Cross-cultural studies. 2. Feminism–India. 3. Feminist theory
Cross-cultural studies. 4. Feminist theory–India. 5. Women–Identity
Cross-cultural studies. I. Title.
HQ1154.G355   1998   99-30084
305.42'0954–dc21   CIP

ISBN 0–415–21586–2 (hbk)
ISBN 0–415–21587–0 (pbk)

Contents

Acknowledgements

Anyone who has experienced the uncharacteristic attractions of house-cleaning or the strange siren call of computer solitaire, when the task at hand was to sit down and write, will understand me when I say that, if left to my own devices, this book would never have been completed. Many people and institutions provided the needed support, assistance and encouragement, as well as the all-important guilt- and discipline-inducing deadlines, which have helped to bring it kicking and screaming into the world. In India, Tanika Sarkar of Delhi University, Urvashi Butalia and Ritu Menon of Kali for Women Press, Kumkum Sangari of the Nehru Memorial Library and, especially, Uma Chakravarti of Delhi University gave most generously of their time in allowing me to conduct extensive interviews with them. Dr Chakravarti's help in organising my programme both before and during my stay in Delhi is also gratefully acknowledged. Discussions with Malavika Karlekar of the Centre for Women's Development Studies, Bina Agarwal and Patricia Uberoi of the Institute of Economic Growth, Prem Chowdhri of Delhi University and Rajni Palriwala of the Delhi School of Economics were also most helpful. Dr Uberoi's logistical support was of great assistance. I am also grateful to the staff at Saheli and CWDS for help in locating important documentation.

The Humanities Research Board of the British Academy provided a studentship which allowed me to pursue the doctoral research on which this book is based, and also granted additional funding to support my travel to India. Supplementary funding from the University of Warwick's Lord Rootes Memorial Fund, for a related research project, also helped make this travel possible.

Members of the Warwick University Feminist Philosophy Group, the Centre for the Study of Women and Gender Research Student Forum and the 'Feminist Theory in a Postcolonial Mode' Reading Group provided important feedback on earlier versions of individual chapters. I particularly want to thank Tonya Blowers and Bibi Bakare-Yusuf for many hours of supportive and stimulating discussion. James Putzel provided helpful comments on more than one version of the manuscript, and invaluable support and perspective on the entire research and writing process. Despite our distance on opposite sides of the Atlantic for many years, Colette St-Hilaire has been enormously helpful. By sharing a trajectory into and through feminist theory, she has been reassuring when we were asking the same questions, and has encouraged me to think a bit harder when we weren't.

Terry Lovell and Avtar Brah were both of great help in turning a doctoral thesis into a book. I hope that I have been able to do some justice to their incisive comments on the weaknesses of its earlier manifestation. Together with her co-editors of this series, Kum-Kum Bhavnani, Ann Phoenix and Gail Lewis, as well as Vicky Peters at Routledge, Avtar has played a particularly crucial role in seeing this project through to completion, and I am especially grateful to her.

I also want to give particular thanks to Shirin Rai, who provided invaluable support in my efforts to understand the complexities of Indian feminisms. Finally, I want to express my deepest thanks to Christine Battersby who, from the moment I began my first Women's Studies course in 1991, has been both demanding and encouraging of my efforts to find my own impure space in the complex landscape of feminist theory. Her intellectual rigour, careful reading, and insightful questions, criticisms and comments were invaluable to the development of this project. Any errors and weaknesses remain, of course, mine alone.

Introduction

It has seemed very rare for feminist theory to hold race,
sex/gender, and class analytically together – all the best inten-
tions, hues of authors, and remarks in prefaces notwithstanding
[...] The evidence is building for a need for a theory of 'difference'
whose geometries, paradigms, and logics break out of binaries,
dialectics, and nature/culture models of any kind. Otherwise
threes will always reduce to twos, which quickly become lonely
ones in the vanguard. And no one learns to count to four. These
things matter politically.
> (' "Gender" for a Marxist Dictionary', in Haraway 1991: 129)

I now want to suggest that feminist theory came into its own, or
became possible as such [...] in a postcolonial mode.
> (de Lauretis, 'Eccentric Subjects', 1990: 131)

Have white Western feminists become any better at maths since
Donna Haraway set us the sum quoted above almost a decade ago?
Thinking about the differences between women while developing
alternative theoretical models of the self, self–other relations,
identity and agency, has proved one of feminism's greatest
challenges. How do we maintain the focus on 'women' that is
feminism's theoretical and political project, while keeping open the
borders we necessarily draw around that category? In particular,
can feminists keep open a space in which to consider the intersections of sex, gender, race, nation and the 'embarrassed *et cetera*' in
constituting identities (Butler 1990: 143), while holding on to a
category 'women' that is sufficiently coherent to form the basis of
effective theory and politics?

Recognising that these intersections exist and need to be taken into account is not a particularly new insight for white Western feminist theory. It is almost twenty years since the growing critiques of theory offered by black and non-Western feminists meant that 'white women [...] discovered (that is were forced kicking and screaming to notice) the non-innocence of the category "woman"' (Haraway 1991: 157). When de Lauretis evokes feminist theory 'in a postcolonial mode' in the passage quoted above, she is arguing for feminist theory that acknowledges that non-innocence of the categories 'woman' and 'women' in two ways. First, in recognising that there is no pure site of identity organised around a single axis of gender or sexual difference, feminist theory needs to problematise the apparent coherence of the category of 'women' by considering the multiplicity of positionings with which women contend. Second, in recognising that there are no pure power-free sites from which to speak and act, feminists need to be attentive to the workings of power differentials between particular groups of women, within their own theorisation and politics (de Lauretis 1990: 131).

In the chapters that follow I will be arguing that, despite twenty years of acknowledging the problem, white Western feminist theory still has difficulty 'counting to four' when it considers women and their relation to social processes of identity-constitution. I focus on identity as what Stuart Hall has called 'the meeting point, the point of *suture*' between the multiplicity of social institutions, discourses and practices which contend to position us as social subjects of a particular kind, and the individual self who emerges from and circulates through that social world (Hall 1996: 5–6). Thus the identity questions that I explore throughout this book centre on that conceptual space where the social and the self meet. How do we conceptualise women's positioning within particular discourses of gender, race, national and class identities? What is the relationship between women's sense of identity 'as women' and other identity categories such as race, nation, ethnicity, class and sexuality? How does women's discursive and strategic positioning within these multiple categories of social identity impinge on their sense of themselves as individual selves and as social agents and actors? What does this tell us about the adequacy of prevailing conceptual models of the self, collective identities and agency and about the possibility of feminist alternative models?

My starting assumption is that the ways in which white Western feminists address these questions can be productively challenged and changed by exploring more fully the possibilities of 'feminist theory in a postcolonial mode'. One way of doing this, which has been neglected by Western feminist theory, is to engage more extensively with the insights of feminist scholars working in non-Western contexts. In this book, I test that assumption by considering the ways in which insights from the work of selected Indian feminist scholars can productively complicate the theoretical models of identity underpinning the work of four important white Western feminist thinkers: Rosi Braidotti, Judith Butler, Donna Haraway and Luce Irigaray.

In choosing to foreground the work of non-Western feminists, I am in no way suggesting that white Western feminism has nothing left to learn from the work of the many non-white feminists in the West. But I am suggesting that another set of feminist voices can bring something additional, and distinctive, to these ongoing critical conversations. I am also suggesting that the particular pertinence of those postcolonial feminist voices to white Western feminist theory is an area which has been left largely unexplored.

Theory in a postcolonial mode

It is still rare for white Western feminists to 'do theory' through an extended and detailed engagement with feminist scholarship emerging from non-Western contexts, or even from diasporic communities in the West. Even when it is recognised that this work is engaged in developing feminist theory, and not just in providing the empirical 'raw material' for white Western feminists to theorise, references to it tend to be brief, general and consigned to footnotes. While there is much Western feminist scholarship that takes the situation of women in non-Western contexts as its object of inquiry, there is still little that attends to the work of non-Western feminists in order to see how it changes, complicates or challenges the theoretical assumptions and models we work with. This project aims to sustain just such an extended and detailed engagement around the theoretical questions of identity, agency and models of the self.

Which 'postcolonial'?

By characterising this project as an effort to develop feminist theory 'in a postcolonial mode', I open it to the highly charged field of contestations over what constitutes 'the postcolonial'. Strong claims have been made for the transformative possibilities of the postcolonial: as the site for a privileged subject-position that celebrates marginality and hybridity, and as a new model for 'doing theory'(see e.g. Ashcroft *et al.* 1989; Adam and Tiffin 1991). These have led to equally strong contestations over how to define 'the postcolonial', who gets to belong to it, what is gained and what is lost by using the term. Is the postcolonial an historical period or a particular theoretical model? Are Australia, Canada and even the United States 'postcolonial' in the same way that South Asia and Africa are? Does the 'post' suggest that the effects of colonialism are at an end, or does it mean that they need to be acknowledged, while moving beyond their constraints? Does evoking 'the postcolonial' lead to an undifferentiated celebration of hybridity and diaspora as features of *the* (singular) postcolonial position? Does postcolonial theory put too much emphasis on discursive processes alone, arguing that a single, overriding 'logic of language' structures social processes, whose complexity is then reduced to a simple mirroring of language as a system? These are just some of the issues that different appropriations of the term have elicited.[1]

My own usage of the term here is both narrower and more open-ended than most of the participants in these debates would accept. First, in referring to 'postcolonial feminists', I use 'postcolonial' as a short-hand (if still contestable) way of referring to feminists in and from non-Western countries that have been on the receiving end of colonialism. While not without its problems, I find the term less problematic than the other available options: 'Third World' begs the question of which are the other two worlds; 'South' or 'East', or even 'non-Western' tend to reinforce the centring of the West as norm and privileged vantage point; 'developing countries' raises yet another highly charged field of contestation and debate over models and standards of development, which is outside the framework of this project.

Second, I find 'postcoloniality' a useful term for designating a specific, historically located time in which we live: after the period of formal colonisation, but still confronted with the effects of colonisation and decolonisation, and with new forms of globalisation, which are still informed by asymmetric power relations. We all have to deal with this generalised state, if from very different locations. For white Western feminists, remembering that we live in a postcolonial world, in this sense, is important if we are to keep to the fore the differences between women that emerge from power relations structured by race, nationality and ethnicity, as well as by economic difference.

Therefore, third, 'a postcolonial mode' is also a conceptual space in which constructs of East and West, margins and centre, as purely discrete and opposed locations, are problematised. For white Western feminism, this suggests an important shift in perspective in terms of what constitutes the 'proper' boundaries for our theorising. To what extent do we still see the 'West' as a hermetically sealed, discrete field on/in which to theorise, as if what happens 'out there' does not impinge on what we theorise 'in here'? If white Western feminism has learned to be cautious about making totalising statements about all women, based on its own limited experiences, it still, for the most part, has not taken on board a second insight of 'a postcolonial mode': that the connections still need to be made, if on a different basis.

Developing that different basis might begin by recognising that we all live in what Avtar Brah has called 'diaspora space', in which the genealogies of dispersal and those of staying put are inextricably entangled. Brah argues that in this impure space, the subject-position of 'the native' is seriously problematised (Brah 1996: 181). White Western feminists need to think about how *their* status as natives, who stay put within the geographical and conceptual space of 'the West', is problematised, and what this can mean for the questions they ask of theory. I will return to this point later on.

Why theory?

A common, and necessary, reaction to recognising the 'non-innocence of the category woman' among white Western feminists has been to be careful not to impose Western theory on non-Western contexts. But this can lead to a position of effectively leaving theory out of the field of cross-cultural dialogue and contestation. For example, in her 1995 book *Feminisms and the Self*, Morwenna Griffiths explains how she chose the cross-cultural material to engage with for her project. In particular, she explains why she decided not to focus primarily on theoretical material from black and postcolonial feminisms. Theory's usefulness is limited,

Griffiths argues, for a number of reasons: because it is the activity of an elite and so doesn't reflect the concerns of the majority of women; because it can be difficult to do it justice when one doesn't know much about the different philosophical traditions from which it emerges; and because, as abstraction, it is even more difficult to situate in its specific context than are descriptions of experience (Griffiths 1995: 34–42).

My point is not to challenge Griffiths' caveats about the difficulties of engaging with theory, nor to challenge her decision to interweave her engagement with a variety of theoretical materials with narratives of personal experience. But I do want to note that her discussion of theory's limitations assumes that there is only one question to be asked of it when we are listening for different voices: does it 'capture' the elsewhere for us in all its complexity, will it allow 'us' to represent 'them' to ourselves in all their complexity? But there are also other questions white Western feminists can ask. If 'postcoloniality' means that there are important connections between 'here' and 'there', then we can also ask how listening to voices from elsewhere might complicate our view of ourselves.

If all we ask of theory is how it can represent the experiences of 'the other woman' in all her complexity, then we always come up against the problem of the multiple mediations through which experience is filtered. So, for example, in evaluating different materials for her project, Griffiths asks, 'where are the voices unmediated by an education in the West?' (1995: 34). If what we are looking for is an 'authentic voice' from elsewhere, then mediation is a problem. But if we want to resist recourse to a logic of authenticity which concepts like postcoloniality, or 'diaspora space' have problematised, and if we want to ask what the 'elsewhere' can tell us about 'in here', then it is precisely the mediated voices that we should be listening to: the voices which share this impure space of feminist theory with us. Feminist theoretical approaches which may have originated in the white West come back to us permanently changed and complicated when they have been put to use outside a white Western framework. These changes and complications can help make more visible the questions that have not been asked, and that still need to be asked by white Western feminists. The answers we arrive at may be very different from those developed by postcolonial feminists, but the first step is to recognise the importance of this impure, mediated space of 'theory in a postcolonial mode'.

Why postcolonial feminisms?

What are the distinctive questions that an engagement with postcolonial feminisms can help us to reframe differently in a white Western context? What can this engagement add to the challenges already being introduced by the work of black and diasporic feminists, and other feminists of colour who are already part of the Western context in which white feminists work? In order to begin to answer these questions, I need first to take a step back to reflect on the ways in which the different non-white Western feminisms have both broken the ground and laid the foundations for the kind of project I am attempting here.

It is clear that, in Donna Haraway's only partially ironic words, white Western feminists had to be 'forced kicking and screaming to notice' the non-innocence of the category 'women', and that it was the critiques and analyses of different non-white feminists in the West which forced this 'discovery' upon us. It is doubtful whether white Western feminist theory today would be engaging at all with the problem of 'intersectionality', of how to theorise 'women' while attending to differences of race and ethnicity, without the challenges to its starting assumptions introduced by the work of black and diasporic feminisms and other feminisms of colour over the last twenty years. Black feminist scholarship in both the US and the UK has made clear that the forms of oppression experienced by women are informed by race and ethnicity as well as by gender. What white feminists had thought of as the constitutive parts of patriarchy or gender relations alone, are instead intimately interlocked with issues of race and ethnicity. Institutions like the family, practices such as sexual violence and the control of reproductive rights, and discourses such as models of femininity all needed to be reconceptualised with a focus on the intersectionality of relations of gender, race and ethnicity.[2] Indeed, even access to the category 'women' can be determined by race and ethnic positioning; some females never become 'women', but rather remain property, or female bodies outside the category, as black feminist scholarship on slavery and colonialism has demonstrated (see Carby 1987; Spillers 1987; Williams 1991).

The widespread concern within contemporary feminist theory with the relationship between identity and location, and with women's multiple positioning between and across a variety of subject-positions, is a second development to which the contributions of different non-white feminisms in the West have been crucial. Concepts such as Gloria Anzaldua's 'borderlands' (1987), Trinh T. Minh-ha's 'inappropriate/d others' (1989) and Avtar Brah's 'diaspora space'(1996) challenge all feminist theorists to work with theoretical models that recognise that multiple positionings of identity are the norm, rather than the exception, for women.

A third crucial insight has been that power relations are always at work within the category 'women', and not just between women and men. From the early critiques of black feminists such as bell hooks (1982) and Hazel Carby (1982) of the 'boundaries of sisterhood' imposed by white feminism, through to Chandra Mohanty's (1991) now-classic exposition of the continuing influence of colonial discourse in white feminism's construction of the 'Third World Woman' as 'other', white feminism has been obliged to recognise the role of race and ethnicity in structuring those power relations. More recently, given the increasing popularity of postmodern celebrations of 'difference' within feminism, I would argue that the focus on power relations within non-white feminisms takes on an added pertinence. Where at least some white feminist appropriations of postmodern or poststructuralist models can result in a de-politicised focus on difference as an 'effect of language', black and diasporic feminist scholarship that explores the continuing effects of racism, slavery and colonialism insists on linking questions of 'difference' with questions of power relations (see e.g. hooks 1982, 1991; Spivak 1987, 1991, 1993; Brah 1996). This insistence on the political stakes involved in 'difference' has had a major effect on the ways in which postmodern and poststructuralist approaches have been developed within feminist theory as a whole, and continues to provide a positive pressure to keep questions of power relations at the heart of feminist theory.

Finally, I would also argue that, because of this continued insistence on questions of power and the political difference that 'difference' can make, non-white feminisms in the West have brought to feminist theory a dual concern to both problematise and positively redefine identity and identity politics. Appropriations of postmodern and poststructuralist theory have led much of current white feminist theory to focus on deconstructing and destabilising categories of identity such as sex/gender and 'women'. While these destabilising moves are also present within non-white Western feminisms, I would argue that they are more often accompanied by a concern to redefine identity on a different basis. Avtar Brah's 'diaspora space' (1996), Gloria Anzaldua's 'borderlands' (1987), or bell hooks' rethinking of 'homeplace' (1991) are just three examples of a trend in black, diasporic and other non-white Western feminisms to simultaneously problematise and reconstruct a space of identity from which a different kind of subject might speak and act. That this approach should take root more easily within non-white than white Western feminisms is not surprising. As Avtar Brah has argued, the diasporic or minoritised/racialised person in the West is still obliged to 'name an identity', to explain where they fit in a hierarchical grid of categories in which they are never the norm, and in which they are never allowed to 'just "be"', living the complexities of their multiple positionings (Brah 1996: 3). As long as racism and ethnocentrism continue to exist, the struggle to resist and problematise those limiting and racist definitions of identity cannot simply sidestep the issue of 're-naming' those identities. White Western feminists, at least in terms of their racial and ethnic positioning, already fit the norm and are not being called upon regularly to account for their racial/ethnic identity. We have the privilege to 'just be' in our unmarked whiteness and Western-ness, and it is perhaps this position of privilege that makes it easier for white feminists to embrace strategies which focus only on destabilising identities. What needs to be considered, however, is whether those unmarked categories of identity can be overturned through destabilisation strategies alone, or whether an analogous process of redefinition also needs to be undertaken.

But what this last point highlights is that white Western women have to take account of their particular positioning in relation to questions of identity. This means that we also need to ask other questions of our relationship to 'intersectionality', which we should not expect those women positioned as 'outsiders' or 'minorities' by racism and ethnocentrism in the West to focus on, or to provide answers for. We need to ask how 'women' continue to be imbricated in processes of constituting racial, ethnic, national and other community identities when they are positioned as 'insiders', 'citizens', as part of the majority or the norm. We need to ask, not only about women's relationship to the dynamics of racist or ethnocentric exclusion, but also about the dynamics of some women's problematic inclusion in the processes through which privileged racial, religious, ethnic, class and national identities emerge. It is on questions such as these that I think the experiences and reflections of postcolonial feminists become particularly pertinent. Postcolonial feminists have had to address a wide range of historical and contemporary issues that focus on women as 'insiders' in this sense: the problematic inclusion of 'the women's question' as part of the anti-colonial nationalist movements of the late nineteenth and early twentieth centuries; women's involvement in the processes of postcolonial nation-building; the postcolonial woman-citizen's problematic relationship to the state; the relationship between women of majority and minority communities in multi-ethnic and multi-racial postcolonial societies. What distinguishes the postcolonial woman as 'insider' from her white Western counterpart is that, given the historical context of colonialism and the contemporary context of global inequalities between 'West' and 'non-West', she cannot so easily forget about her own racial and ethnic positioning. White Western feminisms might, therefore, have much to learn from the ways in which postcolonial feminisms make visible the positioning of 'majority women' in processes of constituting community identities.

I argued earlier that white Western feminists need to think about how their status as 'natives' is problematised in a postcolonial mode. One way of doing this is, as Avtar Brah's concept of diaspora space suggests, to recognise the ways in which genealogies of dispersal and 'staying put' are entangled (Brah 1996: 181); in the context of Western feminist theory, we need to continue to consider the ways in which black and diasporic feminisms, and other feminisms of colour which carry with them 'genealogies of dispersal', are entangled with the white feminist genealogies of 'staying put'. I want to suggest here that the postcolonial feminist, who has also 'stayed put', can contribute something distinctive to this entanglement by drawing our attention to the complex nature of the 'homes' we stay put in. By attending to the ways in which postcolonial feminisms consider locatedness in its historical, political and cultural particularities, white feminisms might find new strategies for theorising 'home' as something that we need to account for as well.

Again, I want to emphasise that I do not expect that the theoretical strategies adopted by postcolonial feminists can simply be applied mechanically to a white Western context. It is not so much ready-made answers that a 'postcolonial mode' of theorising might lead to, but rather an additional set of questions that white feminist theorists might begin to ask, in order to keep visible their own positioning within racial, ethnic, national and other community identities, while sustaining a simultaneous focus on 'women' as a category. In the following chapters, I hope to show that what we can learn from postcolonial feminisms is that these kinds of positionings need to be accounted for, not only when women are excluded or marginalised by their race or ethnicity, but also when they are included, or made central to the 'majority' identity. How we then go about accounting for that positioning, in all its complexity, remains a major and ongoing challenge for white Western feminist theories of identity.

Complexity, impurity and a geometrics of dualisms

Two broad strategies and objectives coexist within contemporary feminist theoretical approaches to identity. The first is to redefine and revalue what is specific to women, what might be called the specifically female, in order to contest the ways in which models of the subject, of agency, of universal norms and 'truths' are, in Irigaray's phrase, 'always appropriated by the masculine'. The second is to rethink, complicate or destabilise the identity category 'gender' in a number of ways. As we have seen, one way of complicating it has been to rethink its interrelationship with other identity categories, such as race, nation, ethnicity and class. Another has been to rethink the apparent usefulness and coherence of the sex/gender, nature/culture, biology/society binaries that much of Anglo-American feminism worked with in the early Second Wave period.

These two strategies are by no means applied in any homogeneous way within contemporary feminist theory, nor are they mutually exclusive. Indeed, as I will argue throughout this book, some aspects of both are necessary if feminist theory is to sustain a simultaneous focus on women and their differences. The four white Western feminists I have chosen to focus on in this project each take up distinctive positions on this strategic spectrum. If Irigaray might be characterised as the strongest advocate of the 'redefinition' strategy among the four, Butler might stand as the staunchest representative of the 'destabilisation' position. Braidotti wants to complicate an Irigarayan feminism of sexual difference by combining it with more attention to multiplicity. Haraway wants to add to the destabilising move a positive redefinition of identity through an 'ontology of impurity'.

In the chapters that follow, I will be looking at how these different strategic positionings make space for the complexity that is required if the double focus on women and their differences is to be sustained. I will be looking for those moves that open up a space in which to consider women's positioning in a complex landscape of gender, race, nation and other community identities. I will also be looking for those spaces where, to borrow Haraway's terms, a geometrics or logic of dualisms reasserts itself in order to reduce that complexity to sameness.

Why 'against purity'?

As my title suggests, I will be arguing that sustaining a space for complexity requires working against conceptual models of purity on a number of levels. In her landmark study *Purity and Danger*, Mary Douglas argued:

> that ideas about separating, purifying, demarcating and punishing transgressions have as their main function to impose system on an inherently untidy experience. It is only by exaggerating the difference between within and without, above and below, male and female, with and against, that a semblance of order is created.
>
> (Douglas 1966: 4)

For Douglas, establishing order in an inherently untidy reality through concepts of purity is a universal and necessary activity of human society. She recognises that dualistic paradigms of purity and belonging are exaggerations imposed to create a semblance of order where complexity continues to exist. But for her, one of the inevitable consequences of 'civilisation' is to establish that semblance of order through ideas of purity.

But as our mathematical and scientific paradigms move from concepts of linear order to the non-linear dynamics of complex systems, in which the relationship between 'order' and 'chaos' or complexity is revisioned, does Douglas' conclusion about the inevitability of purity models still stand? For example, Katherine Hayles has argued that there are two strands within chaos theory. One works with a model of emerging from chaos into order, which sustains the kind of purity model Douglas examines. The second, however, conceptualises 'the orderly descent into chaos' (Hayles

1990: 9). This second approach suggests a model in which the aim is not to re-impose a semblance of order on an inherently complex system, but rather to find ways to live within complexity. If alternative paradigms of impurity are possible, as Hayles' work suggests, then we need to ask what we lose by continuing to establish order through the logic of dualisms that underpins purity models.

Politically, we have seen the tragic consequences of what Paul Gilroy calls 'ethnic absolutism', with its views of immutable differences between pure categories of racial and cultural difference (Gilroy 1993: 2). Theorists of difference such as Gilroy, and Avtar Brah, argue for the more difficult, but possible alternative of a paradigm of identity that begins from the assumption of impurity. For Brah, it is more useful to defy 'the search for originary absolutes, or genuine and authentic manifestations of a stable, pre-given, unchanging identity; for pristine, pure customs and traditions or unsullied glorious pasts' (Brah 1996: 196).

In the chapters that follow I will be looking at how purity models of identity impinge on women's discursive and strategic positioning within unequal relations of power. I will also be looking at how the constraints of purity paradigms can be re-imported into feminist projects to rethink identity through the models of power and language underpinning them. Finally, I will be looking for those alternative models of the self, agency and resistance that emerge when feminist theorists work with the creative possibilities of impurity.

Some impure categories

As part of my own 'orderly descent into chaos', I want to clarify how I will be using some of the highly contestable, but nevertheless crucial, terms that I will be using throughout this book.

Female and feminine; sex and gender

In using these terms I want to hold on to both the distinctions between them, and the problematising of that distinction that has emerged in recent feminist theory.[3] I want to be able to refer to the specifically female, as that which refers to social positioning based on the 'sexing' of bodies. I want to be able to distinguish this from the feminine, as those 'gendered', culturally and historically variable qualities and activities that are usually, but not necessarily, assigned to those persons identified as female. At the same time, I want to resist basing that distinction on any stable nature/culture paradigm. Biology, bodies, sex, and therefore the female, are not pre-discursive and unchanging givens, but are rather historically and culturally mediated productions.

The distinction is of specific importance to this project, because I will be tracking the ways in which both the female and the feminine, the sexed body and the gendered qualities, emerge and are put into play across multiple categories of identity-constitution, ways which do not always converge. I will also be looking for the space that different feminist theoretical models allow for considering the problems and possibilities of specific female embodiment.

Race, nation and ethnicity

I take these three notoriously slippery terms as culturally inscribed markers of difference and belonging that posit boundaries of community based on notions of shared origin. They are all, to borrow and broaden Benedict Anderson's now-famous formulation 'imagined communities', in that the stability of their composition is always contestable, especially in those cases when their composition is framed in terms of immutable, biological givens. However, their effects are no less 'real' in terms of social divisions and individual identities.

Floya Anthias and Nira Yuval-Davis suggest that 'ethnicity' is the broadest of the three terms, referring to a wide variety of constructs of collectivity and belonging postulated through notions of common origin or destiny (Anthias and Yuval-Davis 1992: 2–5). Constructs of 'race' tend to harden their definitions of the boundaries of belonging through 'an immutable biological or physiological difference [...] grounded on the separation of human populations by some notion of stock or collective heredity of traits' (1992: 2). Constructs of 'nation' add claims for separate political and territorial representation to the notions of common origin and shared culture (Anthias and Yuval-Davis 1989: 2). This agrees with Anderson's definition of the nation as 'an imagined political community' which is 'both inherently limited and sovereign' (Anderson 1991: 6).

What holds these three terms together for the particular purposes of this project is that they all work with notions of common origin as the basis for community identities. This focus on questions of origins suggests that women, and the female capacity of birth, will be of particular significance to these social processes of identity constitution. My focus in this project, therefore, will be less on delineating clear dividing lines between claims of national, racial or ethnic identities, but on exploring how women are positioned within the competing and shifting claims about origins and belonging.

It is also because of this particular focus on the relationship between community identities, origins and women that my 'embarrassed *et cetera*' only occasionally includes class. I would agree with some aspects of recent feminist criticisms that the turn to questions of identity in feminist theory has led to losing sight of questions of class and economic inequalities (e.g. Fraser 1995; Coole 1996). But I also suspect that questions of class-belonging and class-positioning, while certainly engaging women in very important ways, might not relate to the question of origins in the same way as do narratives of racial and ethnic identities. As such, questions of class may need more specific attention than this project allows.

A note about 'scare quotes'

In the UK, it is common to put inverted commas around the term 'race', in order to signal the writer's contestation of notions of racial difference as an immutable, biological given. In the US and continental Europe, where the four white theorists I discuss live and write, this convention is much less common. Throughout this book I use race, without inverted commas; however, as the above discussion should make clear, I understand it to be as slippery, culturally mediated and contestable a term as sex, gender, ethnicity or nation.

Perhaps contradictorily, I retain the use of scare quotes for 'women' and 'Woman', when I am referring to the particular discursive versions of the feminine at play in identity narratives ('Woman'), or to 'women' as a category of analysis or as the objects or targets of particular forms of mobilisation, behaviour or activity in identity-constituting processes. I do this because a crucial part of my argument will be that there can be more than one version of the feminine at play in identity-constituting processes, that is, there is no singular 'Woman'; and that these processes engage particular groups of female embodied persons, 'women', in specific ways. More generally, I want to retain, throughout this project, an awareness of the non-innocence of these particular conceptual categories for white Western feminists attempting to make connections with feminist scholarship that emerges from non-Western contexts.

Foucault, productive power and impure subjects

While this book is primarily concerned with conversations among feminists in order to privilege complexity, I need to further complicate my project by introducing an additional voice. Throughout these pages I will be drawing on my reading of the work of Michel Foucault, and in particular on his understanding of power and its relation to subjects and knowledge. My purpose here is not to engage with the large body of feminist scholarship debating the usefulness and problems of appropriating Foucault's project for feminism.[4] Nor is it to follow up on the intriguing possibilities of recent feminist scholarship which employs previously overlooked aspects of Foucault's work linking sexuality and race in order to re-read colonial histories (see Stoler 1996). I will be developing my discussion of Foucault's usefulness for feminist theory throughout the book, and in particular, will be expanding on my version of a Foucauldian feminist model of power in Chapter 7. Here, I want to briefly introduce some of the Foucauldian concepts that I draw on in critically evaluating the feminist theoretical material that is discussed in the following chapters.

The key Foucauldian insight for my argument is his characterisation of power as productive of bodies, knowledges and subjects. It seems to me that neither feminist critiques, nor most feminist appropriations of Foucault, have fully thought through the implications of the conceptual shift that this model of productive power inaugurates. As we shall see, Foucault's move calls for a shift from a logic of repression, exclusion and abjection, to one of proliferation and productivity, in ways that have implications not only for how we conceptualise women's positioning within relations of power, but also for how we conceptualise language, subjects, agency and resistance.

Foucault argued that:

We must cease once and for all to describe the effects of power in negative terms: it 'excludes', it 'represses', it 'censors', it 'abstracts', it 'masks', it 'conceals'. In fact power produces; it produces reality; it produces domains of objects and rituals of truth. The individual and the knowledge that may be gained of him belong to this production.

(Foucault 1977d: 194)

Putting aside the problematic use of the term 'him', Foucault's challenge here is of great significance to feminist theoretical attempts to make space for complexity. Conceptualising power as productive means resisting those models where:

one single and identical 'formula' of power (the interdict) comes to be applied to all forms of society and all levels of subjection [...] [where] power is conceived as a sort of great absolute Subject which pronounces the interdict.

(Foucault 1977b: 140)

Foucault's claim means that power works in complex ways that are not easily contained within binary paradigms:

Power comes from below: [...] there is no binary and all-encompassing opposition between rulers and ruled at the root of power relations and serving as a general matrix – no such duality extending from the top down and reacting on more and more limited groups to the very depths of the social body.

(Foucault 1978: 94)

There is no one general form of domination which is then reproduced 'at the level of individuals, bodies, gestures and behaviours' (Foucault 1977d: 27). Rather there is a multiplicity of networks in which relationships of force take shape and come into play (Foucault 1978: 94). Thus, whilst there may be links and continuity between different forms of power relations, and whilst different networks of power relations may indeed converge in the same bodies, each needs to be considered in its specificity. Foucault resists seeing these multiple forms of power relations as either 'analogous or homologous', as variations of the same theme, repeated in slightly different circumstances (Foucault 1977d: 27).

Thus productive power is not a homogeneous, monolithic force, but is rather local, multi-vocal and diffuse.

Of particular importance to this project is the way in which Foucault situates language and its relationship to the subject within this framework of complex, heterogeneous and multi-vocal networks of power relations. Foucault does not argue for a single symbolic system, whose overriding logic informs the way power is exercised and identities are constituted, in the manner of much current poststructuralist thought. Instead, Foucault works with a model of multiple discursive and non-discursive systems, practices and institutions:

> So it is not enough to say that the subject is constituted in a symbolic system. It is not just in the play of symbols that the subject is constituted. It is constituted in real practices – historically analyzable practices. There is a technology of the constitution of the self which cuts across symbolic systems while using them.
>
> (Foucault 1983: 369)

Power is productive in that it does not sit 'in a position of exteriority with respect to other types of relationships' but is rather immanent in them (Foucault 1978: 94). Crucially, power is productive of knowledge, or rather power and knowledge exist in a state of mutual dependence. Knowledge does not emerge from a suspension of power relations: there are no 'power-free zones', nor is power's sole effect to repress or eliminate knowledge. Rather it produces certain kinds of knowledges and invests them with the legitimacy of 'truths' (Foucault 1977d: 27).

Equally important, power is productive of bodies and subjects. Power is exercised not only *on* but also *through* bodies and subjects: what Foucault has called disciplinary power works by making bodies 'knowable' and 'useful' as power is exercised through them. 'What makes power hold good, what makes it accepted, is simply the fact that it doesn't only weigh on us as a force that says no, but that it traverses and produces things, it induces pleasure, forms knowledge, produces discourse' (1977a: 119). Power 'needs' to be able to make bodies useful in specific ways, to enable subjects of a particular kind, in order to be articulated.

Thus, for Foucault, modern forms of disciplinary, normalising power require, not abjected 'objects', but impure subjects. Within a logic of exclusion and abjection, power is exercised upon that which is refused and designated as part of the 'not-self'. But for Foucault, viewing power as productive puts into question this clear distinction between subject and object. To be a subject is always to be simultaneously 'subjected to' and 'the subject of' (see Foucault 1976: 97; 1982: 212). In other words, individuals are not only the 'inert or consenting target' of power, they are 'always also the elements of its articulation' (Foucault 1976: 98).

Productive power is continuous, in that it is not just a privilege possessed by a dominant social group; it is rather exercised by and through us all, situated as we are in multiple networks of 'nonegalitarian and mobile relations'. As Foucault most famously puts it, 'power is everywhere; not because it embraces everything, but because it comes from everywhere' (Foucault 1978: 93–4). Power is continuous also in that it not only extends into, but emerges from, bodies. What Foucault has called the disciplinary practices of normalisation and surveillance not only fix individual bodies in space, in hierarchical grids of norms and deviations, but also work from the inside out, affecting the way we use our bodies and understand them.

But this also means that power should be understood as fundamentally unstable, incorporating 'innumerable points of confrontation, focuses of instability, each of which has its own risks of conflict, of struggles, of an at least temporary inversion of the power relations' (Foucault 1977d: 27). If one is never outside power, if 'there are no "margins" for those who break with the system to gambol in' (Foucault 1977b: 141), one is also never outside its 'odd term', resistance (Foucault 1978: 96).

As there is no one source of power, there is no 'single locus of great Refusal'. Resistance may indeed at times take the form of great radical ruptures, but it also, and most often, appears in mobile and transitory forms of temporary unities and regroupings, in which even individuals' relationships to their bodies and identities are in a process of flux (1978: 96). This means that, for Foucault, the possibilities of change are 'very urgent, very difficult, and quite possible' (Foucault 1981: 155).

Recognizing that power works by producing impure subjects, by simultaneously enabling and constraining subjects in specific ways, means that both the dangers and possibilities of resistance are highlighted. As Foucault explained:

My point is not that everything is bad, but that everything is dangerous. [...] If everything is dangerous, then we always have something to do. So my position leads not to apathy but to a hyper- and pessimistic activism.

(Foucault 1983: 343)

The Foucauldian emphasis on power's productive aspects should not be taken as a denial that power relations also involve domination, exclusion, control and constraint. What is 'positive' or 'productive' in Foucauldian terms is not necessarily 'good' or desirable, although common language usage, based on binary models, can make these assumptions and slippages difficult to avoid. The Foucauldian move is not to deny that processes of exclusion take place, but rather to challenge that binary logic which takes exclusion as the underlying paradigm or model for all relations of power and social interaction. It questions whether our familiar paradigms of inclusion/exclusion, subject/object, positive/negative, etc., are adequate to the task of conceptualising the complexities of modern power relations and the identities that emerge from those relations. I will be returning to this point, and to its specific implications for feminist theories of identity, throughout the chapters that follow.

Structure of the book

The book is divided into three parts. Part I, 'Indian Complications', introduces the work of a selected group of Indian feminist scholars concerned with issues of the intersectionality of sex, gender, race, religion, nation, caste and class in constituting women's identities. These include feminist historians and cultural, social and political theorists such as Urvashi Butalia, Uma Chakravarti, Amrita Chhachhi, Zoya Hasan, Ania Loomba, Lata Mani, Tejaswini Niranjana, Kumkum Sangari, Tanika Sarkar, Rajeswari Sunder Rajan and Susie Tharu. The theoretical approaches adopted by individual scholars cover a broad range, including appropriations, adaptations and distinctive combinations of poststructuralist, Marxist/socialist, Foucauldian and other feminist frameworks, and combine critical engagements with a variety of white, black and diasporic feminist scholarship produced in the West, and an attention to the specificities of the Indian context.

The work examined focuses mainly, though not exclusively, on two moments in Indian history: the anti-colonial struggles of the pre-independence nationalist movement, and the contemporary rise of communalist conflict between Hindu and Muslim communities. It examines themes such as the relationship between sex, gender, nation and race in identity-constitution, women's positioning within power relations structured around these identities, and models of agency, the self and the collective. Chapter 1 focuses on work exploring women's strategic and discursive positioning in the emergence of these multiple social identities. Chapter 2 looks at Indian feminist discussions on questions of agency, models of the self and collective identities. At the end of Part I, I identify four complications or challenges relating to the category 'women' that emerge from my reading of Indian feminisms, and that I argue Western feminisms need to take on board.

In Part II, 'White Western Feminisms and Identity' I use these insights to critically evaluate the work of four key contemporary white Western feminist thinkers, Luce Irigaray, Judith Butler, Rosi Braidotti and Donna Haraway. My aim is not so much to oppose or contrast these four white Western projects to each other (although some comparative discussion is necessary). Rather, the aim is to read each of these theoretical projects 'in a postcolonial mode', by placing them in critical conversation with insights identified from the work of Indian feminisms in Part I. Drawing on the challenges introduced in Part I, as well as on selected work by black and diasporic feminist theorists, I argue that strategies which privilege sexual difference as primary cannot deal adequately with differences between women, such as race and nation. But I also argue that strategies which privilege deconstructing or destabilising identity can be equally constrained by the logic of dualisms which has made it so difficult for feminists to sustain a simultaneous focus on women and their differences.

In Part III, 'Against Purity', I offer my own strategy for how the insights to be drawn from Indian feminisms might be taken on board by white Western feminisms in order to develop more complex models of power, identity and the self. Chapter 7 works 'against purity' to argue for a feminist model of power and resistance that gives up on the search for pure, power-free zones and works instead with the instabilities power produces as it enables and constrains women. Chapter 8 offers a reading of 'women' in a postcolonial mode as a complex impure category of identity, and as a site for developing alternative models of the self.

This brief description of the book's overall structure will no doubt signal to the reader what has been a persistent concern for me throughout the long process of producing this work. While I can easily name the four individual white Western feminist theorists whose work I focus on, I am forced repeatedly to refer to a much less clearly identified and defined collective category of 'Indian feminists' who provide the insights and complications against which I am reading Butler, Braidotti, Haraway and Irigaray. I am acutely aware that this imbalance persists throughout the book, despite my attempts to give space to the particular arguments and approaches of individual Indian feminists. To some extent, at least, I am helping to reproduce, rather than challenge, the status quo of the field of international feminist scholarship, in which the privilege of individuality is largely preserved for a few white Western 'divas' who perform before the backdrop of a more amorphous chorus of global feminist voices. Given the constraints of that status quo, I have not found a way to avoid this imbalance. I put the spotlight on four white Western individuals, because I am primarily concerned with unpicking the problems in white Western feminist projects, and not with 'speaking for' Indian feminists about their own projects. A more in-depth focus on fewer Indian feminist scholars might have given a better numerical balance between white Western and postcolonial voices. But, given the reality of international publishing practices, and of who gets the time and space to write books that self-consciously 'do feminist theory', my white Western divas would still have ended up with the louder voices. My imperfect solution has been to draw on a wider range of Indian feminist scholarship, in order to introduce a broader and more complex range of issues and theoretical developments than I would have been able to by focusing on the available texts of a smaller number of individuals. Rather than accepting my partial readings as a satisfactory substitute, I hope that readers will be encouraged to engage directly with the work of individual Indian feminists, and other postcolonial feminist scholars, so that the present imbalance in the field of international feminist theory is progressively undermined.

Part I

Indian complications

Chapter 1

Women and community identities in Indian feminisms

Returning home to India after several years studying feminist theory in the US, feminist scholar Mary John ends her 1996 book with a call for Western feminists to see the East as something more than an object of their inquiries:

> Western feminists need to reconsider what they are out to learn from the distant places they visit. Instead of developing ever more theoretically sophisticated twists on the cross-cultural construction of gender, why not attend also to *feminist* voices from elsewhere?
>
> (John 1996: 144, emphasis in the original)

In Part I of this book, I will be taking Mary John's advice to heart, although I would also want to rephrase her formulation. This project is about developing a theoretically more sophisticated understanding of women's identity, *by* attending to feminist voices from elsewhere. Nevertheless, attending to feminist voices from anywhere is not a simple process, and I want first to clarify which Indian feminist voices I am using, what I am listening for and how I propose to put those voices together with the white Western feminist theoretical projects which are the principal object of this inquiry.

This project aims to consider how postcolonial feminisms, such as those being developed in India, can productively complicate theoretical approaches to identity prevalent in Western feminisms. The Indian feminist voices I engage with are, therefore, limited by a number of factors. They are limited, first, to Indian feminists who are interested in engaging in this particular process, who locate themselves in an intellectual space of taking up ideas that may have originated in Western feminist movements, but which they are now in the process of changing to suit a different context. For me, this is part of the multi-directional process of theorising in a postcolonial mode. It is important that white Western feminists make the effort to notice how the theories they work with can be changed and complicated when put to use outside a white Western framework.

Second, I have selected material in which I have been able to identify either an explicit or implicit engagement with theoretical models of identity. This means that I am using some material which is not self-consciously 'doing theory' together with some that is, and that I will be putting different theoretical approaches together and taking them in directions their authors might not have intended, and may well disagree with. I draw on feminist historical studies of India's nationalist movement for independence from Britain, and on studies of representations of women in literature from and about the nationalist period. I also look at political and cultural analyses of women's place in contemporary Indian society, particularly in the context of the recent rise of right-wing communalist movements in the Hindu and Muslim communities. What holds these disparate texts together for me is that they all speak to questions of identity and, more particularly, they focus on identity-constituting sites where intersections between gender, nation and race identities are highlighted. This is a self-consciously selective engagement that is animated by a Western feminist location and a recognition that white Western feminism has had difficulty in dealing adequately with just these intersections.

Third, I have tended to privilege work that is interested both in questions of representation and in material practices and activities that affect women's identities. In my interpretations of the material I have selected, therefore, I try to identify distinctions between 'Woman' and 'women', and between the female and the feminine. Building on the Foucauldian framework established in the Introduction, I work with a sense of multiple discursive systems, rather than a single Symbolic order; thus I am also concerned to identify the different versions of 'Woman' and 'women' at play in identity-constitution processes.

I am, therefore, interested in showing how (specific and limited) groups of women are being discursively and strategically positioned. By discursive positioning, I mean their location in a variety of cultural, political and historical narratives. By strategic positioning, I mean how women's activities, as filtered through those discourses, are located within particular networks of power relations and produce material effects. At the same time I recognise that none of these positionings is ever fully stable, complete or closed, their effects are not always as intended, nor are they homogeneous.

Respecting the complexity and specificity of work produced in another context is always difficult. The material I engage with in these two chapters is, quite rightly, more concerned to speak to the complexities of Indian society than to Western feminists, and recognising and respecting that space is part of what postcolonial theory is about. As Donna Haraway has noted, there is always a 'very fine line between appropriation of another's (never innocent) experience and the delicate construction of the just-barely-possible affinities, the just-barely-possible connections that might actually make a difference in local and global histories' (Haraway 1991: 113). It is difficult to imagine completely avoiding the risk of a Western feminist constructing yet another East to serve Western purposes, and my engagement with Indian feminisms remains open-ended in recognition of this.

But another part of what the postcolonial mode means is that there are no pure spaces called 'East' and 'West', 'centre' and 'periphery', and this inevitable impurity and intermingling is what makes those connections 'just-barely-possible'. I think it also means that the changes and complications effected on feminist theory in a place like India can help make more visible the questions that have not been asked, and that still need to be asked, by white Western feminists in our own impure spaces.

It should be clear by now that this project is not about representing India, or even Indian feminisms, to the West. My purpose is not to attempt a 'complete picture' of the many women's movements in India, nor to argue that such and such a theoretical approach best suits Indian conditions. I recognise that many other intellectual currents, which I do not discuss, exist among Indian women scholars and activists. Thus, for example, I am not engaging with those who argue in different ways for a sharp demarcation from what they identify as 'Western feminism'. While Western feminists no doubt have much to learn from the challenges these women present to our knowledge-claims, they have in a sense placed themselves outside the particular conversation this project is interested in.

Also, I have tried to make clear that when I write about 'Woman', or 'women', I am doing it in relation to a particular discourse under discussion, or a particular feminist's take on a specific group of women's activities, and am not making any universalised claims about (all Indian) women or a singular construct of 'the Indian Woman'. Nevertheless, whilst I am not making any claims to represent the situation of Indian women or the state of Indian feminism, I am seeking to generalise from the selective work I have engaged with. I have tried to identify certain commonalities and connections between these materials, relating to women's discursive and strategic positionings across the categories of social identity such as sex, gender, race and nation, in order to suggest the contours of a more generalised 'economy' or 'logic' with which women need to contend, if always in specific ways, and which feminist theoretical models need to make space for. Finally, I want to note that, whilst I refer to all the feminists discussed in this chapter as Indian, I recognise that they are not all located in India. There is, however, a steady intellectual flow between work produced by 'diasporic' Indian academics and those 'at home', which is yet another condition of the 'postcolonial mode'.

Part I is divided into two chapters. In this first chapter I focus on Indian feminist discussions of the relationship between sex, gender, nation and race in identity-constitution. I begin in the first section by looking at how different Indian feminists take the intersection of these identity categories as a starting point for examining a two-way process: on the one hand, what these different identity categories 'do' to produce women's sense of self; but also, on the other hand, what women do to help produce those categories of identity. Women's productive role in constituting national and raced identities at legal and discursive levels is discussed, as is the importance of the specifically female body. In the second and third sections of this chapter I look in more detail at Indian feminist discussions of how and why the female body becomes a 'useful body' to identity-constituting processes. The second section considers appropriations of birth and the mother-figure, while the third looks at women's positioning in time and space.

Throughout Chapter 1 I suggest a tension in Indian feminisms between tendencies to limit women's 'usefulness' in the emergence of community identities to a passive role, and other approaches that suggest a more active productivity of 'women' at both strategic and discursive levels. In Chapter 2, I discuss these differences of approach more explicitly, when I turn to Indian feminist work on questions of women's agency, and feminist alternative models of the self and collective identities.

Women and identities: sex, gender, nation, race

My reading of Indian feminisms focuses on the question of 'Woman's' and 'women's' discursive and strategic location in the emergence of national, racial, religious and other community identities. Much of the work I have examined from India suggests an approach to identity that keeps women central to the analysis whilst also recognising that what is under analysis cannot be completely accommodated within a frame of gender or sexual difference. Discursive constructs and appropriations of 'Woman', the feminine and the female, as well as the material practices and activities of women, emerge and are put into play within a complex network of 'games of truth' that, while being necessarily and deeply gendered, are also, and at the same time, intimately concerned with national, racialised and community identities and relations of power.

In their introduction to one of the first collections of feminist historical studies of the nationalist movement, Kumkum Sangari and Sudesh Vaid argued that underpinning 'every attempt towards identity has been a redescription of women' (Sangari and Vaid 1990: 9). Many other Indian feminists have shared this interest in tracking the distinct ways in which 'redescribing women' has formed part of redefining national and other community identities. Two historical moments seem particularly significant to the Indian feminists I discuss here for highlighting women's strategic and discursive locations across the apparently discrete categories of sex/gender, race, nation and community. The first of these is the nationalist opposition to British colonial rule through the nineteenth and the first half of the twentieth centuries. Women's status and their participation in the pro-independence struggle became key issues shaping the politics of the anti-colonialist period. But equally, contestations over definitions of the feminine, over the norms and ideals invested in 'Woman', and over the meanings to be read into women's activities and feminised spheres of social life were to bear enormous symbolic weight in the emerging versions of the postcolonial Indian nation.

The second moment of particular significance is the more recent rise of Hindu–Muslim communalism[1] in the 1980s and 1990s. Here again, both the political and the cultural focus are not directly, or not at first glance, on issues of gender or sexual difference. The games of truth emerging in the highly charged context of communal conflict turn around questions of both nationhood and race. On the one hand, the project of the Hindu right pivots around the purifying imperative of a Hindu *rashtra* (Hindu nation) that would reduce the postcolonial Indian sense of nation-ness – always a precarious balancing act between an officially secular state and a complex, multi-ethnic and multi-religious people – to a Hindu component alone. On the other hand, the physical, political and symbolic conflicts that characterise communalism are marked by rival attempts to fix unchanging truths about essential, birth-based differences between the religious groups. In this sense, communalism racialises religious difference, and religion is used as a racial denominator or dividing-line within the broader community of the Indian *polis* (Sarkar and Butalia 1995: 6).

Complexity models

Clearly, neither of these historical moments can be approached adequately through the critical lens of gender or sexual difference alone. Nevertheless, 'Woman' and 'women' remain highly visible, and, some will argue, even central components of these identity-constituting processes. What Kumkum Roy has called this 'curious visibility of women' (Roy 1995: 10) in colonial and postcolonial discourse and practice has led many Indian feminists to work with models of identity that privilege complexity, particularly in terms of the ways in which gender intersects with nation, race, class and caste. As Roy summarises it, there is:

> an understanding that the concern with constructing and re-constructing women stems from a variety of agendas which are not necessarily women-centred, as a result of which women's identities are constituted through processes which are complex and by no means bounded within the framework of a single logic.
>
> (Roy 1995: 10)

Roy suggests here one aspect of working with a complex model of identity, that is, the ways in which women's identities emerge through these competing agendas and multiple categories of social identity. Kumkum Sangari makes a similar point in relation to understanding women as agents when she argues that 'notions of femaleness, self or identity' are so tied up with questions of family, class, religion and other forms of collectivity that they cannot be framed in terms of 'a single unified axis' (Sangari 1993: 871). Sangari argues that it is necessary to work with a concept of 'multiple identities' that emerge 'through several criss-crossing ideologies rather than a single one', and that exist, not as atomised entities, but in close relation with each other (1993: 871).

One of the practical reasons motivating Indian feminists to adopt a complex model of women's identity is suggested by Gabriele Dietrich in her discussion of the impact of the recent rise in communalism on the women's movement. For Dietrich, '[i]f one thing has become clearer over the past few years, it is the fact that caste and religious community are much stronger in women's lives than gender, at least in situations of communal strife' (Dietrich 1994: 43–4). If feminism is to speak to women's lived experience, then it must take this insight on board. But Dietrich's discussion also suggests a second facet that can emerge when feminists take complexity as a starting point; it is not just a question of what various categories of identity 'do' to women, but also how women can be necessary to, and productive of, those categories at the same time. As Dietrich argues:

> As women are crucial in the organisation of the home and the socialisation of children, cultural control over them is funda-mental to the continuity, not only of the race, but of tradition and communal identity itself. [...] The south Indian concept of *karpu* (chastity) is founded on the very real anxiety in men that if women's sexuality is not controlled, actual identities will change in unimaginable ways.
>
> (Dietrich 1994: 44)

It is this second aspect of complexity models, of thinking through how and why 'Woman' and 'women' are key to the emergence of national, raced and other community identities, that provides some of the most distinctive work from Indian feminists and suggests some of the most productive complications that can come from theorising identity 'in a postcolonial mode'.

'Women's work' and community identities

For example, in her discussion of Muslim women in the context of the current rise of communalism in India, Zoya Hasan argues that when religious identities are heightened and gender loyalties subordinated in communal conflict, this doesn't mean that women are less of a focus. They continue to be 'important signifiers of differences between groups; community identities are often defined through the conduct of women' (Hasan 1994a: viii). Hasan takes as her starting point one of the most hotly contested and debated events to focus directly on women in Indian politics in recent years, the 'Shah Bano case'.[2]

The Indian legal system includes a separate sphere of 'personal laws' for each of the major religious communities, dealing mainly with issues of marriage, divorce, inheritance and family. For ten years, Shah Bano, a Muslim woman, had contested the inadequate maintenance terms of her divorce under the Muslim personal law. In 1985 the Indian Supreme Court ruled in her favour. But this ruling then sparked a complex and bitter struggle over the personal law system, the desirability of a uniform civil code that could override or replace the personal laws, and the ways in which the rights and distinctive identities of India's different religious communities should be defined and recognised. The immediate controversy that followed the Supreme Court decision resulted in a compromise Muslim Women (Protection of Rights in Divorce) Act in 1986.

But the issues sparked by the Shah Bano case continue to inform communal conflict, and Hasan contends that Muslim women have remained at the very centre of the communal political imagination and of redefinitions of national identities. Indeed, she argues, in the post-independence period the symbolism of a united Muslim community identity has come to rest entirely on laws pertaining to the family and women (Hasan 1994b: 61). The rights of Muslim women have served as the locus of debates about conservatism versus modernisation, pluralism versus national integrity, secularism and women's equality, a uniform civil code and distinct religious laws (Hasan 1994a: xviii–xix).

For Hasan, issues like the Shah Bano case indicate that it is largely through the regulation of women that attempts are made to homogenise and narrow a definition of Muslim community identity. When identity discourse is locked into a near-exclusive focus on family codes, the main target of which is always women's behaviour, gender interests are set up as opposed to community interests, and women are asked to choose between their gender rights and Muslim identity (Hasan 1994b: 59).

In the Shah Bano case, the success with which major players from both Muslim and Hindu communities managed to shift the terms of the debate from one of women's rights to one of minority rights, had the result of reinforcing the view of those who would subsume women's identities under that of a homogenised and fixed community identity (Hasan 1994b: 65–6). The resultant Muslim Women's Bill ignored the multiple identities which both men and women possess and, in Hasan's view, denied the fact that women might experience conflict between their community and gender identities. By only recognising an ungendered identity for Muslim women, and by foregrounding Muslim personal law as the sole basis of community identity, the state legitimated a narrow interpretation of Muslim community identity, de-authorising other trends of thought and interpretations from within the Muslim community in the process (1994b: 68).

Hasan's concern with tracking the ways in which particular groups of women, and constructs of the feminine, come to 'stand for' the community, and especially for some sense of stable, unchanging truth about the nation or the race, is one that is shared in other recent work by Indian feminists. Like a number of the feminists reviewed here, Amrita Chhachhi draws on Benedict Anderson's landmark study of nationalism, *Imagined Communities* (1991) in her examination of the place of 'Woman' and 'women' in recent fundamentalist and communalist discourse. Despite his own silence on matters of gender, many feminists have found Anderson's understanding of nations as 'imagined communities' a useful starting point for reflecting on how imagined constructs of 'Woman' play a part in delineating the boundaries of community (see also Kandiyoti 1993).

Chhachhi cites Anderson as she discusses how nationalism appropriates the feminised language of 'kinship' and 'home' in order to appear as both natural and given. The merging of nation and community with images of the selfless mother and devout wife evokes the desired response of defence and protection by the male national subject. The linking of nation to 'mother', 'nature' and 'home' reinforces its claims to authenticity (Chhachhi 1991: 163–4).

What Chhachhi adds to this framework is a feminist concern with women's strategic location with respect to these symbolic constructs. Within these paradigms, 'Woman' marks the boundaries and contours of the national community and provides access to its truth about itself. However, those borders, and that so-called 'truth' then work to constrain and regulate the activities of the community's women (1991: 165–7). Fundamentalist or communalist constructs of an imagined community further contract the space for women to act as participants in defining the content of community identity, since their emphasis is on projecting an unchanging and monolithic image of that community (1991: 148).

Chhachhi's work takes a slightly different direction from Hasan's consideration of the relationship between women and community identities under communalism. Hasan wants to identify a distinct gender identity and gender interests, and, both analytically and politically, separate gender from national, raced or community identities. But for Chhachhi, women cannot sidestep their implication in community identity. They need to counter the myth of monolithic community identities, while insisting on their place within the process of defining those communities (1991: 168–9).

Useful bodies

What Chhachhi suggests, but doesn't explicitly discuss, is why 'Woman' and 'women' should prove such useful boundary markers for community identities. One of the points most frequently made in much of the material discussed in this chapter involves some variation on the statement that 'the identity of a community is constructed on the bodies of women' (Kannabiran and Kannabiran 1995: 122). Clearly, it is the female body's capacity for birth that makes women crucial to the preservation of a particular community's integrity and purity.

Urvashi Butalia's exploration of the violence surrounding the 1947 partition of India and Pakistan makes this link between the female body and community identities more explicit. In the partition violence, both the protection and transgression of a community's purity were materially marked on the bodies of its women. Women were killed in order to save them from being 'polluted' and so save the community's purity. Mass suicides of women to protect their own status as pure were valorised as the acceptable face of women's agency. Conversely, the rape and mutilation of women marked them as 'taken' by the other side and made indelibly impure (Butalia 1993: WS14–15). Butalia's discussion of recent communal violence shows many of the same practices at work today (Butalia 1995).

Historical analyses of social practices under contention during the colonial period identify similar symbolic roles invested in the bodies of women. Mrinalini Sinha examines how the gaze of both nineteenth-century colonialists and Bengali nationalists was directed at women's bodies in order to establish norms of femininity and, through them, norms of relative national worth. So, for example, around the issue of child marriage, a whole series of normalising questions were directed at the female body: when does the female body menstruate 'naturally'? Is a body that menstruates earlier than the Western norm 'unnatural'? Who has the right to name the mature body? Is the female body naturally passionless or libidinous? This problematisation of the female body ties the 'naturalness' or propriety of practices involving groups of women to evaluations of norms of both masculinity and nationhood. In the colonial context, contestations over the 'truth' about the female body become the discursive ground for debating whether a male child born of an 'unnaturally' immature mother is effeminate, and whether a nation which carries out such unnatural practices is degenerate, barbaric, and incapable of self-rule (Sinha 1987: 217–31).

Lata Mani's genealogy of the official discourse on *sati* (widow-burning) in colonial India is one of the best-known examinations of the ways in which women can become a focus for games of truth that privilege a male national subject. For Mani, the burning body of the widow is a powerfully contested and multi-vocal symbol at the heart of a number of normalising discourses and practices. Mani shows how the struggle for power between colonialist and nationalist forces produced a new hierarchy of scriptural, legal and traditional knowledges about *sati*, which then became the basis for laws and normalising practices effecting women's lives (Mani 1990: 99–111). Norms of nationhood and womanhood emerge and vie for legitimacy as colonial interests and Indian national supporters and opponents of *sati* sift through, classify, selectively discount and confirm aspects of the past.

What does the widow's burning body say? For the colonialist it becomes evidence of a norm of nationhood that does not deserve to rule itself, and that must be replaced with new, Western norms. For the nationalist opponent of *sati*, it signifies the need to restore to purity a debased and distorted tradition that has been imposed by mis-readers of the scriptures. For the nationalist supporter of *sati*, it already represents that pure tradition. The tremendous malleability of the widow's body in cultural interpretation and in law contrasts cruelly with its absolute fixity – its reduction to ashes – in reality. But then, Mani argues, real women, denied any agency or access to complex subjectivity in any of the norms on offer, are not the proper subjects of this particular debate. Nor are they even the principal objects of the debate. For Mani, norms of womanhood, inscribed on women's bodies, rather constitute the *ground* upon which norms of nationhood, including notions of tradition, authenticity and relative national worth, are contested (1990: 117–18).

I began this section by considering what Kumkum Roy has called the 'curious visibility' of women within colonial and postcolonial discourses and practices that focus on national, raced and other community identities. I end it with Lata Mani's characterisation of women's discursive and strategic positioning as the ground upon which groups of men contest norms of national identity. Clearly there are important differences between these two ways of conceptualising women's location within processes of identity-constitution. To speak of women's visibility is to suggest that they are foregrounded in these processes. As Zoya Hasan puts it, it is to suggest that women are at the very centre of redefinitions of national or community identities. To speak of women as the ground of identity-defining processes can suggest that women's location is characterised by exclusion and abjection, by invisibility.

Hasan's approach suggests a focus on the female body as a useful body, in the Foucauldian sense, both enabled and constrained within specific relations of power. Mani's formulation, if applied too unilaterally, suggests that the female body is only useful when it is abjected and objectified, made to serve as a passive ground for 'games of truth' which concern only men. Too simple or monolithic a reading of this move can result in a view that women always disappear; that all discourses objectify women; that there is no difference in the end between, for example, the nineteenth-century reformers who wanted to abolish *sati* and those who wanted to preserve it; that it makes no difference whether the women in question live or die.[3] Mani herself has argued against such a view, insisting that feminists must not concede to colonial or patriarchal discourse what it has at times attempted to achieve – the erasure of women (Mani 1992: 403).

On the other hand, only to speak of women as visible and foregrounded carries the risk of covering over the fundamental asymmetry in male–female power relations that makes women's bodies useful in highly constrained ways. The Indian feminist material I find most productive holds these two moves together, combining an attention to women's subordination with an acknowledgement of the ways in which they are also enabled, foregrounded and made central to processes of identity-constitution. In the following sections, I look at two specific themes in which this double focus on the useful-but-constrained female body emerges in Indian feminist scholarship. In the next section I look at appropriations of birth and the mother-figure. In the following one, I look at the female body in relation to questions of time and space.

Appropriations of birth for nation and race identities

As we have seen, many Indian feminists seem to share an understanding that the female body, and especially its capacity for birth, plays an important symbolic and material role in the emergence of national or community identities. But there are also differences over how to define, or where to locate, that importance: is it only a question of 'domesticating' birth and evoking the maternal as passive in order to appropriate it for other purposes? Or is there a more complicated 'managing' of the maternal at work, that acknowledges a certain female or feminine power, in order to have something powerful to serve particular identity-building processes?

One site for these debates is scholarship on the place of the mother-goddess and concepts of birth in the metaphysical and mythological groundings of Hindu culture. It should be noted that almost all Indian feminist discussions of cultural images of birth and the mother-figure take place in a Hindu context; these are mainly feminists from the Hindu community reading both Hindu culture and its appropriations within nationalist and communalist movements. Indeed, one of the problems raised in this material is the way (mainly upper-caste and mainly Bengali) Hindu icons of mother-goddesses take over the space of the nation through their reincarnations as Mother India.

This occurs most obviously in contemporary Hindu communalist projects; but it was also a problem historically within the nationalist movement that claimed to promote a secular inclusiveness of all India's religious/racial communities. The women's movement has also at times been complicit in using specifically Hindu cultural images to represent all Indian women (Agnes 1995). During demonstrations in support of Shah Bano, for example, Muslim women were placed in the front lines, but were asked to march alongside predominantly Hindu cultural symbols (Butalia 1995: personal interview).

Stepping into this complex discursive space for someone who is neither an expert in Hindu metaphysics nor in Indian history, is not easy. But there is a significance here that goes beyond the space of Indian feminisms, which makes it worth negotiating the risks to identify a number of points. Discussions of the place of the mother-figure in Hinduism suggest that there can be a variety of metaphysical models in which the specifically female is managed in identity-constituting processes that continue to privilege men. This is important for three reasons. First, it is a warning to Western feminists who may still be tempted to look beyond the West for pure alternatives to the metaphysical models that bedevil them.[4] Second, it suggests that the specifically female needs to be attended to when considering how differences like race and nation emerge; it is not something that feminists can discount. Third, it suggests that the margin, or the excluded and repressed outside, is not the only 'proper' space for 'Woman' within symbolic or social systems that subordinate women.

Indian feminists are, it seems, faced with a chorus of maternal voices in 'the Hindu tradition', especially since the latter is not, in fact, a single tradition but 'a mosaic of cults, sects and deities [...] constituted through plurally authored, multiply motivated myths which must be read not only as alterations and reinterpretations but also as appropriations and contestations' (Pathak and Sengupta 1995: 288). Feminists too are involved in these multiply motivated appropriations and contestations.

Some Indian feminists tend to privilege those voices which link the originating power of the universe – *shakti* – with female birth.

Kamala Ganesh, for example, looks at a wide variety of powerful mother-goddesses in Hindu scriptures and iconography, and argues that at least some of these goddesses are never fully domesticated or constrained by male gods (Ganesh 1990). For Ganesh, such manifestations of the mother-goddess, which bind together dualities of life and death, nurturing and destruction in the female body, and which are represented as unconstrained by lineage, husband or family, can be a persistent disturbing presence (Ganesh 1990: WS59–63).

Other feminist scholars focus on traditions that posit the mother as passive field sowed by the active seed of the father (Dube 1986; Bhattacharji 1990), or that subordinate the potentially unruly mother-figure to the domesticated figure of the wife (Chakravarti 1983). Kumkum Roy notes that spiritual birth, defined as masculine, often takes precedence over physical birth, as in those initiation ceremonies where upper-caste Hindu boys are 'reborn' from their spiritual priest-teachers (Roy 1995: 16). These appropriations of birth may acknowledge its power, but only by distancing birth from specifically female physicality, and under conditions over which women are expected to have little or no control (Roy 1995: 15–16). The symbolic distancing of birth from women is also suggested by the small number of important mother–child relationships in classical mythology,[5] and the lack of any significant myths about mother–daughter relationships (Chakravarti 1983: 68).

When the debate turns to ways in which this chorus of maternal voices has been put into play in nationalist and communalist movements, there are again some differences of approach. Some feminists privilege the image of a self-sacrificing Mother India that constitutes a passive, nurturing ground for a nationalism that is largely defined by and for men. Jasodhara Bagchi, for example, looks at what she describes as the ideological mobilisation of motherhood in the service of nationalism in late-nineteenth-century Bengal. Her reading of the Bengali tradition of maternity stresses an 'undying spirit of self-sacrifice for the family' (Bagchi 1990: WS65) which is then pressed into service by the nationalist movement in two ways. On the one hand, it glorifies motherhood for actual women, displacing movements to reform women's social status. On the other hand, it glorifies an abstract motherhood as the ground for asserting national selfhood and identity against the colonial presence – the mother-nation becomes a 'domain one could claim for one's own' (1990: WS65–6).

At the same time, Bagchi notes how the incorporation of a Hindu mother-goddess figure into the centre of the emerging sense of Indian nation-ness helps to exclude Muslim Indians from that 'imagined community' (1990: WS70). As this particular appropriation of the mother-figure excludes Muslim anti-colonialists from its frame of reference, so too, for Bagchi, does it exclude most women. For her, what lies behind this glorification of the mother is largely the anxieties of men, and their need for authentication and valorisation in the face of the colonial rulers. The legitimacy – a revalorised national identity – that emerges from the process is passed on to their sons, and not their daughters (1990: WS71).

Bagchi is one of a number of Indian feminists to acknowledge the importance of the mother-figure to national identities; but for Bagchi and many others, that importance seems to derive largely from the supposed passivity of the maternal-feminine.[6] In these narratives, those unsettling, excessive voices of the mother-goddess seem to have been completely domesticated. But as Ania Loomba has argued:

> For the Indian woman to be cast as Mother India and to serve a wide spectrum of political interests in colonial times, she had to be rewritten as more-than-victim. As an agent of Hindu tradition, or nationalist interests, a certain amount of volition, and even desire had to be attributed to her.
>
> (Loomba 1993: 216)

Tanika Sarkar complicates the reading of nineteenth-century Bengali nationalism given by Bagchi and others to suggest instead ways in which the strong mother-goddess figure is acknowledged, put into play and managed within a discourse that still foregrounds the male subject. In her examination of nationalist discourse as expressed in nineteenth-century Bengali poetry and literature, Sarkar stresses the flexibility of nationalist appropriations of the mother-figure, and the many meanings read onto the image of the mother. By tapping into both sides of the life–death duality discussed by Ganesh, these nationalist appropriations draw on traditional evocations of the mother as both power and powerlessness. They also engage with new meanings of the maternal introduced by the colonial presence and discourse (Sarkar 1987: 2011).

Sarkar focuses on the evocations of country as mother-land and the different strains woven into this image. On one level, she argues, the glorification of country as female, as Mother India, is a defiant response to the colonial power that represents itself as Imperial (male) lion, and that denies masculinity to the colonised Bengali which it characterises, by its own value system, as 'effeminate'. But this defiant image can only work because it draws on those traditions of female originating power (*shakti*) and of mother-goddess worship which retained their resonance in nineteenth-century Bengal (1987: 2011).

At the same time, the mother-figure is also being evoked as authentic, stable, unchanging origin, to whom the male Indian subject can return in his quest for authenticity, shaken by his failure in the terms of the West's discourse of progress (1987: 2011). Thus Sarkar notes a never fully resolved tension between evocations of those aspects of militancy and sexuality in the mother-goddess as icon of anti-colonial struggle, and the desire to contain this militancy within the safer frame of the innocent, nurturing and healing mother-figure who passes power back to her sons (1987: 2012).

In the twentieth-century independence struggle, Gandhi also adopted for himself a powerful maternal persona as a way of heightening his authority, evoking what Meena Alexander calls the 'virile Mother-India' figure (Alexander 1989: 371). For Sarkar, the theoretical discordance between the powerful, militant mother-figure Gandhians helped to promote, and their resistance to following through on the implications of that image for reordering gender relations, remained a key unresolved tension of the nationalist movement (Sarkar 1987: 2014).

In the context of the contemporary Hindu communalist movement, that virile Mother India persona can also be directly taken up by women. Sarkar notes how, in some of the recent literature of the Hindu right, motherhood is 'emptied of its customary emotional and affective load and is vested with a notion of heroic political instrumentality' (Sarkar 1995: 188). Communal women leaders take up the same strain of heroic mothers willing their children to die for the Hindu nation, and the rank and file mothers of the communal movements are mobilised as pivotal 'political creatures and agents' in the right's bid for hegemony at the level of everyday relations, personal habit and domestic ritual and practice (1995: 189).

Sarkar makes the point that this kind of symbolic and strategic appropriation of both the Mother-India figure, and of the activities of real mothers, has a directly political significance in the context of the communal movement (1995: 189). This is not just something which happens in a separate or ancillary ideological or cultural field. I want to suggest that Sarkar's point might apply beyond the specific context of communalist politics. Discursive and strategic appropriations of birth such as this might be understood as examples of the kind of productive bio-power Foucault describes. Here, the specifically female body, and its capacity for birth, becomes a useful body in the Foucauldian sense, invested with particular truths and engaged in producing particular material effects, as it is enmeshed in specific power relations. In the following section, I will look at how this theme is further expanded through considering women's location in time and space.

Purity models – time/tradition and space/home

One recurring issue in the Indian feminist scholarship I have examined is the different ways in which 'Woman' has been linked with notions of timeless tradition in both the colonial and postcolonial periods. This reinforces the sense of 'Woman' as stable, unchanging ground upon which an active male subject rebuilds a sense of self shaken by the uncertainties of colonial and postcolonial societies. So, Sangari and Vaid argue, 'the recovery of tradition throughout the proto-nationalist and nationalist period was always the recovery of the "traditional" woman – her various shapes continuously readapt the "eternal" past to the needs of the contingent present' (Sangari and Vaid 1990: 10).

It is a familiar argument among both feminists and non-feminists that women play a key role in preserving and transmitting cultural traditions, especially in Third World societies. Anthias and Yuval-Davis have argued, for example, that since women have less access to the public sphere, they are often less assimilated socially and linguistically into the wider society with all its 'modern' or Western influences. And since they tend to have primary responsibility for child rearing, they are particularly well placed to transmit this heritage of traditional symbols and ways of life (Anthias and

Yuval-Davis 1989: 3). The equation 'women = tradition' thus seems quite straightforward and unproblematic.

But the work of a number of Indian feminists suggests a rather different, and certainly more complex, understanding of the woman–tradition connection. Sangari and Vaid note that neither tradition nor modernity is available in a value-free or unproblematic sense. Rather, they argue for a focus on:

> how change is made to appear as continuity [since] the ideologies of women as carriers of tradition often disguise, mitigate, compensate, contest actual changes taking place. Womanhood is often part of an asserted, or desired, not an actual cultural continuity.
>
> (Sangari and Vaid 1990: 17)

Uma Chakravarti's study of the re-scripting of India's past in the colonial period argues that women do not simply transmit a self-evident already-constituted body of tradition; tradition is rather being constantly reinvented, woman's place in that tradition is constantly reinterpreted, and contemporary women's self-definition is being reproduced in relation to that invented tradition (Chakravarti 1990: 27–57). Chakravarti focuses on the complex intersections of caste, class, gender, national and imperialist interests that converged in the process of 'scripting' a lost Vedic-Aryan Golden Age and placing it at the centre of Indian historical consciousness. She argues that for women in particular, this perception of a lost glory has 'led to a narrow and limiting circle in which the image of Indian womanhood has become both a shackle and a rhetorical device that nevertheless functions as a historical truth' (1990: 28).

In Chakravarti's account, a version of a pure unchanging tradition, which places a pure traditional Woman at its centre, emerges and claims its continuity from a decidedly impure and discontinuous field of contestations. The sometimes convergent, sometimes contradictory agendas of Western Orientalist scholars (both male and female), and upper-caste Hindu literati, who were also sometimes Hindu revivalists and/or nationalists, meet in the apparently still space of this traditional Indian Woman (1990: 29–45). The pure space occupied by this Traditional Woman is only secured by covering over a multiplicity of caste, class and religious differences between women, and by disqualifying those counter-discourses which question whether the Golden Age 'she' embodies ever existed (1990: 66–76).

Nevertheless, 'she' is presented as the unbroken link back to that lost Golden Age, ready to take on active roles to preserve family or caste honour in times of crisis, and to produce children as part of the physical regeneration of the weakened Aryan race (1990: 50–60). Both aspects suggest variations on the militant mother-goddess figure we examined earlier, whose power and privileged access to origins, both in terms of spirituality/tradition and birth, is at once acknowledged and contained within the framework of a community or national agenda.

In the postcolonial context, Rajeswari Sunder Rajan points to popular cultural representations of the 'new Indian woman', a construct that aims both to reconcile, in her person, the conflicts between tradition and modernity in Indian society, and to deny the actual conflicts that women experience in their lives (Sunder Rajan 1993: 129). As an example of this process, Sunder Rajan looks at advertisements on Indian State Television that promote the 'pan-Indian' subject, as opposed to specific regional, religious or communal identities. She notes that this is only achieved, ironically, by 'westernizing' the Indian male consumer, whose project of 'modernization-without-westernization' is saved by the presence of 'the Indian *woman*, perenially and transcendentally wife, mother and homemaker' whose specific role is to balance (deep) tradition and (surface) modernity (1993: 133).

In these representations, according to Sunder Rajan, 'Woman' and religion occupy the same conceptual space; in both cases, the traditional is defined as timeless, and hence able to embrace, and make space for, modernity as a transitional phase disguising the permanent essence of tradition. 'Woman' is made to serve as the harmonious symbol of historical continuity, rather than being recognised as a conflictual subject (1993: 134–5). Women's emancipation (the 'new' part of the 'new Indian woman' construct) is made to appear as a matter of individual women's achievement and choice, in ways that fit comfortably with a tradition preserved intact in an idealised conjugal and domestic sphere. Again, as in the re-scripting of the Golden Age examined by Chakravarti, this version of tradition can only survive by what it excludes. Here, Sunder Rajan argues, this is achieved by redefining precisely those aspects of 'tradition' that are the most frequent sites of women's oppression – sexual harassment, domestic work, dowry demands, marriage rituals. By sanitising, glamorising or trivialising these moments, the advertisements project them instead as sites for 'remaking female identity'(1993: 132).

Sunder Rajan identifies this same move at work in Hindu communalist support for recent cases of *sati*, where 'modern', educated young women are represented as being able to negotiate their way through modernity and, through the act of *sati*, reconfirm the timeless, authentic identity of their communities (1993:17–18). But it is not just through such highly charged and visible acts as *sati* that the Hindu right mobilises the woman–tradition–authenticity package. Sarkar notes that, in projecting itself as a religious rather than political movement, the Hindu right draws on the notion that faith is timeless and above historical change and political manipulation. Demands made in the name of religion, then, refer back to this timeless faith and not to any modern variant that is open to political appropriation. Women become central to this argument because they are seen as the custodians of this timeless faith (Sarkar 1995: 209).

V. Geetha and T.V. Jayanthi note that in Hindu communities, it is often through activities for which women are responsible that a community's structuring of time marks it as Hindu. Women are responsible for the observance of pollution and purity rituals; for breaking up calendar time into fasting and festival days, or auspicious and inauspicious moments; for patterning meals to suit these sanctified blocks of time. All this inscribes religiosity into women's lives and bodies in caste- and culture-specific ways (Geetha and Jayanthi 1995: 245).

But, in turn, women's activities in time also become markers for the community of these religion- and caste-specific identities. The Hindu right seeks to displace and reproduce these women-specific activities outside the household, both mobilising women's 'private' rituals in a public cause and grounding its claims to authenticity in women's presence and activities (1995: 247). A pure, 'timeless time' of Woman lends legitimacy to the impermanent moment of political contestation.

The related spatial move in both nationalist and communalist movements that has interested Indian feminists is the conflation of 'Woman' with 'home'. There is, of course, nothing particularly new in feminists looking at the ways in which women have been associated with concepts of the private, 'home' or 'inside'. One complication that Indian and other postcolonial feminisms have brought to this question is their insistence that the feminised space of home is productive not only of gendered but also of raced, national and other community identities.

Ania Loomba, for example, looks at the shifts introduced to the meanings of public and private by the colonial presence. She argues that, to some extent at least, a Western reading of public/private spheres is introduced to Indian nationalist discourse through the power struggle over spheres of influence between the colonial government and the indigenous elite. In instituting a division of labour in which certain 'social issues', designated as dealing with moral or cultural questions, were de-linked from the institutions of public (colonial) power and handed over as a sphere of influence to the indigenous elite, particular Western concepts of a private realm of moral conscience were also being taken on. And, of course, many of these issues defined as private centred around women (Loomba 1993: 213).

Samita Sen also explores this redefinition of the private, in which women became the arena for playing out agreements and conflicts between the colonial bureaucracy and the colonised middle class. 'Home' became designated as the private space where the colonised subject retreats from his master; neither collaboration nor protest were to impinge on the hearth where 'Woman' is constituted as the repository of traditional values and upholder of the moral order of the subject-race. For Sen, nationalism inherits a language that links and sets up a series of connected binary oppositions between 'the "home and the world", the nursery and the nation, the private and the public' (Sen 1993: 233).

In both Sen and Loomba's discussions, then, we see the familiar public/private binary extended beyond gender to include questions of nation or race. But I think it is possible to suggest other ways in which Indian feminist scholarship complicates the way we think about the relation between women and space. Perhaps because this particular reading of 'Woman' as home was born out of the very public anti-colonial struggle, this 'private' was also very evidently a presence in the public sphere. There is a sense here of nationalism constructing a private sphere which women can then carry around with them into the public sphere, so that women are mobilised and contained at the same time.

On this question, as in her consideration of the mother-figure, Tanika Sarkar points to the tension between moves to enable and constrain women. On the one hand, there is the promise of reordering gender relations implicit in a certain 'feminisation' of nationalist discourse, and in the political mobilisation of real women. On the other hand, there is the containing of women by the nationalist movement within its own patriarchal norms.

This 'feminisation' of the movement through a public discourse of home worked through this tension on several levels. For example, the move to invest moral authority and purity in the feminine-home sphere represents a potential challenge to patriarchal perceptions of women's actual authority in the family. But investing women with this moral ascendancy was often linked to rejecting the importance of formal education for women, so that the household, centred around domestic work and an oral tradition of stories from the epics, becomes woman's religious text, sufficient to her needs (Sarkar 1987: 2013).

The foreign presence, in the form of false knowledge and foreign goods, was often characterised as a foreign parasite attacking the body; in these nationalist discourses, health and life therefore depended on women's authentic knowledge and traditional healing, shopping and feeding skills, in the interior space of the household (1987: 2013). Gandhi also took over traditional home-based rituals as rituals of the public movement. Sarkar argues that, on one level, this utilisation 'extended domestic, feminine ritual into the world of men and public affairs. There was a mingling of male and female spaces and practices. The sharing opened up possibilities for the reordering of gender relations' (1987: 2014).

But, although Sarkar does not put it in these terms, because 'Woman' has to *be* the pure private space of home, and not just *visit* it as 'Man' does, women can never stand in the same relation to this 'privatised' public movement as its male participants and leaders do. Sarkar notes the tendency in nationalist literature to conceptualise home and women's bodies as integrally linked, and as the one safe hiding-place for the national subject's battered independence:

> Very often, an implicit continuum is postulated between the hidden, innermost private space, chastity, almost the sanctity of the vagina, [and] political independence at state level; as if, through a steady process of regression, this independent selfhood has been folded back from the public domain to the interior space of the household, and then further pushed back into the hidden depths of an inviolate, chaste, pure female body.
>
> (Sarkar 1987: 2014)

But if Woman *is* the pure, chaste body in which the independent self lives, then there is no space for female desire, either sexual or political, and the self that needs a hiding place, or a ground to stand on, must be male.

What emerges is a complex sense of women's location that is actually not that easily contained within the familiar man-world-public/woman-home-private binary which Sen and Loomba suggest. Woman, and women's activities may often figure as the home men can retreat to, but women's activities also bring that home into the world in complicated, impure ways. Women are enabled as participants in political contestations, but their presence is also used to claim an authenticity of identity for the national or raced subject who remains stubbornly Man.

Beyond the frame of nationalist or communalist politics, Seemanthini Niranjana also suggests a more complex locating of women in space in her study of the mapping of cultural spaces in a village community. Niranjana found that much of what was said in the village about femininity, the female body and the activities of women was governed by a strong spatial narrative. But at the same time, descriptions of space, the community and its identity are, in turn, mediated through references to female morality, shame, honour and rules of movement (Niranjana 1994a: 5).

The manner in which women inhabit space becomes a key to preserving the physical and moral parameters of particular groups. This is, first, because considerations of female honour and sexuality both inform the rules underlying women's use of space and are the hinge along which groups such as households, castes and villages draw their boundaries. Second, it is women who are often the central actors in this process of cultural reproduction (1994a: 13).

Additionally, what appears at first sight to be a simple echo of the public/private split, with men's space designated 'outer' and women's 'inner', turns out to be more complex. Notions of inner-ness and outer-ness are flexible and shifting. The 'inner', as women's space, can, depending on context, mean the village, the shared space of kinship or caste group, or the household; women's presence lends an inner-ness each time to a different configuration of relations. What remains constant is that female sexuality and its regulation remain both the target of and the medium through which not only female identity, but also the boundaries of community space, come to be negotiated (Niranjana 1994a: 14–15).

My reading of the Indian feminist material examined in this chapter suggests a complex discursive and strategic positioning for women. First, discursive constructs of 'Woman' and women's activities are seen as productive of, and often central to, the emergence of national, raced and community identities. Second, one of the ways in which 'Woman' and 'women' become necessary to the emergence of these identities is through acknowledging and appropriating the privileged access to origins that the female capacity of birth represents. But third, the stability of these community identities relies on locating 'Woman' and 'women' as pure origin, as timeless tradition and the fixed place of home. The female body becomes a highly useful body, in the Foucauldian sense, by linking it to models of purity and unchanging, authentic identities.

This complex positioning of 'Woman' and 'women' raises two important theoretical issues for feminism. The first is whether the familiar binary logic of self/other, inclusion/exclusion, public/private divisions, on which so much of feminist theory relies for its paradigms, can adequately reflect this complexity. In particular, is the familiar characterisation of women as marginalised, excluded, or abjected, one that can be sustained? Or do we need to look also at how women are foregrounded, made visible and useful in the constitution of specific community identities?

This leads to the second issue we need to consider: how does this complex positioning impinge on questions of women's agency? If we move away from simple inclusion/exclusion paradigms, then we cannot posit women as ever fully passive and without agency. But at the same time, the particular ways in which women emerge as 'useful' bodies and subjects will make some forms of agency more acceptable than others within prevailing relations of power. How have Indian feminists dealt with these questions of women's problematic visibility and problematised agency? What do they propose as feminist alternative models of the individual self, of the subject-agent and of collective identities? It is to these questions that I turn in Chapter 2.

Agency, the self and the collective in Indian feminisms

As I argued in Chapter 1, one of the issues to concern Indian feminists in recent years has been the 'curious visibility of women' in colonial and postcolonial discourses and practices centring on national and other community identities. This has raised a number of conceptual challenges for Indian feminists when they turn to the question of women's agency and resistance. How are feminism's claims for women to be distinguished from other discourses and practices that might focus on 'Woman' and 'women', but which don't seem to advance the cause of women very much? Do these discourses and practices always constitute 'Woman' and 'women' as a passive, silenced and powerless ground upon which national or raced identities are constructed? Is this only a question of women being objectified across a more complicated set of networks, but with the same moves of exclusion, repression or objectification being enacted across those different categories? And conversely, is any foregrounding of women as active agents necessarily a form of resistance to this subordination?

In the first section of this chapter I suggest that different theoretical starting points can affect the ways in which Indian feminists have answered these questions. I begin by discussing two contrasting Indian feminist analyses of women's active presence in the contemporary Hindu communalist movement. This debate suggests broader theoretical differences within Indian feminisms over how to characterise women's agency and positioning within predominant power relations.

The second section explores a number of Indian feminist discussions of when and how women's agency is valorised within discourses and practices that centre on community identities. The third section links the limitations placed on women's agency with the ways in which the female body is conceptualised. In the next section, I consider how women's location within specific communities problematises their access to subject-positions that are not defined by a single community. In particular, I consider Indian feminist discussions of women's access to the status of citizen. This leads, in the final section, to a consideration of the problems and possibilities for alternative feminist models of the self and the collective.

Visible women

The foregrounding of women as militants and leaders within the right-wing Hindu communalist movement has sparked some important theoretical reflections on the question of agency, and has revealed some significant differences of approach within Indian feminisms. The feminist historian Tanika Sarkar has been researching the question of women leaders and militants within Hindu communalism for a number of years (Sarkar 1991, 1995). Sarkar presents a many-layered picture of women's complex location within the discourses and practices of the Hindu communalist movement.

This is in part because of the complex nature of the movement itself, its versatility and its use of shifting icons, images and versions of Hindu 'tradition' (Sarkar 1995: 192). But it is also because, in at least some versions of the communalist project, women are being offered a space within the movement as militant, actively and radically political beings, in ways that depart from conventional norms of domesticity and that add political dimensions to more traditional norms of femininity (Sarkar 1995: 188–9).

Sarkar argues, for example, that in previous national and communal movements, the 'fetishised sacred or love object to be recuperated has been a feminine figure' (1991:2057), a 'Mother-India figure'. However, in the contemporary movement that position can also belong to a specifically male deity, the god Ram, and women are being pressed into action to liberate him:

> The reversal of roles equips the communal woman with a new and empowering self image. The woman has stepped out of a purely iconic status to take up [an] active position as a militant.
> (Sarkar 1991: 2058)

Sarkar's research suggests that it is not enough to view women active in the Hindu right as victims of false consciousness or as pawns being manipulated in a movement which goes against their interests. Indeed, the involvement of these women has complex consequences which suggest the need to constantly problematise the whole question of interests, and whether it is at all useful or even possible to demarcate a distinct and stable category of gender interests. While recognising that the ways in which women have been mobilised in the Hindu right's various organisations is class- and caste-specific, Sarkar finds that, for those touched by the movement, there has been an enabling effect that needs to be acknowledged. In part, this can be because religion gives women a forum in which to discuss a world of meanings beyond their immediate and limited experience; these discussions are then given a political dimension through the organisations of the Hindu right (1991: 2060).

Sarkar also suggests that, in projecting the communal woman as militant warrior, the movement opens a space in which issues of women's self-protection and respect within their own environment can come to the fore (1991: 2061). Sarkar has found that political involvement in the right-wing Hindu organisations can give women unprecedented bargaining power within their families, and that their example leads other local women to feel dissatisfaction with early marriages, or with the burden of housework which keeps them from political engagement (Sarkar, personal interview 1995). This sense of an increased room for manoeuvre on domestic issues for women militants of the Hindu right is echoed in other studies (see, for example, Bacchetta 1994b).

How to understand this foregrounding of women in the Hindu right is a subject of some debate within Indian feminisms, in ways that suggest the importance of theoretical starting points in terms of models of power, identity and the subject when feminists aim to theorise women 'in a postcolonial mode'. For Sarkar, the foregrounding of women, and its possible enabling consequences for some women, is something that needs to be acknowledged. But acknowledging this does not mean that she concludes that the Hindu right is a feminist movement, or that it represents a qualitative challenge to women's subordination. On the contrary, she argues against any simple belief that women in the Hindu right will eventually 'see the light' and turn it into a feminist movement (Sarkar, personal interview 1995). If the Hindu right has offered an alternative version of normative femininity within some of its women's organisations:

> the thrust of the transformation is to obliterate the notion of selfhood, to erase concern with social and gender justice and to situate the public, political, extra-domestic identity on authoritarian community commands and a totalitarian model of individual existence, every particle of which is derived from an all-male organisation.
>
> (Sarkar 1995: 188–9)

Thus, while some Indian feminists have read Sarkar as identifying some kind of 'bourgeois feminism' within the Hindu right (see, for example, John 1996: 140), I would argue that she is instead trying to clear an analytical space in which every foregrounding of women does not necessarily refer back to a feminist project.

Sarkar does not make her theoretical allegiances explicit, but in my reading, she is working with an underlying understanding of power that enables as it constrains all subjects, including women. There is no pure space where unproblematically defined gender interests can be separated off from other, historically specific networks of power relations. As a consequence, notions of the subject, agency, interests, and categories of social identity such as gender, race, class and nation, are all problematised. Within such a framework, foregrounding women as agents can be one way of constraining them within power relations that continue to privilege men.

Kumkum Sangari has also argued, more generally, that patriarchies work in part through obtaining consent from women and not just through coercion. Granting women agential capacities may be one of the ways in which this consent is obtained. She sees consent as 'part of this uneven process of the reconstitution of patriarchies' (Sangari 1993: 869), and wants a more complex understanding of both patriarchies and women's place in them, linked to specific modes of production, class structures, and caste/class inequality. While Sangari does not mention questions of race, nation and community specificity in this context, her argument that 'women's consent may itself be one of the nodes of the condensed articulation of patriarchies with other social structures in specific historical conjunctures' (1993: 869) does suggest a space in which to consider women's productive implication in constituting these different categories of social identity.

In contrast, other theoretical approaches operative within Indian feminisms seem to find it much more difficult to deal with this double move of enablement and constraint. Because of their pertinence to the Western feminist projects I will be examining in future chapters, I want to focus here on how that difficulty is expressed in some Indian feminist appropriations of poststructuralist models.

In one of the most direct recent attempts by Indian feminists to apply postmodern and poststructuralist theory to Indian politics, Susie Tharu and Tejaswini Niranjana look at a number of recent cases where 'Woman' and 'women' are foregrounded in problematic circumstances. These include women's involvement in Hindu communalist organisations, and the appropriation of a language of women's rights and agency in communalist, caste and class politics. In each of the cases they look at, a particular image or version of the 'model Woman' is projected in ways that cover over caste, class or religious differences between women (Tharu and Niranjana 1994: 96–109).

On one level, Tharu and Niranjana's examples, or 'metonyms', as they call them, can be read as another reflection of women's complex location across a variety of categories of social identity: women's activities and discursive constructs of Woman emerge as crucial to the elaboration of caste/class, national and community identities. In this sense, Tharu and Niranjana provide more examples of the picture of women's complex location that emerges from the work of Sarkar, Hasan and others, which I discussed in Chapter 1. They also quite rightly point to the limitations of a liberal feminist framework that asks only that women be included as citizens, agents and subjects without problematising the terms within which such categories are defined within the prevailing social order.

But it is what Tharu and Niranjana do with their appropriation of postmodern and poststructuralist theory that does make a difference. They take as a starting point, the now familiar narrative that the 'subject' of modernity, or of 'Western humanism' (1994: 95–6), is produced through exclusion – exclusion of women, of lower classes and castes, of minority or other 'othered' communities. Underpinning this narrative is a view that power also works primarily through exclusion and through making those who are excluded invisible. Feminism has contested this invisibility and insisted on women being included among the visible. Women's visibility is, in their view, therefore inevitably linked to feminism.

But wherever Tharu and Niranjana look, Woman's and women's 'new visibility' places them in some highly contestable situations, with less than admirable allies. The problem for them then becomes feminism, along with the concepts of secularism, democracy, rights and citizenship that emerge together with the humanist subject (1994: 96). The only kind of political resistance they seem comfortable with is a celebration of the micro-politics of the local (1994: 114–15).

A number of consequences flow from this analysis. Where Sarkar works to hold on to the complexities of situations in which women's foregrounding or even centrality are both acknowledged and problematised, for Tharu and Niranjana every foregrounding of women is conflated with feminism. The direct and necessary line they seem to draw from 'Woman' to feminism to the subject of feminism (1994: 101) flattens out the ways in which 'Woman' can also be productively invested with a variety of meanings in ways that continue to subordinate women.

Nor is this 'new visibility' necessarily completely new. While Sarkar does suggest certain unprecedented particularities in the 'model Woman' of the contemporary communalist movement, her own work on the anti-colonial nationalist movement (Sarkar 1987) indicates that the foregrounding of women can also be found in earlier historical periods. The work of Mani and Sinha discussed in Chapter 1 also suggests this.

In addition, while there is no doubt that feminism *can* be complicit with moves to exclude, objectify, 'other' or oppress, this is not to say that any move which foregrounds women in problematic ways is also, by definition, feminist. Similarly, if feminism's language of women's rights, agency and choice is appropriated by non-feminist social forces for a variety of political ends, this does not necessarily disqualify feminism's use of that language; it only suggests that the meanings of these terms are never fully stable, embedded as they are in a field of socially specific power relations.

Recognising this instability would seem more consistent with Tharu and Niranjana's desire to dispense with the 'humanist subject', and the notion of pre-discursive, pre-social or pre-symbolic 'essences' or 'truths', than does their insistence on connecting every evocation of 'Woman' or 'women' to feminism.

Instead, by suggesting that the language of rights, citizenship, democracy and secularism, and of women and feminism, is indelibly tainted by stain of humanism, they actually ascribe a certain stability of meaning to these terms. At the same time, they concede the macro-political terrain of contesting and redefining these concepts, and retreat to the 'safer' ground of local micro-struggles.

Finally, Tharu and Niranjana's work suggests another danger of some appropriations of poststructuralist models. In granting primacy to the linguistic and social gesture of exclusion, they can overstate the degree to which women are, in fact, erased from view. For example, in Chapter 1 we saw how Hasan's work on legal constructs of 'the Muslim Woman' within the context of communalism suggests ways in which women become central to the communal political imagination. In contrast, Tharu and Niranjana's appropriation of poststructuralist language models leads them to claim that the Indian Muslim Woman becomes unrepresentable, a linguistic non-possibility (Tharu and Niranjana 1994: 108). If meaning is secured only through exclusion, as in the language model that underpins their approach, then 'Indian'-ness and 'Woman'-ness need to exclude 'Muslim'-ness in order to make sense to the communalist.

Here again, Tharu and Niranjana seem to be flattening out the complexity of women's location to a single move of marginalisation. Their starting premise is the need to capture the ways in which the apparently stable category 'women' can cover over caste, class and community differences. But in the end their approach seems to create less space in which to consider the specificities of differences between women. This is because Tharu and Niranjana's approach reduces those specificities to the single binary of exclusion versus inclusion.

In contrast, Sarkar works with a more complex model of power in which women's positioning is not easily contained within this exclusion/inclusion binary. By acknowledging the ways in which women can be simultaneously enabled and constrained within the communalist project, she turns attentions towards the ways in which women are both implicated in the emergence of national and racialised differences, and are affected by those differences. At the same time, she takes questions of agency outside the simple frame of 'true' and 'false' interests, and turns attention to the need to situate women's agency in the impure field of specific power relations. Within this more complex frame, women are never fully invisible or passive, but specific constraints are placed on their access to subject-agent status. Their agency can be legitimated or disqualified in context-specific ways.

Valorised agencies

Urvashi Butalia raises the question of the conditions under which women's agency is valorised or dismissed in the context of the violence surrounding the 1947 partition of India and Pakistan. During this period, individual and mass suicides by women, in order to prevent forced conversion or capture, were seen as a valorised form of agency. Butalia argues that these actions were approved because women were protecting the purity of the community whose borders they constitute (Butalia 1993: WS 15–16).

Butalia also shows how this process worked differently when, after partition, it came to deciding the repatriation of women caught on the wrong side of those borders. Those who resisted repatriation, whether because they were settled in a new life, or feared a hostile welcome as 'soiled goods', now found that exercise of choice disqualified (1993: WS 16). Of course, the whole concept of 'choice' is further problematised by the complex conditions of intersecting gendered, racial-religious and national conflict in which women found themselves. But the particular point that Butalia focuses on here is that women's agency is often seen as problematic when it threatens to complicate the simple equation of 'Woman = community'. When women act in ways that suggest that they might want to, or might have to negotiate a more complex set of locations, their actions are seen as 'inauthentic' agency that must be disallowed (1993: WS 19).

Kumkum Sangari looks at militant women leaders of the contemporary Hindu right to discuss another form of valorised agency for women: female incitement, or women entering the public sphere in order to call upon men to act (Sangari 1993: 872–3). She argues that it is only when the female militant is projected as fully submerged within the interests of the community that her power and agency can be safely recognised. By contrast, when women name themselves as women, and insist on the right to name their interests as women, this is viewed as 'dangerous incitement' (1993: 880). This suggests not only that the articulation of distinct gender interests by women is considered dangerous to the stability of community identities, but also that women's access to an individual sense of self is seen as threatening.

Uma Chakravarti also analyses the place of the powerful Hindu woman in myth and literature. She argues that, in these narratives, women may be invested with the power to preserve and regenerate the nation or the community, but that power often depends on a simultaneous obliteration of the self (Chakravarti 1983: 73).

Problematic bodies

That it is a specifically female self that needs to be obliterated is suggested also when the female body is viewed as something to be overcome if women are to be recognised as agents. Amrita Basu, for example, notes that the three most powerful female orators of contemporary Hindu nationalism, Vijayraje Scindia, Uma Bharati and Sadhvi Rithambara, are all celibate and promote their chastity publicly in order to heighten their iconic status and present themselves as pure representatives of community spirituality (Basu 1995: 161). Scindia is a widow, and therefore marked as past the dangers of sexuality, Bharati and Rithambara both wear the orange robes of the Hindu *sanyasin* (renouncer). Thus they draw on a well-established narrative in both Hindu metaphysics and mythology, and its appropriations by the anti-colonial nationalist movement, of the Hindu woman who becomes heroic by sublimating herself and transcending her sexuality (Chakravarti, personal interview 1995).

Uma Chakravarti provides an example of this narrative persisting even within oppositional discourses in her 1989 article 'The World of the Bhaktin in South Indian Traditions – The Body and Beyond'. The *bhakti* movement, which began in south India in the sixth century AD, developed as a counter-tradition to the highly hierarchical ritual order of Brahmanical Hinduism. It asserted that all souls were equal before god, that self-realisation was accessible to even the lowliest of persons (including women), and that this could be accomplished, without the medium of a priestly class, through individual devotion to a personal god (Kishwar 1989: 3–8).

Chakravarti looks at the legends that have emerged around the lives of four sixth–twelfth-century women saints within the *bhakti* tradition in south India, and at their poetry. She considers both the space this tradition provided for these particular women to expand their own selfhood, and the manner in which the female body shaped or impinged upon their sense of identity as agents. In each of the cases Chakravarti examines, the woman must in some way deny her specifically female body in order to attain that sense of complete selfhood which is expressed as union with a personal god, and which gives her the right to act as a subject-agent: to teach, to formulate a code of ethics, to assume a social position of authority over men (Chakravarti 1989: 24).[1]

One, Avvaiyar, passes over the stage of female fertility by being transformed into an old woman. The second, Karaikalammaiyar, gives up the female form altogether to be turned into a monster. A third, Andal, refuses to marry any living man, and is absorbed into a stone replica of the god Vishnu when married to him. The fourth, Akka Mahadevi, follows a more complicated trajectory. Rejecting her earthly husband, she throws away her clothes and uses her nakedness to defy the earthly norms imposed on her sexuality that signify the female body as vulnerable. Of the four, Chakravarti argues, only Akka Mahadevi works her way towards complete selfhood from within the female body, approaching her god, not as a domesticated wife but as a more equal lover. Yet she too is, in the legends, finally absorbed into the image of her god (1989: 19–27).

Chakravarti notes that these myths offer women a different ideal for living than that offered *bhakti* men. On the social level, women had to choose either marriage and the household, or devotion to a personal god (1989: 23). By contrast, the male sage-poet could rely on the unqualified devotion of a wife to do the 'body work' for him (1989: 21) while he acted as a social and ethical agent in the world. On the symbolic level, *bhakti* men are portrayed as achieving union with their god at a metaphoric level; it is a metaphysical union which leaves the body intact. For these women, the union is much more explicit in requiring a sacrifice of bodily existence (1989: 28). Thus, despite the increased space afforded these women within the *bhakti* tradition as social and ethical-religious agents, they are still working within a model of selfhood that takes the male body as norm, and for which the female body is a problem to be overcome.

If we recall the Indian feminist material discussed in Chapter 1 on how the female body becomes a useful body to identity-constitution processes, we can see why the notion of a female embodied agent-self becomes so problematic. As we saw in Chapter 1, the female capacity for birth, and the privileged access to origins this represents, are repeatedly appropriated within narratives of community identities. But they are appropriated as the site of pure origin, as timeless tradition, as the fixed place of 'home'. The female body is a highly useful body to these 'games of truth', but its usefulness requires that this body 'stays put'. The mobility required of the individual self as agent does not fit with the kind of work women and women's bodies are being asked to do within these discursive frames.

Women and/as citizens

Another way of looking at this dissonance between women as agents and the 'body work' they are being asked to do is through women's problematic relationship to the concept of citizen. Vasanth Kannabiran and Kalpana Kannabiran, for example, have argued that while men become citizens and claim democratic rights in the public space of modern civil society, they still depend for their identity on a sense of rootedness in older forms of community, which, in modern India, tend to centre on the family and what they call a 'religio-cultural fringe'. Maintaining the stability of these older forms of community is seen as the primary responsibility of women (Kannabiran and Kannabiran 1995: 124–5). A tension is therefore set up between women's identity in/as the closed and stable space of community and their demands for democratic rights as citizens in the open-ended space of civil society.

Similarly, Mrinalini Sinha has argued that the modern community of the nation represents its constituents as citizens, that is as abstract individuals not bound by a particular family, religious or community group (Sinha 1995: 49). But the modern nation continues to legitimise itself by appropriating to itself the particularism of pre-modern, 'organic' ties like the family, caste and religion (1995: 50). An uneasy relationship is thus sustained between the supposedly 'free' individual-citizen of the public domain of civil society, and a private domain of sexualised, racialised, and class subjects (1995: 49).

The move which Sinha does not make, but which is strongly suggested by the preceding discussion, is to consider how men and women might be differently located within this model of the citizen's relationship to national and other community identities. If, as we have seen, women are often called upon to serve as key markers of both the nation and the 'pre-modern' or 'private' categories that Sinha says are still being accommodated and reconstituted within conditions of modernity, it becomes more difficult for their claim to the status of unbound individual-citizen to be acknowledged.

If the issue of personal laws and a uniform civil code discussed in Chapter 1 is placed in this theoretical context, we can see why it has become a focus of such intense contestation. If, as Hasan has argued, in the context of communal conflict, personal laws and the normative 'Woman' they produce can come to bear the symbolic weight for a community's united identity (Hasan 1994b: 61), then a community which perceives itself as beleaguered will insist even more on the fixity of 'Woman' as its protective border. This strengthens the hand of fundamentalism and attempts to project a homogeneous narrative of community identity that, as in the Shah Bano case, places further constraints on that community's women.

However, as we have seen, community identities are not just imposed on women; women help to constitute them in turn. There is no simple way of separating women's identity 'as women' from their location in specific communities. Therefore, simply opposing the personal laws in the name of a generic category of 'women's interests' covers over the differences between women. In the context of unequal power relations between majority Hindus and minority Muslims (and other religious groups), treating all women the same in the name of equality can result in treating minority communities like the Hindu community. This would have the effect of subordinating them to Hindu norms and practices.

It is in precisely this way that the Hindu right can support a uniform civil code, couching their project in the language of equal rights (Kapur and Cossman 1995: 101). But when feminists do not take seriously the interdependence of gender and specific community identities, they too have been complicit in this kind of hegemonising move, both by relying on exclusively Hindu cultural images in their counter-narratives of Indian women, and by positing a pure gender unity outside the context of specific community differences (Agnes 1995: 139–54).

One result of attempting to negotiate this conceptual minefield has been, for some Indian feminists, to focus on the concept of citizenship that underpins the question of a uniform civil code. Without going into all the details of the different positions on the civil code that have emerged – for these are beyond the constraints of this project – I want to point to some of the productive complications this debate has generated. These complications take the form more of questions than of firm answers at this stage, but they are questions that may also be pertinent to feminists outside the particular conditions of contemporary Indian politics.

At issue in these debates is the conflict posed for women between attempts to fix singular birth-bound identities on and through their persons, and their access to the more fluid and multi-layered space of civil society (Menon and Butalia, personal interviews 1995). The challenge posed by an egalitarian civil code is to find ways of insisting on the same recognition of complexity for women as might be available for men. All citizens need the space in which to negotiate between the 'personal' and the many layers of the 'public' realm, and an egalitarian civil code is one way of acknowledging that space.

This would not free women from the need to negotiate their way through the complex networks of power relations in society, any more than it would free men, who are also differentially located within those power relations. Women in different communities would still need to struggle with men regarding those traditions that subordinate women, and that are encoded in the personal laws (Chakravarti, personal interview 1995). But the demand for an egalitarian civil code can become a site for demanding the same 'privilege' of complex subjectivity for women as for men (Mani 1992: 397). It raises the question of how legal definitions of women might start from an assumption of social heterogeneity rather than the singular fixities of birth-bound identities (Sangari, personal interview 1995). Ultimately, it foregrounds the questions of women's access to the status of 'citizen' and of their role in redefining concepts of citizenship. I will return to this point in Chapter 8.

Collective identities and models of the self

The tension between moves to fix 'Woman' as the ground of community identities, and the mobility required of women as agents, has also led some Indian feminists to rethink the relationship between the individual self and collective identities. Some of them start from the assumption that, if the individual subject-as-agent model on offer proves problematic for women, then perhaps the solution is to rethink identity and agency in terms of collectivity.

Rethinking the collective

Sikata Bannerjee, for example, in reflecting on the dangerous attractions of communalist discourse to provide a sense of belonging to women, argues that feminism needs to offer women an alternative but equally compelling sense of collective identity (Bannerjee 1995: 228–9). Seemanthini Niranjana has suggested that the concept of the individual self is fundamentally a Western imposition, at odds with Indian metaphysical preferences for a more relational model of agency and subjectivity (Niranjana 1994b: 32).

For Rajeswari Sunder Rajan some concept of the collective subject is one of the necessary moves feminism must make if it is to break out of the impasse of viewing the subject of feminism as either the powerless subaltern woman-as-victim or the powerful individual modelled on hegemonic paradigms of agency (Sunder Rajan 1993: 119–20). Sunder Rajan argues that the postmodern move to decentre the autonomous subject of Western modernity needs to be accompanied by an attention to the role of solidarity and collectivity in forming subjectivities, an attention we can draw out of the Marxian tradition (1993: 120).

While not wanting to simplistically over-idealise collective life, nor to lock concepts of collective praxis into Marxist paradigms of social change, Sunder Rajan argues that models of collective social agency and leadership should be reclaimed for feminism. She points to examples of all-women village-governing bodies in certain parts of India, which, in admittedly modest ways, are both changing the political agenda in gender-specific ways and altering models of agency-leadership (1993: 122).

Ania Loomba has also argued that feminists need to frame the question of agency in terms of collective subjectivity, although her reasons for doing so are somewhat different from Bannerjee's, Niranjana's or Sunder Rajan's (Loomba 1993: 220). Loomba wants to stress a notion of a collective subject, first, as a way of getting beyond the constraints of framing agency in terms of individual will alone. So, for example, contemporary episodes of *sati* – which are often discussed only in terms of their voluntary nature – need to be connected to the politics of the community and the nation, and to the articulations of gender within each of them. They need to be seen as part of a context in which various types of violent and oppressive practices have been constructed as questions of female choice; these include dowry murders interpreted as suicide and the disproportionate abortion of female foetuses read simply as expressions of the mother's choice (1993: 221–2).

But, second, Loomba wants to focus on the notion of a collective subject in order to denaturalise it; it is important that feminists, as an organised political movement intervening 'for' women, do not take their right to represent women as an unproblematic given, but rather reflect on the nature and limits of the collective subjects they construct. Collective female agency is, for her, 'wrought out of precariously achieved political intervention' (1993: 222).

Loomba's reflections on the potential dangers of an unproblematised celebration of collective identity are particularly pertinent given the ways in which notions of collectivity inform communal politics. As we have already seen, the Hindu right offers a version of collective identity that is underpinned by an obliteration of the individual self, and this is particularly dangerous for the women who have to 'stand for' that community. Sarkar argues that, in a number of Hindu communalist narratives, theories of individual rights are characterised as the alien and alienating effects of colonialism, and are counterposed to 'traditional' notions of community obligations and mutuality. An indigenist reasoning is then used to oppose notions of civil liberties, democratic rights, social equality and gender justice (Sarkar 1995: 213–14). Without a concept of the individual self, and an attendant theory of individual rights, it becomes difficult to counter the homogenising and hegemonising imperatives of such a version of the collective (Sarkar, personal interview 1995).

More generally, given the ways in which the stability of national, racialised and other community identities seem to depend on a conflation of 'Woman/women' with community, and on the disallowing of a specifically female self, it seems important that feminists insist on holding on to some concept of the individual self for women. At the same time, and for the same reasons, it seems important that this model of the self proceeds on a different basis, one that will not posit the female body as a problem to be overcome, but which also resists yet another variation on the models of purity which have proved so problematic for women. One way of doing this is, as I discussed above, to rethink the individual self-as-citizen, and to insist that women have access to this complex, mobile and 'impure' subject-position, rather than remain fixed in/as the pure space of community identities. Another source for such alternative models of the self is to re-work the impure spaces assigned to 'women' in contemporary cultural forms. I want to conclude this chapter by looking at a speculative experiment in tracing the contours of an alternative model of an impure, female self from one of these cultural spaces.

A female self?

Vidya Rao offers an intriguing glimpse of an alternative model of the self, based on a morphology of the specifically female body, in her 1990 article '*Thumri* as Feminine Voice'. *Thumri* is a small, intimate form of singing, with an erotic or romantic content, generally written by men and performed by women for men. For Rao, therefore, it is constructed in the male gaze, and articulates female desire as patriarchally constructed (Rao 1990: WS31).

Nevertheless Rao will argue that *thumri* contains a subversive edge, to be found in its structure and form, which defy easy classification by the predominant norms of traditional Indian music, and which can be read as specifically 'feminine' (1990: WS32). I understand Rao to be referring here to a 'feminine' which cannot be fully contained within a patriarchal order and which thereby contests that order. If the following summary of Rao's description of *thumri* is fairly detailed, it is not because I wish to defend her interpretation as definitive (I am in no position to make this kind of judgement) but because I am interested in the language she uses, in what she, as a feminist working in a context which is not my own, is looking for as a specifically female voice.

Rao begins with notions of space within the *thumri* form, and what would appear to conform with traditionally feminine allocations of space in society; she describes it as working on a small canvas, with a limited repertoire of tunes and lyrics, a smaller number of notes than in the regular scale, performed in an enclosed space, with singer and listener in close proximity. But then she points to uses of space which contest this sense of enclosure: the music expands the space available to it, not linearly but laterally, not outwards but inwards, 'relentlessly questioning the established and accepted structures of music' (1990: WS32). It both shares and subverts the consensus of ideas about what is and is not musical (1990: WS32), suggesting, if music is a form of language, a space both in and not-in a particular discursive frame.

For Rao, *thumri* does this in a number of specific ways. It multiplies the forms of improvisation available to the singer, increasing the number and modes of acceptable points of departure from the 'text', so that 'all meanings exist together, reflect each other, create further meanings' (1990: WS33). The singer uses vocal texturings to create different voices within a piece, repeating lines in different voices, or with a different stress, or both combined, in order to multiply both space and meaning, thereby creating a drama which moves away from simple first-person narrative to a dramatic narrative with multiple viewpoints (1990: WS33–4).

Other texts are inserted into the body of the main song as quotations, thus playing with notions of ambiguity and certainties of meaning (1990: WS34). This is not done according to the conventions of classical Indian music, in which two songs are combined to create a third, or in which one distinct melody follows another. Rather, 'the points of weakness – the margins and boundaries – in the *raga*'s structure are used as points at which other *ragas* are allowed to enter into the 'body' of the main *raga*' (1990: WS35). For Rao, this is done in a playful, humorous spirit of transgressing the boundaries and dangerous thresholds erected to keep pollution at bay.[2]

According to Rao, the listener can be fooled into thinking he is hearing a different scale each time: 'the point is that several scales can and do co-exist at the same time harmoniously – that there is no one truth, each voice speaks it differently but without contradiction' (1990: WS35). This playing with structures suggests an always shifting standpoint, in which the ground, centre or starting point is always changing. *Thumri* laughs ironically at the pedantic differences set up between different *ragas* or forms of music, like 'the foolish third child of the fairy tales, or the trickster'. It is a play of 'traps, rows upon rows of reflecting mirrors', in which all certainties are disordered (1990: WS36).

All this leads Rao to draw links between *thumri*'s form and the female body – an open body, incapable of closure, both always vulnerable to pollution and, at the same time, the source of life and continuity. And this recovered female body and feminine voice, Rao suggests, should lead us to question not just the identity of the individual, but the nature of identity itself. For her, *thumri* suggests a model of identity which does not seek to close the border and guard against transgression, but rather to remain open and vulnerable, and through this, to expand the space available to it, according to its own rules for negotiating those transgressions

(1990: WS37). The self is not dissolved (it has rules, it can negotiate), but neither is it defined by containment or closure.

Rao's feminine voice does seem to speak to the complex location of 'Woman' and 'women' delineated by the Indian feminists I have discussed in Part I. It redefines the self by breaking out of the confined and fixed place of origin or 'home' to travel across the apparent certainties and stabilities of community identities. Yet it also holds on to a sense of locatedness in the impure space of complex power relations.

Reading Rao from the perspective of white Western feminisms, there are also clear resonances between her work and some of the theoretical projects I will be exploring in Part II. The language of non-linear flows and multiplicity in identity, the desire for a position that is both in and not-in a discursive order, the images of mirrors and laughing tricksters will all be revisited – in differing degrees – in the work of Irigaray, Haraway, Butler and Braidotti. What remains to be seen is whether the landscape in which these figurations are located in these Western feminist projects is complex enough to take differences of nation, race and community into account.

In the two chapters of Part I, I have identified four ways in which a critical engagement with Indian feminist scholarship can complicate our theoretical approaches to the question of identity and differences between women:

• first, women play a simultaneously productive and subordinated role in the emergence of multiple categories of social identity, including gender, nation, race and other communities;
• second, women's location within this intersecting landscape of gender, nation, race and community identities is a complex one, that is not easily contained within an exclusion/inclusion binary;
• third, it is not only discursive constructs of the feminine that are important to the emergence of nation, race and community identities – the female body, meanings invested in the specifically female and women's activities also need to be taken into account;
• fourth, destabilising the concept of an individual self may not be sufficient if feminists are to develop models of agency that take women's differences into account – redefining models of the self and its relation to collective identities may also be necessary.

In Part II, I will bring these complications to bear in examining four Western feminist theoretical approaches to identity and evaluating to what degree these approaches keep a space open for considering the differences between women. I begin, in Chapter 3, with the work of Luce Irigaray.

White Western feminisms and identity

Luce/loose connections

Luce Irigaray, sexual difference, race and nation

At first sight, the theoretical project of Luce Irigaray is a difficult place to look for ways to open up the space within feminist theory for consideration of the differences between women. A feminism of sexual difference suggests an in-built hierarchy of differences, an irreducible privilege being accorded to the question of sexual difference as 'the issue of our age' (Irigaray 1984: 5). Irigaray has little to say herself about the differences race and nation may make, and some of the few references she has made to these issues are, as we shall see, problematic. To date, there has been little discussion within feminist theory of the problems and possibilities of bringing issues of race and nation into a sexual difference framework. Rosi Braidotti's attempt to open up a space for these issues will be explored in detail in Chapter 5. In the next chapter, I will look at Judith Butler's work in *Bodies that Matter* (1993a) to bring questions of race into conversation with both Irigaray and Lacan. But in general, engagements with sexual difference feminism have tended either to ignore the questions of race and nation, or simply to note that their absence within the framework is a problem that will need further exploration (but not in the article or book in question). Tina Chanter has made the stronger claim that Irigaray's project to think otherness 'otherwise' (Chanter 1995: 176) actually opens up a space for considering other differences such as race (1995: 126), although, as we shall see, there are problems with the way she develops this argument, and it remains a very small part of her overall consideration of Irigaray's work.

In this chapter, I want to explore some of the problems that Irigaray's theoretical framework creates by insisting on an absolute privileging of sexual difference. But I also want to argue that some of the issues and theoretical moves that she has had a major part in bringing onto the Western feminist theoretical agenda have their parallels in certain developments in postcolonial feminisms, and that these resonances can suggest productive directions for thinking about 'women' while attending to differences such as race and nation. As this chapter's title suggests, however, these aspects of Irigaray's work need to be 'shaken loose' from the sexual difference framework in which they are anchored.

I will look at these two aspects of Irigaray's project through three points. First, I discuss the relationship between sexual difference and other differences in her overall theoretical framework. Second, I look at her explorations of 'Woman' and 'women' as the outside and ground of male-centred theory and of an 'economy of the same', focusing on her early work in *Speculum of the Other Woman* (1974) and *This Sex Which is Not One* (1977). I concentrate especially on Irigaray's discussions of how an economy of the same relies on masculine appropriations of the female capacity of birth and, through it, of access to origins. Third, I examine Irigaray's discussions of alterity and the need for an 'economy of the interval', looking especially at her work in *Speculum* and *An Ethics of Sexual Difference* (1984). In this context I consider the alternative model of the self that emerges from her work, and what possibilities this model of the self offers for feminist politics.

Sexual difference and other differences

Tina Chanter has argued that, far from closing down considerations of the differences between women, Irigaray's feminism of sexual difference offers a new way of bringing these differences into feminism. At the outset of her book *Ethics of Eros*, Chanter claims that 'Irigaray's questioning of sexual difference, rather than precluding serious consideration of other differences, requires that they be taken into account' (Chanter 1995: 8). According to Chanter, this is because of the way Irigaray approaches the question of sexual difference; by insisting on the need for radical alterity, to think otherness 'otherwise', Irigaray is pointing to the need to develop models of self–other relations that go beyond the prevailing Western model of an 'economy of the same', in which difference is always cast as the poor cousin of sameness (1995: 11–12). Thus, Chanter argues, Irigaray's model can move beyond the question of sexual difference because it recognises 'the importance of specifying multiple ways of existing in a society' (1995: 126).

In support of this view, Chanter points to Irigaray's refusal, from her earliest works, to close down definitions of 'what it means to be a woman', or to determine the 'truth' of the feminine. She cites those passages in *This Sex*, where Irigaray emphasises that each woman's struggle will be different, and will depend on which form of oppression is 'for her most immediately unbearable', and distances herself from attempts by the Women's Liberation Movement to 'condemn women who might have immediate objectives that differ from theirs' (Irigaray 1977: 166–7 quoted in Chanter 1995: 175).

On one level, I would agree with Chanter's argument. Irigaray's exposure of the economy of the same, and her insistence that difference can and must be thought within another model of self–other relations, does provide feminism with an important insight on which to build models that approach the differences between women as a positivity to be explored, rather than a problem to be overcome. But I would also argue that Irigaray has not, herself, provided those models, nor can she as long as sexual difference remains her privileged entry point to the question of sameness and difference.

In support of her argument, Chanter notes a number of places where Irigaray refers to questions of race, but if we actually look closely at what Irigaray is saying in these passages, we see that she is not actually saying very much – and that this is more an exercise in 'spotting the word race' than in serious analysis. For example, Chanter quotes Irigaray's comment in *Je, Tu, Nous* (1990), that 'sexism is the most unconscious form of racism' (1995: 302 fn 8). But why should sexism be an unconscious form of racism? Why unconscious? What does this really mean? Is it enough, or even necessarily appropriate, to simply draw analogies between the two forms of oppression? In this context, we might remember Irigaray's own critique of Freud's use of analogy as the 'time-honoured device' of an economy of the same (Irigaray 1977: 72). Taking seriously into account the differences between women must mean more than making a few undeveloped links between racism and sexism; it means actually spending the time working out how race and sex might be interconnected in an economy of the same. But Irigaray spends all her time looking for, and working out that economy in relation to sexual difference alone.

Joanna Hodge takes a slightly different approach to Irigaray's handling of the relationship between sexual difference and other differences, but ends up in a very similar space to Chanter. Hodge argues that for Irigaray, the parameters of the Western philosophical tradition, what it includes and excludes as its 'proper' field of investigation, are determined by its founding gesture of matricide (Hodge 1994: 194). By contesting this 'originary matricide', Hodge suggests, Irigaray is opening up lines of possibility that philosophy has closed down:

> Once the figures of the other/woman and of the mother have ceased to be the hidden other, some further layer of conceal-ment in the text of European culture can perhaps be uncovered: perhaps the questions of race, imperialism, neocolonialism, indeed of being European.
>
> (1994: 207)

But what Hodge's argument makes even clearer than Chanter's is the hierarchy of differences underpinning the Irigarayan project – first we need to uncover the figures of woman/mother, then we can move on to other differences. If sexual difference is 'originary', are other differences derivative? And if other differences derive from sexual difference, then there always remains the suggestion that they can be subsumed within sexual difference, and need not be taken into account in terms of their own complexities and role in constituting bodies, knowledges and subjectivities.

In the next section, I will be arguing that Irigaray's focus on the exclusion of the maternal and the specifically female can be made to open a space for considering differences between women. But I want to note here that this will not be achieved by leaving a hierarchy of differences intact, in which sexual difference (or gender) is tackled first, with other differences to follow, a strategy which both Hodge and Chanter seem to leave unchallenged. While Irigaray rarely addresses this strategic question directly, her later work suggests that she does adopt such a hierarchy of differences. For example, in *Thinking the Difference*, Irigaray seems to suggest that, while the struggles of other minorities remain within the limits of the dialectical logic of patriarchy, women alone can, to some extent, stand outside this logic (Irigaray 1989: 6). While she does not take this analysis very far, it remains a problematic assumption that separates the struggles of (undifferentiated) women out from other struggles against oppression, and invests these women's struggles with inherently superior transformative possibilities.

It remains unclear to what degree Irigaray is conscious of the ethno-specificity of her own project, as speaking to a white Western tradition and counter-tradition. On the one hand, in articles like 'The Poverty of Psychoanalysis' (in Whitford 1991a), Irigaray is scathing in her critique of the 'gentlemen psychoanalysts' of the Lacanian school who deny the cultural and historical specificity of both their theory and practice, and who claim for it the status of universal truth (Whitford 1991a: 80). She rejects their attempts to define the symbolic as a 'universal innocent of any empirical or historical contingency' and instead argues that it is their fantasies which 'lay down the law', their 'imaginary transformed into an order, into the social' (1991a: 94). To the extent that Irigaray's project is about subverting and re-working psychoanalysis from within psychoanalysis (Whitford 1991a: 5), then she, too, must be bound by the cultural and historical locatedness she wants its theoreticians and practitioners to acknowledge.

On the other hand, Irigaray's work displays at times a lack of vigilance regarding both offensively racialised remarks and the pitfalls of an orientalist reading of the East as exotic other. For example, in recounting the myth of Kore/Persephone, she refers twice to Hades as 'the black man all little girls fear', without feeling the need to comment on the racist genealogy of such a statement (Irigaray 1989: 104). In the same text, she projects a version of India which seems to derive more from her need to construct an other for the West, and its refusal to allow women access to the divine, than from any serious investigation of that culture's complexities. India here is reduced to the function of counterpoint to the West, and is simply affirmed as a place where sexuality is sacred; where women's divinity is recognised; where the mother–daughter couple is accorded a symbolic relation to the divine; and where women's relation to time and memory is valorised (1989: 11–13). Not surprisingly, Irigaray reaches these highly simplistic conclusions without any reference to the work of Indian feminists.

More fundamentally perhaps, there remains the question of how deeply Eurocentric Irigaray's project is in terms of its intense dialogue with, and embeddedness within, an exclusively European narrative of the history of European philosophy; no voice from outside that tradition gets a look in within her project. I see this as a problem in two registers: first, it relates to questions of style and the accessibility of feminist theory to feminism as a political project; second, there is the problem of uncritically inheriting a Western narrative of 'the West' in which race has been written out.

Irigaray's style of refusing to 'mark off' the references to the words of other philosophers in her own texts with the familiar conventions of references, quotation marks or footnotes, is part of a strategy she shares with other poststructuralist philosophers. One purpose of this strategy is to subvert the claims to authority and impartiality that such conventions represent, and so keep the text contestable and open-ended (Hodge 1994: 200). The problem is that the game of contesting authority can only be played once one is familiar enough with the authorities, and this requires a considerable engagement with a particular tradition of continental European philosophy on the part of the reader. Doing theory in this way means cutting oneself off from the large number of people in the world who will not (or cannot) make the necessary investment of time and effort that would be required to get 'inside the frame' and understand *what* is going on. Only then can one begin to form an opinion about *how* it might help feminism's political project of change. The open-endedness and contestability of the text only work, to a certain extent, from within the boundaries of the Western philosophical tradition. The boundaries themselves – and especially the exclusions of the non-West, the non-European, that are part of their constitution – are not seriously troubled by such a textual strategy.

Here, the question of style merges with the second register of exclusion. Theorists like Said (1978) and Gilroy (1993) have argued that orientalism and racism must be seen as not merely accompanying certain periods of European history, but rather as part of the constitutive ground of modern Western European thought. Work like Martin Bernal's *Black Athena* (1987) suggests some of the ways in which exclusions of Africa and blackness might lie at the heart of those modern philosophical narratives which construct a purely European Greece as their point of origin.

Whatever the strengths and weaknesses of such arguments, which cannot be my focus here, the work of postcolonial theorists clearly suggests that the boundaries of what constitutes Western European thought need to be troubled, even by those whose principal target of investigation lies within those boundaries.[1] In the case of Irigaray, for example, I think it needs to be acknowledged that the privileging of sexual difference that she takes as her starting point leaves untroubled a specifically European narrative of how subjectivity is constituted. To what degree is her strong claim that sexual difference is *the* issue of our age and that *the* originary crime is matricide, a function of the success with which other constitutive exclusions have been covered over? If, as a number of theorists have argued, 'whiteness' and 'Westernness' function as norms principally through their invisibility (hooks 1992a; Frankenberg 1993; Dyer 1997), we need to ask if Irigaray is not perpetuating the erasure of race by insisting on an exclusive focus on sexual difference.

Ironically, some of the ways in which Irigaray works with the word 'white' (*blanc* in French) are very evocative of recent theoretical discussions of whiteness, and could have given her an entry point to a more direct and productive consideration of race within her overall project. In playing with the homonyms *sang blanc* (white blood) and *semblant* (semblance/same), and by contrasting the *sang blanc* with the red blood of female birth and menstruation, Irigaray enlists whiteness to the cause of a masculine economy of the same (Irigaray 1974: 220–2). In the triumph of white over red blood, whiteness is associated with death:

Blood is burned to cinders in the writing of the text of law whereby man produces (himself) at the same time (as) the double [...] and the color of blood fades as more and more semblances are produced, more atoms of individual egos, all bloodless in different ways. In this process, some substance is lost: blood in its constitution of a living autonomous subjectivity.

(Irigaray 1974: 221–2)

Linking whiteness to the draining/fading of colour and to death is evocative of bell hooks' discussion of representations of whiteness in the black imagination. For hooks, both the experience and writing of American blacks provide powerful evidence of the ways in which an absence of colour can signify not the benign invisibility white people so often accord their own whiteness, but rather the presence of terror and the possibility of death (hooks 1992a: 341–2, 344–5; Dyer 1993).

Without making any explicit connections between race and the economy of the same, Irigaray evokes whiteness both in contexts where sameness is achieved through a violent silencing of difference, and where its association with truth is achieved through its invisibility. So, for example, in the chapter 'Volume without Contours' in *Speculum*, Irigaray speaks of the 'still immaculate white spaces' that remain after Woman has been 'devoured and torn apart inside' (Whitford 1991a: 54).[2] Furthermore, in her re-reading of Plato's myth of the cave, Irigaray emphasises the '*white* light that cannot be seen as such but allows us to see and gives us an awareness of the black' (Irigaray 1974: 258, emphasis in the original). For Plato himself the sun and light stood for truth; Irigaray's linking of this 'truth' to an invisible whiteness suggests a resonance with theoretical discussions of 'whiteness' as the unmarked norm against which difference is constituted. Ultimately, however, these remain intriguing suggestions of where Irigaray might have complicated her understanding of the economy of the same by considering race, and she does not allow them to distract her from her primary focus on sexual difference.

We also need to ask how critical Irigaray is of the universalising aspects of the poststructuralist model of language that underpins the Lacanian narrative of subjectivity. This narrative's focus on Language as a system (*langue*), rather than on languages or on cultural and historical specificities, carries a powerful universalising charge that suggests that there is only ever one way for the human to come into language and subjectivity. Irigaray complicates this model by specifying that what Language as a system particularly requires is the exclusion of the feminine and the female. She also goes beyond a single language model when she suggests that there can and must be two ways for the human to become subject and that we need two symbolics – the 'masculine' and the 'feminine'.

As I will discuss further in the final section of this chapter, Irigaray also unsettles the model of a univocal Language by insisting on the possibility and presence of those subversive incursions when women 'speak (as) woman'. But the absolute privileging of sexual difference in this model of language makes it difficult not to hear only an unspecified woman, undifferentiated by race, nation and other specific locations, speaking (as) woman. The move from one to two symbolics, using only the axis of sexual difference to differentiate them, also strongly suggests a universalised female/feminine that embraces all the differences between women within a closed system.

For all these reasons, I would argue that there are significant problems with the view that Irigaray's framework is one that opens up space for considering other differences. But the resonances with the postcolonial mode remain, ironically, at the level of particular theoretical moves within the overall framework. I believe that it is more productive to look at these individual moves for what Irigaray can bring to feminist theoretical attempts to sustain a dual focus on women and their differences.

An economy of the same and the 'still silent ground' of theory

In a 1995 interview, Luce Irigaray discussed some of the differences between her project and that of Simone de Beauvoir. Her focus is on their differing attitudes to the question of 'the other':

> Simone de Beauvoir refused to be the Other because she refused to be second in Western culture. [...] What I myself say is that there is no true Other in Western culture and that what I want – certainly I don't want to be second – but I want there to be two subjects.
>
> (Hirsch and Olson 1995: 99)

For Irigaray, the strategy is not to overcome otherness as it might be defined within the terms of an already existing system, but to 'demand to be radically Other in order to exit from a horizon' (1995: 114) that she defines as an economy of the same.

De Beauvoir's characterisation of Woman-as-Other in *The Second Sex* (1949) remains tremendously influential for feminist theory in both Western and non-Western settings. Unlike Irigaray, she also does try to make links between women's and other 'othering' processes, to suggest how sexual and racial economies might be connected, although this work is not without its critics.[3] But I will argue in this section that it is Irigaray's departure from the Woman-as-Other model, and her delineation of 'Woman' and 'women's' positioning within an economy of the same, that produces unexpected openings to conversations in a postcolonial mode.

Irigaray shares the idea of an economy of the same with Derrida, who uses it to expose the exclusionary processes at work in language, and by extension the Western metaphysics limited by that language (e.g. 'Différance' in Kamuf 1991: 70). But while for Derrida the economy of the same is principally an effect in/of language, where the *'féminin'* is another name for the disruptive potential of *différance*, for Irigaray it is an economy in which real women are constrained by their symbolic exclusion and reduction to a 'specular feminine' defined by a masculine subject.

As Margaret Whitford explains, Irigaray asks us to 'look for the resistances and defences which conceal the original crime of matricide [...] to look for the specular relationship, to uncover the buried mother' (Whitford 1991b: 34). Irigaray moves beyond de Beauvoir's insight, now taken as almost a commonplace within feminism, that woman is constituted as man's other – the weak pole of the binary. Instead, Irigaray argues that woman is not just marginalised or made secondary within Western philosophical thought, but is made to disappear altogether. Her exclusion from the world of meaning and from the social contract fashioned out of that world of meaning, is the *necessary condition* for philosophy and the worlds we build with philosophy.

Just as the child, in the Lacanian framework, must exclude the mother to take its place in the world of signification as a subject, Western philosophy begins by placing woman outside the frame of reference altogether: this is the crime of matricide to which Whitford refers. The woman that exists within the frame – the weak side of the binary – is defined by and for man, his own poor reflection in a mirror: this is the specular relationship Whitford discusses. This is why Irigaray names both patriarchal society and phallocentric thought as an 'economy of the same' or as 'hom(m)osexuality'. The woman within the frame is always a woman defined by the needs, values and desires of man. Men are always speaking about men, even when they are speaking about women. Putting these two moves together, Irigaray then looks for the ways in which woman constitutes the excluded but necessary ground upon which the male speaking-subject stands in order to make sense of, and act upon, the world, the 'mute outside that sustains all systematicity [...] [the] maternal and still silent ground that nourishes all foundations' (Irigaray 1974: 365).

Derrida's work to trouble the economy of the same in language has been picked up and developed within a particular strand of postcolonial and black theory.[4] Perhaps ironically, Irigaray's feminist take on this 'mode of semblance', with its sharper political edge of insisting on women's material (bodily) specificity and on both symbolic and strategic exclusions of 'Woman' and 'women', has been much less discussed in relation to postcolonial feminisms.

In part, this is probably a reflection of the problems of exclusion discussed above, in the sense that the conversations Irigaray has engaged in in her work are so intensely centred in the West and in a particular tradition of Western philosophy (although the same could certainly be applied to Derrida). In part, it is probably also due to the politics of publishing practices, so that what is most easily available to feminist intellectuals outside the West is still the earliest Anglo-American reception and interpretation of a very partial selection of Irigaray's early work.[5] And yet, despite the fact that neither side seems to be speaking directly to the other, in reading both Irigaray and a variety of postcolonial feminists for this project, I hear a conversation in progress. And it is particularly around Irigaray's mapping of the specular economy that the resonances occur. I want to suggest three sites on the Irigarayan map that can also be re-located in a postcolonial space.

Woman as ground for debates among men

In naming the specular economy as hom(m)osexual, Irigaray extends and enriches our understanding of the 'exchange of women' as a founding point of human society. 'Woman' becomes the ground for all kinds of debates and exchanges among men, the ground upon which men gain access to, and define, their truths. Women's subordination, then, comes not only from finding themselves on the weaker, losing side of the dialectic, but from being outside the field of play altogether:

> What the anthropologist calls the passage from nature to culture thus amounts to the institution of the reign of hom(m)osexuality. [...] From this point on, patriarchal societies might be interpreted as societies functioning in the mode of 'semblance'.
>
> (Irigaray 1977: 171)

> Hom(m)m-osexuality is played out through the bodies of women, matter, or sign, and heterosexuality has been up to now just an alibi for the smooth workings of man's relations with himself, of relations among men.
>
> (Irigaray 1977: 172)

As I argued in Part I, locating 'Woman' and 'women', and especially the 'bodies of women [as] matter or sign', as the ground for exchanges between men, is a recurring theme for a variety of Indian feminists when looking at the ways 'Woman' and 'women' circulate across the categories of sex/gender, race, nation and community. Lata Mani's formulation of women's location within the official discourse on *sati* in nineteenth-century India as 'neither subject, nor object, but ground'(Mani 1990: 118) is a particularly clear expression of the resonance that exists between Irigaray's work on this question and a number of the Indian feminists I have already discussed.

However, as I also discussed in Part I, there remains the question of whether this characterisation of woman as ground does not lead to an over-emphasis on women as excluded, passive and absent, and whether this in turn, by reducing the complexity of women's symbolic and strategic locations to a single move, does not end up covering over differences between women. The work of Paola Bacchetta, an Italian feminist who has spent several years researching in India, is an interesting example of the resonances between Irigaray's work and the concerns of a number of Indian feminists, as well as the potential problems of adopting an Irigarayan approach.

Bacchetta's work has focused on the relationship between women and particular organisations of the Hindu right, and on representations of Muslim women in Hindu communalist discourse. Bacchetta draws frequently on Irigaray in developing her conceptual framework to argue that Hindu communalist discourse positions both Hindu and Muslim women, in different ways, as the excluded ground of a hom(m)osocial project concerned with the production of an ideal Hindu male identity (Bacchetta 1994a: 191–6, 221 fn 46).

But, like those Indian feminists discussed in Part I who rely on poststructuralist language models, Bacchetta's stress tends to be only on the way women are made to disappear in this project. Both Hindu and Muslim women are, she claims, absent from the material world as constructed by the discourses of the Hindu right that she examines; in the symbolic realm, Hindu women figure in order to represent idealised Hindu culture, but Muslim women are 'totally invisible' (1994a: 196). Elsewhere, Bacchetta argues that Muslims, and especially Muslim women, stand for that which is 'unrepresentable'; the 'debt that cannot be acknowledged'; a 'screen upon which the fantasy of evil threatening the integrity of the Hindu nation is projected' (Bacchetta 1994b: 154–5 fn 8).

Bacchetta compellingly appropriates recognisably Irigarayan moves in order to shed light on one aspect of the ways in which communalist discourse and practice positions women. But at the same time, her reading of Irigaray seems to leave no space for considering the different ways in which communalism makes Hindu and Muslim women central, both materially and symbolically (see Hasan 1994; Sarkar 1995). Irigaray's 'woman as ground' model, while clearly finding a resonance in the Indian context, needs to be complicated in at least two ways if it is to take into account insights from Indian feminisms. First, the characterisation of 'woman as ground' needs to be supplemented with an understanding that, as Tanika Sarkar has argued, particular women can also be fore-grounded as 'political creatures and agents' (Sarkar 1995: 189) in some forms of community identity politics. The results of this active foregrounding, in Hindu right-wing politics in India or in Christian fundamentalist and 'family values' movements in the West, may be no more desirable to feminism than women's positioning as a 'still, silent ground'. Nevertheless, it needs to be understood in its particularity. Part of that particularity relates to women's positioning across multiple categories of identity, which include, but which cannot be reduced to, sexual difference or gender alone.

Second, Irigaray's 'woman as ground' model can be productively complicated by work such as Uma Chakravarti's exploration of the 'scripting' of India's 'Golden Age' and of the Traditional Hindu Woman who stands as its apparently stable ground (Chakravarti 1990). Work such as this complicates the 'woman as ground' model by pointing to the intersections of gendered, class, race and national interests that contribute to its production. But it also suggests that the 'still, silent ground' is produced over an impure and discontinu-ous field of contestation, in which different agendas, sometimes convergent and sometimes contradictory, meet to produce a temporary and apparent stability. As Chakravarti argues, that apparent stability is only produced by covering over caste, class, religious and other differences between women (1990: 66–76). Irigaray asks, 'If the earth turned and more especially turned upon herself … what would there be to rise up from and exercise his power over? And in?' (Irigaray 1974: 133). One way of meeting that challenge, of highlighting the instability of that ground/earth, is to focus on the discontinuities and differences that have been covered over to produce 'Woman as ground'. This might prove more effective than producing an alternative version of unspecified 'Woman' which rejects her positioning as ground for men, but remains equally silent about those differences. It also draws attention to the multi-vocality within and beneath apparently stable traditions of thought, which can help counter the sometimes overly homogeneous portrait of the history of Western philosophy that Irigaray's model can suggest.[6]

Female birth and origins

The 'mode of semblance' that Irigaray identifies works particularly through the denial of the specifically female nature of birth and the masculine appropriation of access to origins. Throughout *Speculum*, one of Irigaray's concerns is to locate those moments where philosophy 'cuts up and re-works *the subject's links to his archives*. And *to his process/trial of engendering*'; where the subject severs 'the cord' (Irigaray 1974: 182) in order to both deny female birth and to appropriate to himself the creative power of origins. Woman/Mother needs to be fixed as body, as earth or ground, stripped of her creative possibilities, in order to clear a space for the:

> singular subject who is charged with giving birth to the universe all over again, after he has brought himself back into the world in a way that avoids the precariousness of existence as it is usually understood.
>
> (1974: 182)

For the 'great male thinkers' of Western philosophy, it is, according to Irigaray, 'better to work the Earth on the Father's account than to return to it' (1974: 352): 'clearing land that still produces its own fertile growth, that is still virgin of (his) proper names' (1974: 352). For her, this same move recurs through all the philosophical projects she interrogates: 'it is in search of the lost roots of the same that the place is always being ploughed over again in this way' (Whitford 1991a: 54). This recurrent search for the 'lost roots of the same' suggests a dual understanding of the importance of this move to exclude the mother, one which I think touches a theme I discussed in Chapter 1: on the one hand, the recognition of the power of that moment of connection between self and (M)other;

on the other hand, the absolute need to deny the specifically female nature of birth and to subsume that specificity within a regime of sameness. This is the triumph of a 'logos that claims to reduce the power of the maternal back to the same – the Same – in itself and for itself' (1991a: 55).

This is one of the spaces in Irigaray's work where the potential to connect with postcolonial feminist insights is at its strongest. Wherever group or community identities are 'imagined', to use Benedict Anderson's phrase (1991), to be wholly or partly birth-based – and this remains largely the case wherever nations, races, castes and many other forms of community are imagined – then exercising the power to define those identities must, in part at least, pass through both a symbolic and strategic appropriation of birth. As we saw in Chapter 1, Indian feminists have charted such symbolic appropriations of birth through the use of mother goddess/Mother India iconography and imagery in both the nationalist movement of the anti-colonial period and the contemporary Hindu communalist movement. Some interpret this appropriation as providing a passive nurturing ground for a nationalist movement defined largely by and for men (Bagchi 1990; Lakshmi 1990; Sen 1993). Others complicate this analysis by arguing that these identity narratives also draw on the mother as a source of inciting, mobilising power (Sarkar 1995; Sangari 1993; Loomba 1993; Alexander 1989). But both approaches suggest that an active discursive management of the maternal is involved in the constitution of national and community identities. That this appropriation is seen, by at least some Indian feminists, in terms akin to Irigaray's model of a specular economy, is suggested by Kumkum Roy's (1995) and Uma Chakravarti's (1983) discussions of the symbolic distancing of birth from women, discussed in Chapter 1, and by Chakravarti's (1989) and Amrita Basu's (1995) reflections on the ways in which the specifically female body is discursively constituted as a problem for selfhood and agency, discussed in Chapter 2.

This is, therefore, one of the spaces in Irigaray's work where I think it is possible to read her resonance with postcolonial feminist projects in a more nuanced way than Bacchetta does. For Irigaray, the maternal is not only excluded; its potency, its privileged access to origins, is both mobilised and contained through its appropriation by the masculine. The move that Irigaray does not make, unlike those Indian feminists discussed above, is to think about what specific origins, what particular racialised or national community identities, are at stake that require this harnessing of the 'power of the maternal' to a regime of sameness. If her overall framework did not privilege sexual difference over all other differences, she might have made more of her observation in 'Volume without Contours' that the father's appropriated 'wealth [...] can take the form of a family, a horde, a community, a people' (Whitford 1991a: 62), to think about the ways in which other categories of identities ('a community, a people') also work through appropriations of birth.

Woman as place

It is also via this dual understanding – to both mobilise and contain the power of the mother – that Irigaray approaches the question of the relation of 'Woman' to truth within an economy of the same. Woman is the necessary place, or receptacle within which both power and truth reside, the condition for their existence, but without any influence on the form they will take. Man 'continues to feed on her undefinable potency of which *place* would be, some say, the most extraordinary store' (Irigaray 1974: 166). Because Woman constitutes place for the male subject, she cannot take her place as a subject in her own right:

> Woman is still the place, the whole of the place where she cannot appropriate herself as such. Experienced as all-powerful where 'she' is most radically powerless in her indifferentiation. Never here and now because she is that everywhere elsewhere from whence the 'subject' continues to draw his reserves, his resources, yet unable to recognize them/her.
>
> (Whitford 1991a: 53)

This linking of the figure of Woman/mother with the question of place opens Irigaray's project to a key concern within postcolonial feminisms. For example, in exploring the evolution of nationalist discourse in pre-independence India, Samita Sen (1993), Tanika Sarkar (1987) and Ania Loomba (1993) all highlight the nationalist reliance on a feminised concept of home/place as the pure space unsullied by colonial influence. In her examination of the recent rise of the Hindu right, Sarkar sees a similar move to locate norms of Woman and women's activities as the site of resistance to a more generalised 'Western' or 'modern' influence (Sarkar 1995). In these narratives of national, religious or community identities, the Woman/mother stands for the place of authenticity in which an independent self can affirm itself against a variety of alien others. But if Woman is the pure and stable place in which an authentic national, racial or religious self lives, there is no space for female desire, either sexual or political; the self that needs a hiding place, or a ground to stand on, remains stubbornly masculine. On the one hand, the maternal-feminine is invested with certain 'truths' about access to origin, to timeless tradition or to a purity that sustains community identity. On the other hand, men appropriate the right to define those truths, and control access to that origin through controlling the activities of women. While Irigaray's own treatment of 'place' remains unspecified in this respect, this remains a third point on which her specular economy is both reflected and refracted in the work of postcolonial feminists. Again, we also see a nuancing of the position of woman-as-ground, in which Woman does not simply disappear, but is both 'all-powerful' and radically powerless at the same time.

If the different forms of the economy of the same that Irigaray explores in *This Sex* and *Speculum*, and the language that she uses to evoke them, can be heard echoed in very different feminist projects, it is, I think, because Irigaray has identified a process that is also at work outside the frame in which she is looking for it. Irigaray has helped provide feminism with a map and a vocabulary for the process of saming. For her, this map continues to bear the contours of the Lacanian original that she is in the process of re-drafting, in that she continues to privilege questions of sexual difference. Nevertheless, many of the locations of saming that she identifies can, I believe, be usefully re-visited within a landscape complicated by considerations of race and nation. The complications introduced in Part I suggest that 'Woman' can be understood as the necessary but excluded, 'still silent ground', not only for Man's truths about himself as Man, but also for truths about the nation, the race, the community.

Privileging the interval and alternative models of the self

Resonances with Indian feminist projects can also be heard when Irigaray turns to the possibilities of feminist resistance to the 'mode of semblance'. As part of her project to destabilise the economy of the same, and find a space from which women can begin to speak as subjects, Irigaray returns repeatedly to the concept of the interval – the space between self and other and all the binary oppositions around which, in her view, Language as a system is structured. In both *Speculum* and *An Ethics of Sexual Difference*, we can see Irigaray turning to the 'space between' as the space in which difference might be able to exist without being constrained by a logic of binaries. Privileging the interval becomes a way of countering the economy of the same, in which the space of the other is always appropriated or colonised by the One.

In her re-reading of Plato's myth of the cave in *Speculum*, Irigaray says that Plato's account leads the reader to forget two things. The first is the cave itself, and its connections to the womb, earth and matter. This founding myth of Western metaphysics is, therefore, based on the exclusion of the mother-womb-ground (Irigaray 1974: 243–4). The second thing that is forgotten is the passage between the prisoners and the men casting their shadows upon the back wall of the cave. Forgetting the passage and the space 'between' is what founds and sustains:

> the hardening of all dichotomies, categorical differences, clear-cut distinctions, absolute discontinuities, all the confrontations of irreconcilable representations.
>
> (Irigaray 1974: 246)

By locking difference into this structure of dualisms, Plato's myth initiates a process whereby 'all divergencies will finally be proportions, functions, relations that can be referred back to *sameness*' (1974: 247). Irigaray reads Plato's myth as an endless play of sames, likenesses, resemblances, repetitions, all of which begin by forgetting the 'space between' (1974: 247–8). Against Plato and his heirs, Irigaray suggests that recovering the forgotten transition and allowing the 'spaces between the figures' that have been 'fixed in oblivion' to 'come to life' might have the result of 'turning everything upside down and back to front'(1974: 138).

In *An Ethics of Sexual Difference*, 'betweenness' is named 'the interval' and is evoked as an undecidable threshold space, that can be seen as both the unspoken condition for the binary pair of self and other, and as excessive to the logic of a binary economy. It is 'both entrance and space between' (Irigaray 1984: 12). The famous 'two lips' of *This Sex* are a similar attempt to defy and exceed binary structures: for Irigaray they are both inside and out, one and two, and can evoke the undecidability at the heart of a possible alternative female imaginary and symbolic order that might be able to replace a binary logic of saming. In *An Ethics*, Irigaray links the two lips to other concepts that cannot be contained within a logic of dualisms, the sensible transcendental, and mucous (Irigaray 1984: 17–18).

On one level, this move to privilege the interval could be read as a continuation of the deconstructive strategies Irigaray adapts from Derrida, also seen in *Speculum* and *This Sex*. Like Derrida, part of Irigaray's aim in adopting these strategies is to destabilise binary structures and make visible the indeterminacy that is covered over by attempts to fix meaning in logocentric, or phallogocentric, language and thought. But while recognising her Derridean trajectory, it is also important to note that Irigaray's theoretical and political impetus is quite distinct from Derrida's. Irigaray locates 'Woman' and the feminine within these strategies in order to find a way out of phallogocentric thought, in order to find a speaking-position for women as subjects. This is a theoretical and political project which she opposes to Derrida's deployment of a disembodied *'féminin'* that becomes yet another way to allow men to speak.[7]

For Irigaray, then, privileging the interval and other spaces of indeterminacy is not only about guerrilla attacks on the machinery of Language. It is also about finding a speaking-position for women as subjects in the social order, and about finding a model of the self and self–other relations that can transform that social order, by not adhering to a logic of dualisms, which, in the end always folds difference back into sameness. These are both philosophical and political issues, and politically, the interval is about recognising the play of power relations between self and other.

Recognising and respecting the space between selves is a way of contesting the power effects underpinning most models of human interaction, in which the space of the self is secured by denying, encroaching upon or circumscribing the space allocated to the other. Respecting the interval therefore becomes part of a move to rethink alterity outside of an economy of the same, to respect otherness in its own terms. For Irigaray, the other in question is 'Woman': 'The question being how to detach the other – woman –

from the otherness of sameness' (Irigaray 1977: 169). But if saming occurs outside the landscape of sexual difference as well, then this move to leave the other his/her right to otherness can and should be taken beyond the sexual difference frame as well.

For example, Tina Chanter describes the view of alterity that exists within prevailing self/other models as follows:

> To render the unknowable knowable, to contextualise the *foreign* by placing it within the familiar comfortable world of the subject's experience is to grasp everything *exotic* – all that is other to oneself – and to make it available for use according to one's own purposes and projects.
>
> (Chanter 1995: 220–1, emphasis added)

Chanter defends Irigaray's privileging of the sexual difference frame as a way out of this view of alterity, but Chanter's reliance on such terms as 'the foreign' and the 'exotic' to make her point suggests that the problem needs to be addressed within a broader frame that takes differences of race, nation and other community identities between women, and between men and women, into account.

Irigaray's earlier work does include some aspects of this more political view of 'the space between'. For example, in discussing her experience as an analyst in 'The Limits of Transference', Irigaray stresses the need for a relationship between women analyst and analysand that is not based on models of merging or fusion (Whitford 1991a: 108). There needs to be a 'space or site of liberty between two bodies, two flesh, which protects the partners by giving them boundaries' (1991a: 115). In both this article and her later *Je, Tu, Nous* (1990), Irigaray points to the placental economy as a possible model for self–other relations that goes beyond the fusion/aggression dichotomy. The placental relation involves a continuous negotiation between self and other, through which both are actively modified, while remaining distinct (Irigaray 1990: 39–41). Clearly, Irigaray is concerned here with keeping the space between selves intact in a situation where she, as analyst, needs to recognise her position of relative power. This suggests that, while Irigaray's principal concern is to create and sustain that intact space for women and the feminine, in and beyond a male-centred specular economy, she is also aware of the need to secure that space in terms of relations between women.

In *An Ethics of Sexual Difference*, Irigaray continues to develop this question of boundaries between self and other. Irigaray is looking for a model of relationships between self and other 'which weds without consum(mat)ing' (Irigaray 1984: 186). In 'The Fecundity of the Caress', Irigaray returns repeatedly to this notion of a relationship between self and other that affirms, indeed, in a sense, *creates* the boundaries of each self while going beyond the limitations of the individual self. She writes of 'the other's hands' which 'give me back the borders of my body' (1984: 187), and also of 'giving the other her contours [...] inviting her to live where she is without becoming other, without appropriating herself' (1984: 204). Later on she also evokes 'that subtle palpable space that envelops each of us like a necessary border' and that enables one to become 'capable of more than the "I can" of the body itself' (1984: 207). One can only move to a model of self–other relations that welcomes porosity or multiplicity *through* respect for this space of difference: 'porosity, and its fullest responsiveness, can occur only within difference' (1984: 191).

Irigaray's position here reminds us of the concerns of some Indian feminists, discussed in Chapter 2, to retain some notion of the individual self if women are both to contest attempts to submerge them within community identities and to resist the reproduction of power differentials between women in the name of a 'collective feminist subject'. As Flavia Agnes (1995) and Ania Loomba (1993) have discussed, in the context of racial, religious, ethnic and other community differences between women, claims for a collective sexed or gendered identity will always run the risk of reproducing and indeed reinforcing those differences. In Irigaray's terms, the 'porosity' of a collective feminist subject can only emerge through respecting and preserving the space of difference. Additionally, given the prospect of right-wing or communalist versions of community identity which depend on an obliteration of the individual self, and particularly the female self who has to 'stand for' the authentic traditions and values of that community (Sarkar 1995), we can see the political pertinence of Irigaray's insistence on some kind of borders for the self.

Irigaray's position also bears certain similarities to Haraway's notion of the 'semi-permeable self' which will be discussed further in Chapter 6. As we will see it also leads to an understanding of the relationship between separation and alliance that is very similar to Haraway's, and that is pertinent to the question of how to rethink feminist politics in ways that respect the differences between women:

> What is missing is the double pole of attraction and support, which excludes disintegration or rejection, attraction and decom-position, but which instead *ensures the separation that articulates every encounter and makes possible speech, promises, alliances.*
>
> (Irigaray 1984: 9, emphasis added)

In this model, alliance and connection are premised, not simply on the merging of selves, but on a different kind of separation of the self, that does not appropriate the other to the needs and desires of the one (1984: 74). Feminist alliances, especially when they attempt to impose unity around a fixed and exclusionary definition of woman or women, need to bear this risk in mind.

The space between selves needs to be privileged in Irigaray's view, in order to find an 'elsewhere' to the economy of the same that prevails in a logic of dualisms. But this alone is not enough if women are to find that radically other elsewhere from which women can speak and act as subjects. A different model of the self, based on a morphology of the specifically female body, is also necessary. In 'Volume without Contours', Irigaray characterises that alternative model of the female self as '*in-fini*', both infinite and unfinished (Whitford 1991a: 59). It is less than the One-Self model of an economy of the same:

> unable or unwilling to close up or swell definitively to the extension of an infinite. [...] Metamorphoses [...] where the systematicity of the One never insists. Transformations, always unpredictable because they do not work towards the accomplishment of a telos.
>
> (1991a: 59)

But it is also more than One; there is a 'plurality of the female commodity' that the (male) subject is always trying to gather up into a One (1991a: 60), a multiplicity that cannot be contained within a logic of dualisms:

> Now, the/a woman does not have *one* sex [...] cannot subsume it/herself under *one* term, generic or specific.
>
> (1991a: 59)

The/A woman is never closed/shut (up) in one volume.

(1991a: 65)

She cannot relate herself to any being, subject or whole that can be simply designated. Nor to the category (of) women. One woman + one woman + one woman never will have added up to some generic: woman.

(1991a: 55–6)

As elsewhere in Irigaray's work, women's multiplicity is continuously referred back to a morphology of the female body: the 'sex organs more or less everywhere' (Irigaray 1977: 28); the indeterminacy between separation and touching, between closure and openness; of the two lips; the multiple flows from women's bodies that make her 'an other difficult to grasp [...] woman: the fluent' (Whitford 1991a: 64). There are strong resonances here with Vidya Rao's elaboration of a feminine voice and an alternative model of identity patterned on the Indian musical form of *thumri*. Rao, too, draws links between the female body and a model of identity that works with non-linear flows and multiplicity, in which the self is not dissolved, but is not defined by containment or closure either (Rao 1990). But additionally, the insights I have drawn from Indian feminisms suggest that women's multiplicity can be referred back, not only to a morphology of the female body, but also/rather to the ways in which the female, the feminine, 'Woman' and 'women' circulate across and between the discourses, practices and institutions that produce gender, race, nation and community. If we shake Irigaray's 'woman as *in-fini*' loose from the sexual difference framework in which she is anchored, she can perhaps speak both to women's specificity and to their differences.

Irigaray's lyrical evocations of a transgressive feminine economy that privileges fluidity, undecidability and uncontainability, in writings like 'Volume without Contours', or 'When Our Lips Speak Together' (Irigaray 1977) have elicited a varied response within feminism. For those unsympathetic to her project, they are the space where she falls most seriously into essentialism and surrenders to the patriarchal logic that reduces 'woman' to her body (see Moi 1985: 145–7). More sympathetic readings focus on her utopian quality, her mode of speaking 'as if', in order to help bring about a desired future (Whitford 1991b: 51), or on Irigaray's tactical deployment of mimesis in order to subvert a discursive order which positions woman as lack (Braidotti 1991: 257–8).

While I would agree that it is important to recognise both the utopian and tactical aspects of Irigaray's work, what is less often stressed is how at least some of Irigaray's lyrical flights into an elsewhere remain rooted in an understanding of how the specifically female is socially and discursively located in the here and now. To Irigaray the utopian visionary and Irigaray the tactical jammer of the machinery of phallocentric Language, it is possible to add an Irigaray with some sense that, politically, women need to redefine the female self. In 'Volume without Contours', for example, it is clear that women need alternatives to the model of the One that depends on reducing woman to 'the cohesion of a "body"' or to 'the solidity of a land, the foundation of a ground' (Whitford 1991a: 64). In Chapter 1 we saw Woman/women positioned as body-land-ground in highly political ways. At a point where one might expect Irigaray to be of least use in an immediate and political way – in her 'utopian' mode – she nevertheless has a definite political pertinence. At a point where one might expect her to be at most risk of positing a universal Woman that overrides women's particular location within specific communities, she speaks to one aspect of that location quite clearly.

In this chapter I have argued that Irigaray's absolute privileging of sexual difference as 'the issue of our age' presents significant difficulties for thinking about identity in ways that take seriously the differences between women. I have also suggested that her reliance on a model of Language as a system that works primarily through exclusion of the feminine may have the result of folding difference back into a model of sameness, by reducing the complexity of women's social and discursive positioning to a single move. At the same time, however, I have argued that there are strong resonances between some aspects of Irigaray's work and some of the concerns of Indian feminists regarding the location of women in the emergence of national, raced and other community identities. Perhaps ironically, these resonances are at their strongest when Irigaray insists on the importance of the specifically female, both in terms of how appropriations of birth and access to origins play a crucial part in underpinning an economy of the same, and in terms of what a specifically female model of the self and of self–other relations might look like. Reading Irigaray through the refracting prism of postcolonial feminisms suggests that the specifically female may be as important to the emergence of raced, national and other community identities as it is to categories of gender or sexual difference. This in turn suggests possible new directions for feminist theoretical projects that aim to sustain a simultaneous focus on women or their differences.

Yet for many Western feminist theorists, attempts to create a greater space for considering differences such as nation or race have focused on the need to destabilise, rather than redefine, our concepts of the female and the feminine. One of the best-known proponents of this alternative trajectory is Judith Butler, whose work is considered in the next chapter.

Chapter 4

Female trouble

Judith Butler and the destabilisation of sex/gender

As we saw in Chapter 3, Irigaray works within and against the sexual (in)difference of poststructuralist models of language and subjectivity in order to make a space for the specifically female. She wants to work towards a future where sexual difference is recognised on a different basis. In contrast, Judith Butler works within a poststructuralist framework in order to destabilise the logic of sexual difference. Butler's strategy brings elements from the work of Lacan and Derrida together with insights drawn from Foucault, in order to complicate feminism's understanding of identity by undermining the apparent coherence of such categories as sex, gender and race. While Butler's complex and demanding engagement with these three theorists produces some important insights, it also produces an unresolved tension in her work between incompatible models of power and language.

In this chapter I will argue that Butler addresses important issues for feminist attempts to rethink identity in ways that keep a space open for differences between women, but that, in the process, she turns away from considering women's specific location in the emergence of identity categories such as race and nation. At the same time, she closes off consideration of possible alternative models of the self and self–other relations that take a specifically female subject-position as a starting point.

I will look at these tensions in Butler's work through four issues. First, I discuss her approach to the question of identity through the concepts of materialisation and performativity. Second, I focus on her re-reading of Lacan in order to destabilise the symbolic, and with it, a logic of sexual difference. Third, I look at the implications of her approach to identity for questions of feminist politics, resistance and agency. Finally, I explore how Butler's strategy leads her to reject a focus on the specifically female, and discuss some of the implications of this rejection. Throughout, I look back to the four major insights from Indian feminisms identified in Part I, to gauge the extent to which Butler's strategy speaks to these concerns.

Performativity, materialisation and the subject

Michel Foucault's work on the productive and normalising effects of power in constructing subjectivities is one of Butler's key reference points. Her reading of Foucault underpins the genealogical critiques of gender (in *Gender Trouble*) and sex (in *Bodies that Matter*) that inform her approach to questions of identity-constitution, and, to a large extent, her understanding of the need to rethink the basis of feminist politics and resistance. I will return to Butler's reading of Foucault on the question of politics in the third section of this chapter. Here, I want to look briefly at how the Foucauldian strand in Butler's work can enable an understanding of the sexed/gendered subject that is open to both the possibilities of resistance and to the permeability of other categories of identity, such as race.

Like Foucault, Butler wants to resist the notion of a subject that exists before the taking on of such norms as sex; rather, she is arguing that the subject, the speaking 'I', is formed through the process of assuming a sex, together with other regulatory, productive norms. Her introduction to *Gender Trouble* presents her project in clear Foucauldian terms:

> A genealogical critique refuses to search for origins of gender [...] a genuine or authentic sexual identity that repression has kept from view; rather, genealogy investigates the political stakes in designating as an *origin* and *cause* those identity categories that are in fact the *effects* of institutions, practices, discourses with multiple and diffuse points of origin.
>
> (Butler 1990: x–xi)

Butler draws on Foucault's argument that the law and its transgression, sexuality as norm or 'perversion', are signified on and through bodies. By being made to appear to be internal to the self, these norms are solidified, reproduced and developed by the self as it aspires to subjectivity. Like Foucault, Butler argues that modern power is at its most effective in this 'capillary' mode:

> If the 'cause' of desire, gesture and act can be localized within the 'self' of the actor, then the political regulations and disciplinary practices which produce that ostensibly coherent gender are effectively displaced from view.
>
> (Butler 1990: 136)

When, in *Bodies that Matter*, Butler turns to the question of the 'materiality of sex', she argues, similarly, that sexual difference 'is never simply a function of material differences which are not in some way marked and formed by discursive practices' (Butler 1993a: 1). This does not mean that discourse causes sexual difference. 'Sex' is a normative category, a regulatory ideal and practice that produces, 'materializes', the bodies it governs. 'Sex' becomes one of the norms by which the 'one' becomes viable, that which qualifies a body for life within the domain of cultural intelligibility (1993a: 2). Rather than seeing sex as the raw material or 'matter' out of which gendered identities are fashioned, Butler wants to rethink the concept of matter itself not as site or surface, but as:

> *a process of materialization that stabilizes over time to produce the effect of boundary, fixity, and surface we call matter.* That matter is always materialized has [...] to be thought in relation to the productive and [...] materializing effects of regulatory power.
>
> (1993a: 9–10)

Like Foucault, Butler will argue that both regulation and the possibilities of resistance are produced through this process. Because norms need to be continuously reiterated and re-articulated, because bodies need to be rematerialised, there is always the possibility for re-articulations that call into question 'the hegemonic force of that very regulatory law' (1993a: 2). It is also, in part, this Foucauldian understanding of power as working through 'institutions, practices, discourses with multiple and diffuse points of origin' that leads Butler to question whether the regulatory norms of sex/gender can be viewed in isolation from other norms, such as race (1993a: 243 fn 1).

Immediately, we can note some clear resonances with the insights emerging from my reading of Indian feminisms. First, Butler's insistence on the productive role of power, and on viewing such regulatory norms as sex, gender and race in interconnection, provides a conceptual opening for considering the ways in which women play a simultaneously productive and subordinated role in the emergence of multiple categories of social identity. Her problematising of the stability of origins gains an additional importance when considered in the light of work by Chakravarti (1990), Sarkar (1987, 1995) and other Indian feminists who have explored the problems that arise when women are symbolically and strategically linked to notions of stable origins and timeless tradition in models of national or religious identity. In arguing that 'sex' is not a fixed raw material, but is rather materialised in order to produce 'viable subjects' within the context of specific productive power relations, Butler opens up a possible space in which to consider the third of the insights discussed in Part I – the importance of the specifically female to the emergence of nation, race and community identities. In defining 'sex' in this way, Butler suggests a framework in which to consider how female sexed specificity comes into play in constituting multiple categories of identity, although, as we shall see in the fourth section of this chapter, Butler stops short of this herself for particular reasons.

Butler is best known for conceptualising the subject in terms of 'performativity'. Performativity is not in itself a Foucauldian concept, but remains, in Butler's usage, in some sort of conversation with a Foucauldian understanding of the relationship between power, knowledge and subjects. In a 1994 interview, Butler makes this link herself when she describes her trajectory to the concept of performativity:

> I begin with the Foucauldian premise that power works in part through discourse and it works in part to produce and destabilise subjects. But then, when one starts to think carefully about how discourse might be said to produce a subject [...] it's useful to turn to the notion of performativity, and performative speech acts – understood as those speech acts that bring into being that which they name. [...] Then I take a further step, through the Derridean rewriting of Austin, and suggest that this production actually always happens through a certain kind of repetition and recitation. [...] Performativity is the vehicle through which ontological effects are established.
>
> (Butler 1994: 33)

Like Foucault's genealogical project, performativity suggests the need to contest and problematise the notion of the subject as an ontological given. For Butler, identities are 'fabrications manufactured and sustained through corporeal signs and other discursive means' (Butler 1990: 136). The categories of that identity – sex, gender, race, etc. – are neither essentially true or false, but are rather produced as the 'truth effects' of a discourse of primary and stable identity. For Butler, recognising that the gendered (or raced) body is performative 'suggests that it has no ontological status apart from the various acts which constitute its reality' (1990: 136). Rather, the notion of the performative suggests 'a dramatic and contingent construction of meaning' (1990: 139), where 'gender is an identity tenuously constituted in time, instituted in an exterior space through a *stylized repetition of acts*' (1990: 140).

Nevertheless, and against many of the readings of her work that followed the publication of *Gender Trouble*, Butler argues that understanding identity as performative does not imply that one can voluntaristically remake bodies and identities as a kind of radical, improvisational theatre (Butler 1994: 33). Butler returns to her reading of Foucault to consider the constraints on performativity, as a 'specific modality of power as discourse' in which certain reiterative chains of discursive production have become norms 'without which no bearing in discourse can be taken. The power of discourse to materialize its effects is thus consonant with the power of discourse to circumscribe the domain of intelligibility' (Butler 1993a: 187). There are, thus, always constraints on what can be 'performed' and the terms within which it can be performed or materialised.

However, while identities cannot be simply 're-performed' for Butler, this materialisation through the regulatory power of norms is never fully stable. This is for two reasons: first, because the norms one is called to identify with (e.g. 'masculine' and 'feminine') are not themselves fully stable or exhaustive (1993a: 187–8); and second, because the normative force of performativity works, not only through reiteration, but also through exclusion and through constructing a 'constitutive outside'. These exclusions 'haunt signification as its abject borders or as that which is strictly foreclosed: the unlivable, the nonnarrativizable, the traumatic' (1993a: 188).

This is where Butler steps aside from Foucault who, she argues, does not lend sufficient weight to this gesture of exclusion (1993a:

35). I think it is significant that she chooses this point to diverge from a Foucauldian trajectory. Many feminists take their distance from Foucault primarily because of his failure to take sexual difference sufficiently into account, and for his strategy of destabilising gender or sex binaries (see Foucault 1977c: 219–20). But as we shall see in the fourth section of this chapter, Butler holds on to this latter strategy. She moves away from Foucault, to both Lacan and Derrida, in order to focus on the gesture of exclusion. But in doing so, she turns to models of language, and of power, that produce an unresolved tension with the Foucauldian strands that remain in her work. It is as if, having problematised ontology through the notion of performativity, Butler concludes that there are no more interesting ontological questions to ask. All the interesting questions can only be asked through epistemology, through what is representable, 'thematizable', 'narrativizable'. But this move to an exclusive focus on language is, as we have seen, one that Foucault resists. Instead, Foucault argues for a simultaneous focus on 'historically analyzable practices' and the symbolic systems they use (Foucault 1983: 369).

The focus on exclusion also sets up an unresolved tension in Butler's work, between Foucault's understanding of power as productive, multi-vocal and diffuse, and one which conceptualises power in terms of the taboo and the negative (Foucault 1978: 150). For Foucault, Lacan's model of the 'I' (like other psychoanalytic models) posits a single formula of power that is made to apply to all forms of society and to all levels of subjection. This model is predicated on the power of an absolute Subject, such as the 'Law of the Father', to pronounce a founding interdict (Foucault 1977b: 140). Against such a model, Foucault argues that truths, including the truth about the self, are never just related to a gesture of repression or exclusion, but also to the proliferative and productive interplay of power and knowledge. Butler tries to bring the apparently incompatible Lacanian and Foucauldian conceptions of power together in her work. She does this, in part, through a series of moves to re-locate and complicate the sites of those exclusions, which I will examine in the next section.

In my discussion of Indian feminisms in Part I, I suggested the importance of a theoretical framework that would hold together the ways in which women are foregrounded and made central to processes of identity-constitution with those ways in which they are excluded and marginalised. In Chapter 3, we saw that at least some aspects of Irigaray's post-Lacanian model of sexual difference can lead to over-emphasising the ways in which women are 'made to disappear'. Does Butler's strategy of bringing together Foucauldian and Lacanian models of power offer a more successful response to this challenge?

Relocating the gesture of exclusion

Butler's work returns repeatedly to two moves which she draws from a psychoanalytic framework: first, the necessary failure of the process of identification, so that the subject 'never quite inhabits the ideal s/he is compelled to approximate' (Butler 1993a: 231); and second, that 'what is exteriorized or performed can only be understood with reference to what is barred from the signifier and from the domain of [...] legibility' (1993a: 234). With these two moves, Butler brings into play all the elements of what Alice Jardine calls 'Lacan's four-cornered topology' (Jardine 1985: 123):

> a logic of the real, imaginary, symbolic and 'the subject in his reality'. This subject [...] is put into movement around the four corners of a square [...] according to a series of displacements over which 'it' has no control; the substitution and displacement of signifiers, the differential process of language.
>
> (Jardine 1985: 121–2)

Yet I would argue that while Butler is using this Lacanian topology, she is also constantly trying to undermine it, in three different ways. She does this, first, by displacing each of the elements in the system. Thus, at various points in *Bodies that Matter* Butler will argue that the symbolic is an imaginary construct (Butler 1993a: 79); that the imaginary is constructed in the symbolic (1993a: 13–14); that the Real also is in fact part of the symbolic (1993a: 207). Here, Butler performs a classic deconstructive reading of Lacan's system, displacing each of the terms in the system to show how the borders of each are secured by their exclusion of and differentiation from the other, while continuing to be troubled by the 'trace' of the other.

But at the same time, there is a second, more directly political move that Butler makes. She seeks to destabilise the Lacanian system by insisting that all the elements in it are constructed within the realm of the social and within specific, historically constituted power relations, in ways that leave these elements subject to social change. This second move, which I think owes more to Butler's reading of Foucault than to Derrida, accompanies the first in a sort of uneasy tension with it, as Butler moves back and forth between a focus on Language as a system (*langue*) and on the social field which is in part constructed through language, but which cannot be completely reduced to it.

Butler also makes a third move, which derives mainly from debates within feminism around respecting differences between women. She seeks to contest the privileged place given to sexual difference within the Lacanian system, and to broaden the field of constitutive exclusions to consider other differences, especially, in Butler's case, sexuality and race. I will look at how Butler uses these three destabilising moves in her treatment of the Lacanian symbolic.

Butler argues that it is not enough to locate a space of feminine resistance in the realm of the imaginary, while leaving the status of the symbolic intact as immutable law, structured by the Law of the Father, in the manner of some feminisms which appropriate Lacan (1993a: 106). This move valorises feminine resistance in its specificity, but at the same time renders resistance no more than a temporary escape from 'the constituting powers of the law', without fundamentally altering the symbolic or its structural sexism and homophobia (1993a: 106).

Butler's alternative strategy is to destabilise the symbolic itself. She argues that the distinction between the symbolic and the imaginary cannot hold, and that 'what operates under the sign of the symbolic may be nothing other than precisely that set of imaginary effects which have become naturalized and reified as the law of signification' (1993a: 79). Further, she argues, we need to read the symbolic performatively, as producing that which it declares. Butler's argument here relies heavily on her appropriation of Derrida:

> Is there an original authority, a primary source, or is it, rather, *in* the very practice of citation, potentially infinite in its regression, that the ground of authority is constituted as perpetual *deferral*? In other words, it is precisely through the infinite deferral of authority to an irrecoverable past that authority itself is constituted.[...] The pointing to a ground which is never recovered becomes authority's groundless ground.
>
> (1993a: 107–8, emphasis in the original)

Of particular interest for this project is Butler's rethinking of the symbolic in ways that bring sexual difference and race together. She argues that 'the order of sexual difference is not prior to that of race or class in the constitution of the subject; [...] the symbolic is also and at once a racializing set of norms' (1993a: 130). Further, she claims, the entire psychoanalytic paradigm needs to be subjected to this insight (1993a: 130). Butler suggests three ways in which this might happen.

First, she asks, what happens if we take the assumption of masculine and feminine positions to occur not only through a heterosexualising symbolic, but also through a complex set of racial injunctions, operating in part through the taboo on miscegenation? What if homosexuality and miscegenation converge as the constitutive outside of a normative heterosexuality which also serves to regulate racially pure reproduction (1993a: 167)? Butler also questions Irigaray's reading of Western philosophy which sees the feminine as monopolising the sphere of the excluded from the time of Plato onwards. Butler points to Plato's construction of racialised others (the non-Greek-speaking, the slave) whose nature is considered less rational than 'man's', and whose exclusion is also essential to 'Plato's scenography of intelligibility' (1993a: 48).

Second, and related to the above, Butler questions the Lacanian model's linking of Language as a system exclusively to questions of sexual difference. Lacan's notion of the symbolic as the set of laws conveyed by language itself, which compel conformity to notions of 'masculinity' and 'femininity', has been taken by many psychoanalytic feminists as the point of departure for their work. From this, Butler argues, they have claimed that sexual difference is as primary as language, that there is no speaking/writing without a presupposition of sexual difference. It is their claim that sexual difference is more fundamental than other differences which, for Butler, marks so much of psychoanalytic feminism as white, since what is assumed is that there is such a thing as sexual difference unmarked by race (1993a: 181). What requires radical rethinking for her, therefore, is what set of particular social relations compose the domain of the symbolic: what convergent set of historical formations of racialised gender, gendered race, sexualisation of racial ideas, racialisation of gendered norms, make up both the social regulation of sexuality and its psychic articulations (1993a: 182).

Third, Butler suggests that 'Woman's' place in the symbolic needs to be seen in relation to raced as well as gendered identities. In her reading of the film *Paris is Burning*, Butler explores the ways in which gender becomes the site of articulation of race and class, and shows how the sign 'woman' 'constitutes the site of the phantasmatic promise of a rescue from poverty, homophobia, and racist delegitimation' (1993a: 130). Through each of these points, Butler is identifying processes which concern many of the Indian feminists discussed in Chapter 1 – the construction of 'Woman' as a way into constituting categories of class, race, community (Mani 1990; Sinha 1987; Hasan 1994b) and the need to control women's sexuality in order to maintain the purity of those categories (Chhachhi 1991; Agnes 1995; Butalia 1995). Butler's approach thus builds on an Irigarayan concept of 'Woman as ground', and opens it out to the broader landscape of the intersections of sex, gender, race, etc., that Irigaray herself resists.

However, it is important to note that, in making this argument, Butler seems to shift from a focus on the symbolic as the system of Language itself, to a focus on the symbolic as a set of particular social relations and the impact of these relations on the individual psyche. Of course Butler would argue that these two aspects are inseparable, since our only relation to the social is through language. However, here it seems to me the tensions between the Lacanian, Derridean and Foucauldian strains in Butler's work are highlighted. Clearly, she is working with a more destabilised view of the symbolic than Lacan's, but it remains unclear whether she is privileging a Derridean view that still focuses on a symbolic system in itself, or a Foucauldian insistence that 'historically analyzable practices [...] cut across symbolic systems while using them' (Foucault 1983: 369). To what degree is the subject defined by the laws of language alone, and to what degree are the laws of language changeable? Perhaps most importantly, to what degree does Butler's turn to language models over-privilege the gesture of exclusion, to the detriment of a focus on the productivity of power? As we saw in Chapter 2, in discussing the work of Tharu and Niranjana, a focus on Language and its logic of exclusion can actually turn attention away from the differences between women. Butler's move to displace the gesture of exclusion may not be sufficient to capture the complexity of women's relationship to the emergence of different community identities. As we will see in the next section, these tensions between incompatible models of power and language re-emerge when Butler turns to questions of feminist politics and resistance.

Politics, resistance and agency

Many Western feminist theorists have raised the question of whether postmodern or poststructuralist theories threaten the possibility of feminism as a political project of resistance and change. Much of this debate has focused on definitions and redefinitions of postmodernism, poststructuralism and feminism. Judith Butler is one of the few feminist theorists to take this debate as an occasion to rethink the other key terms involved in the question – politics and resistance. Butler asks if we need to theoretically assume a subject with agency before we can articulate the terms of a political process of change (Butler 1992: 13). She asks if feminism would not do better to dispose of its attempts to pre-define and describe its subject, the category 'women', the 'we' of feminism, since 'the "we" that is supposed to be presumed for the purposes of solidarity, produces the very factionalization it is supposed to quell' (1992: 14):

> The minute that the category of women is invoked as *describing* the constituency for which feminism speaks, an internal debate invariably begins over what the descriptive content of that term will be.
>
> (Butler 1992: 15)

For Butler this means we need to rethink the limitations of identity politics in general. More specifically, she wants feminism to rethink the category of 'women' as a political signifier, as well as the relationship between this category and others like race, ethnicity and what she has memorably called the 'embarrassed', 'exasperated' and 'illimitable *et cetera*' (Butler 1990: 143). She suggests that the whole process of forging political unities, formulating political demands and taking political action needs to be rethought so that feminist politics do not simply reproduce, in slightly new forms, the power relations they are trying to contest.

If, following Foucault, identity categories are never merely descriptive, but always normative, what normative constraints underpin constructions of the feminist subject (Butler 1992: 14–15)? If the subject is always both regulated and produced through the workings of power relations, then its agency cannot derive from some pure space, defined by primary identities, but only from the possibilities that emerge within those power relations (Butler 1993a: 12–15). These possibilities emerge in part from the instabilities of those normative power relations, whose results are not always predictable and which can therefore produce unintended consequences (1993a: 122–3). They emerge in part as well from the fact that power can only regulate those subjects it produces while also enabling them, so that it is possible to turn:

> power against itself to produce alternative modalities of power, to establish a kind of political contestation that is not a 'pure' opposition, a 'transcendence' of contemporary relations of power, but a difficult labour of forging a future from resources inevitably impure.
>
> (1993a: 241)

All these are identifiably Foucauldian moves, that also speak to a number of the issues discussed in Part I. Butler's view of the possibilities of an *im*pure collective political action can be heard to resonate with Ania Loomba's concern to problematise the collective subject of feminism as one 'wrought out of precariously achieved political intervention' (Loomba 1993: 222). Her concern to rethink identity politics in ways that don't close down definitions of 'women' is of great importance when we consider that feminisms can be complicit with the kinds of identity politics that exacerbate communal conflict (Chhachhi 1994; Agnes 1995). Yet despite her awareness of the dangers and difficulties involved, Butler seems to share Foucault's conviction that 'if everything is dangerous, then we always have something to do' (Foucault 1983: 343); she seems to be suggesting that rethinking identity politics, and therefore redefining the self and collective identities on a different basis, remains 'very urgent, very difficult, and quite possible' (Foucault 1981: 155).

However, as we have seen, Butler also wants to interrogate the ways in which identity categories rely for their apparent coherence on the construction and exclusion of an abjected outside, and on the impossibility of identity categories to satisfy their promise of immediate self-presence and completeness. For this, she turns away from Foucault to both psychoanalytic and Derridean frameworks. Feminism, Butler argues, has been faced with the problem of reconciling the apparent need to found its politics on a category of 'women' and the demand to problematise that category and interrogate its exclusions. Identity politics seems to promise full recognition. But a psychoanalytic approach suggests that identity categories, based on exclusions, can never fulfil their promises of full recognition, unity and universality. Disaffection with identity politics, then, can be understood as following on from this failure to deliver the promise.

For Butler, political signifiers such as 'women' are not describing pre-given constituencies, but are rather empty signs which come to bear phantasmatic investments. It is the signifier's inevitable failure to fully describe the constituency it names that opens it to new meanings and possibilities of political re-signification. Butler argues that 'it is this open-ended and performative function of the signifier that seems to me to be crucial to a radical democratic notion of futurity' (Butler 1993a: 191). Furthermore, it is because categories of identification are produced through processes of exclusion and abjection, which continue to haunt those identifications, that these categories remain unstable. Thus, while political contestation has tended to rely on identifications for advancing political goals, Butler is suggesting that the persistence of *dis*-identifications may be as crucial to a politics of change, and that dis-identificatory practices need to be mobilised within feminist politics (1993a: 4).

It is, therefore, not a question of giving up on such political signifiers as 'women', but rather of finding ways in which they can be 'repeated in directions that reverse and displace their originating aims' (1993a: 123). Feminists cannot stand at an instrumental distance from such terms; we are always, to some extent, being used by them as we use them. But they remain 'an occasion to work the mobilizing power of injury, of an interpellation one never chose' (1993a: 123), as an affirmative response to violation. It is the repetitions 'which fail to repeat loyally' that constitute resistance (1993a: 124).

Butler's model of resistance is perhaps best known through her privileging of parody. Parody destabilises the symbolic system by resisting any notion of an 'original' identity (Butler 1990: 138). Parodic speech acts expose the 'ground' of identities as groundless (1990: 141). For Butler, the boundaries of the symbolic system can be extended or displaced by:

the enunciation that *establishes* a position where there was none, or that marks the zones of exclusion and displacement by which available subject-positions are themselves established and stabilized.

(Butler 1993a: 114)

This type of 'parodic proliferation' challenges the stability of identity categories and insists on their permanent 'openness to resignification' (Butler 1990: 138).

Rethinking identity categories also means rethinking the connections between apparently discrete categories of analysis and resistance. In *Bodies that Matter*, Butler includes her own earlier work among those feminist positions that she judges to have 'problematically prioritized gender as the identificatory site of political mobilization at the expense of race or sexuality or class or geopolitical positioning/displacement' (Butler 1993a: 116). It is not a matter of relating race, sexuality and gender as if these were separate categories. Rather, what appear as separate categories are revealed as the conditions of articulation for each other. This means that notions of political unities need to be rethought, outside of the 'logic of non-contradiction by which one identification is always and only purchased at the expense of another' (1993a: 118).

For Butler, then, what we need is to 'map out interrelationships that connect, without simplistically uniting' (1993a: 114–15), and to find a way:

both to occupy such sites *and* to subject them to a democratizing contestation in which the exclusionary conditions of their production are perpetually reworked (even if they can never be fully overcome) in the direction of a more complex coalitional frame.

(1993a: 115)

For Butler this means questioning the notion of coherent identity as the starting point for political alliance, for to do so is to presume:

that what a 'subject' is is already known, already fixed, and that that ready-made subject might enter the world to renegotiate its place. But if that very subject produces its coherence at the cost of its own complexity [...] then that subject forecloses the kinds of contestatory connections that might democratize the field of its own operations.

(1993a: 115)

I think Butler is raising important questions here about rethinking the nature of coalition politics and about how the constituency of feminist politics might be developed in new ways. If the 'we' of feminist politics must always be determined beforehand, and if consolidation of a 'we' always involves an exclusionary process of setting boundaries, then spaces for the differences between women will always be closed down. If we think about the 'we' emerging through the process of coalitional politics, it may be possible to keep that space open to new possibilities. And yet I think Butler avoids two crucial questions which her discussion of these issues invites.

First, her reliance on a poststructuralist language model closes down the field of identity constitution so that she increasingly focuses only on the question of exclusion. If subject-positions are, as she says, established and stabilised through exclusion and displacement, then opening up the subject-position of 'women' as a 'site of permanent openness and resignifiability' (Butler 1992: 16) can be a radically democratising move. However, this move cannot address those effects of productive power that have already taken 'women' as such an open site of 'resignifiability'. As we saw in the analysis of Indian feminisms in Part I, there is already a proliferation of definitions and redefinitions of 'Woman' and 'women' which help to produce community identities that, in turn, continue to subordinate women. The overall effect of Butler's turn to exclusionary paradigms is, then, to under-emphasise both the way women can be constrained by these workings of productive power, and the instabilities and possibilities of resistance that can emerge from them.

Second, if we want to 'rework a logic of non-contradiction in which one identification is always and only purchased at the expense of another', do we not also need to think about positively redefining alternate models of the self, and self–other relations, in which to ground new ways of relating politically? Furthermore, is it possible to do all this work at the level of signification alone, without recourse to either an alternative ontology or an alternative ethics? And does not the closing down of her focus to the level of signification mean that Butler also closes down the possibility of seeing possible sources for those alternative models? In the next section I will argue that this is what, in fact, happens as a consequence of Butler's failure to redefine a specifically female subject-position.

Losing the female

In *Bodies that Matter* Butler questions whether recourse to the materiality of sex is necessary 'in order to establish that irreducible specificity that is said to ground feminist practice' (1993a: 29). She wants to establish a Foucauldian genealogy of materiality and, as a feminist, wants to uncover the 'problematic gendered matrix' (1993a: 29) that serves as ground for that materiality. She seeks to uncover the exclusion and degradation of the feminine that underpins prevailing concepts of materiality, so that feminists do not take on board this exclusion when they turn to concepts of the 'body's irreducible materiality' as a 'necessary precondition for feminist practice' (1993a: 30).

But what we need to pay attention to in Butler's trajectory, is whether, in destabilising notions of materiality, she also does away with any recourse to 'the sexed specificity of the female body'. In some places at least, Butler does seem to link female specificity *necessarily* with a notion of materiality that has been excluded and degraded (1993a: 28). In particular, I would argue that we need to see what happens within her framework to the female body, the maternal body and the specifically female capacity for birth. If, as my reading of Indian feminisms has been suggesting, the specifically female and especially the female capacity for birth are key to the emergence of raced, national and other community identities, then feminist theoretical models of identity need to take this on board if they are to attend to differences between women. It seems to me that both in Butler's reading of Irigaray, and in her reworking of Lacan to produce 'the lesbian phallus', this female body disappears. Furthermore, what disappears with this body is the possibility of feminist strategies of resistance that take a specifically female subject-position as the starting point for alternative models of the self, self–other relations and identity.

Butler's Irigaray

In *Bodies that Matter*, Butler's reading of Irigaray centres on the chapter in *Speculum* entitled '*Une Mère de Glace*', which consists of a selection of extracts from Plotinus' Sixth Tractate, 'The Impassivity of the Unembodied'. Here, Plotinus discusses Plato's concept of matter, also referred to elsewhere in *Speculum* as 'first matter', the 'receptacle' and the '*chora*'. All these terms refer to a concept of absolute impassivity and unchangeability, of absolute absence, within which substance, reality or existence can be contained.

For Butler, this kind of concept of matter, or materiality, is paradigmatic of the constitutive exclusions she is interested in: what must be placed outside signification and outside the realm of the intelligible, in order for signification to proceed. Thus, what interests Butler in Irigaray's work is the way she links this 'unthematizable materiality' to the feminine, whose exclusion becomes the necessary condition for philosophy to proceed and for a phallogocentric economy to posture as internally coherent (Butler 1993a: 37–8).

As part of her argument that feminism needs to contest the constitutive exclusions that ground hegemonic discourses, Butler focuses on this linking of the feminine with materiality. She wants to alert feminism to the dangers of grounding its project in appeals to notions of materiality that bring with them the abjection and exclusion of the feminine. However, at the same time, she wants to contest Irigaray's privileging of the feminine as monopolising the sphere of the excluded (1993a: 48). While I have argued in Chapter 3 that Irigaray's project needs to be opened up to consider other differences, I want to argue here that Butler's way of proceeding to do so creates its own problems. Butler opens the space for other differences only by de-authorising any focus on the specifically female.

It is clear from her first discussions of Irigaray in the chapter 'Bodies that Matter' that Butler's reading will emphasise the similarities between Irigaray's project and Derrida's. For Butler, Irigaray's strategy is not to find a place for 'her' voice, but rather to effect:

> a disruptive *movement* which unsettles the topographical claim [...] a taking of his place, not to assume it, but to show that it is *occupiable*, to raise the question of the cost and movement of that assumption.
>
> (1993a: 36)

Thus, Butler says that, for Irigaray, the excluded/excessive matter functions like the Derridean supplement in language (1993a: 38). This constitutive outside is internal to the system as its 'nonthematizable necessity' which re-emerges within the system, as both incoherence and as threat to systematicity. The feminine is thus 'set under erasure as the impossible necessity that enables any ontology' (1993a: 39).

These are all very Derridean formulations which focus on the feminine as a position in language, or rather as the outside of language. Irigaray is frequently mentioned in tandem with Derrida in this section, and Derrida is the chief point of reference and comparison in Butler's discussion. Never is any distinction made between Derrida's disembodied *'féminin'* and Irigaray's insistence on making links between the position of the feminine in language and questions concerning both real women, and the possibility of an embodied, specifically female subject-position. However, as we have seen in Chapter 3, Irigaray's strategy is not just a deconstructive 'overreading which mimes and exposes the speculative excess in Plato' (1993a: 36) and other philosophers. By only asking Derridean (epistemological) questions about representability, intelligibility and thematisability, Butler closes off consideration of the (ontological) questions about subject-status and models of self–other relations, which are also part of Irigaray's project. Indeed, Butler will argue against seeing Irigaray's work as looking for alternative origins in, for example, the maternal (1993a: 41), or as being grounded in a 'rival ontology' (1993a: 45).

This very Derridean reading of Irigaray gets Butler into trouble when she tries to track Irigaray's position on questions of the maternal body and the female capacity for birth. On the one hand, she wants to argue that Irigaray, like Derrida, would resist linking the abjected, excluded outside of Matter/the receptacle/the *chora* to the maternal body. However, on the other hand, Butler has to concede that, for Irigaray, philosophy's constitutive exclusions are bound up with a masculine appropriation of origins and of the female capacity for birth. Thus, Butler refers to 'the female power of reproduction that is taken over by the phallogocentric economy and remade into its own exclusive and essential action' (1993a: 42), and a 'phallic phantasy of a fully self-constituted patrilineality [...] effected through a denial and cooptation of the female capacity for reproduction' (1993a: 43).

By the end of this section of *Bodies that Matter*, Butler's attempt to conflate Irigaray with Derrida is straining at the seams. On the one hand, she is still only asking questions about the 'feminine in language' (1993a: 47) and reducing Irigaray's multi-layered project to this one move; on the other hand, she now claims that Irigaray *does* take the link with the maternal body as a symbolic model for an alternative relationship between the self and origin, and between self and other (1993a: 46–8). But at the same time, Butler continues to try to contain this link within a deconstructive register. Irigaray is, for Butler, still largely concerned with the 'linguistic operation of metonymy, a closeness and proximity which appears to be the linguistic residue of the initial proximity of mother and infant' (1993a: 48). The focus on the female in Irigaray is lost once again.

It is at this point in her argument that Butler takes issue with Irigaray's privileging of the feminine, as monopolising the sphere of the excluded, and criticises Irigaray for not following through on the 'metonymic link between women and [...] other Others, idealising and appropriating the "elsewhere" as feminine' (1993a: 49). Yet I find it ironic that Butler chooses to make her stand for 'other Others' at this point. In my own reading of Irigaray, which insists on maintaining a double focus on her treatment of both the feminine in language and the specifically female, this is one of the points at which Irigaray's project is most conducive to being opened up to a consideration of differences between women. As I have already argued, Irigaray's tracking of masculine appropriations of birth, of constructions of the mother as 'receptacle' or 'place' within which a male-defined 'truth' resides, and of the 'Woman-Mother' as the ground for exchanges among men, all find their resonances in the Indian feminist work discussed in Part I. However, these convergences only become visible if we look for the female in Irigaray and are willing to consider 'woman's' disruptive possibilities, an option Butler has already closed down.

Indeed, one of the most striking things about Butler's treatment of Irigaray is the degree to which Irigaray is not allowed to speak. After the conflation of Irigaray with Derrida, we have what is announced as Butler's reading of Irigaray's reading of Plotinus' reading of Plato in 'Une Mère de Glace'. But, as already noted above, 'Une Mère de Glace' is not 'written' in any conventional sense by Irigaray; it consists entirely of extracts from Plotinus, a point which Butler never makes clear. Without a consideration of this point any conclusions drawn about Irigaray's voice, or her project, become problematic, to say the least. A further irony is added when Butler uses this chapter of Speculum as evidence of Irigaray's 'penetrative textual strategy' of 'writing with and through the language of phallic philosophemes' (1993a: 45). It could be argued conversely that, in this chapter of Speculum, Irigaray never penetrates the phallic text at all, since her voice is deliberately not there – like the Mother-Matter-receptacle which can have no voice of its own. Finally, what is announced as a reading of '*Une Mère de Glace*' includes only one quote, of part of the last sentence of the chapter. The rest of this 'reading' is Butler's own discussion of Plato. In fact, Butler enacts her own set of displacements whose effect is to erase Irigaray's voice altogether. First we have Derrida as Irigaray; then Plotinus as Irigaray; and finally we have Butler herself speaking in the space she announces as a reading of Irigaray. Perhaps this is a clever comment on Irigaray's view on the difficulty of speaking (as) woman in an economy of the same, but the result is unsatisfactory in what purports to be a conversation among feminists.

I have said that Irigaray's voice is not present in '*Une Mère de Glace*', but of course she is present to the extent that she has chosen which extracts of Plotinus to include, and how to structure them. And if we read Irigaray's choices politically (as I have argued in Chapter 3), and in the overall context of *Speculum*, it becomes clear that what is at stake is not only the position of the feminine in language, but also the barring of a subject-space for women and the construction of a particular version of '*female-ness*' that serves the economy of the same. Irigaray's hidden presence in the text stands not only for the 'unspeakable' feminine within language, but also as an incursion from – and an insistence on the possibility of – a specifically female subject-space.

'*Une Mère de Glace*' follows three chapters dealing with the location of women in the work of Plato and Aristotle. '*Une Mère de Glace*' proceeds slightly differently. Women are hardly mentioned at all as Plotinus works his way through a variety of arguments in which he progressively rids the concept of matter of all remaining vestiges of dynamism, visibility, activity, and any part in the generation of things. Irigaray leaves to the very end the selection from Plotinus where matter is equated with the Mother. But this is clearly a particular construct of the Mother and of female-ness, stripped of any part in generation, 'sterile [...] female in receptivity only, not in pregnancy', with the 'impregnating power' assigned 'only to the unchanging masculine' (Irigaray 1974: 179).

At the same time as she has constructed the text to build up to this final connection of matter to the maternal/female, Irigaray scatters the text with indications that this is the direction in which Plotinus is heading. Throughout, Irigaray has chosen extracts in which Plotinus has recourse to the language of mirrors, echoes and reflecting vessels (see especially 1974: 169–70, 174–6). Each evocation of the mirror refers the reader to the many levels on which Irigaray deploys these terms: woman as mirror to reflect man's other of the same; the woman/mother behind the mirror, supporting the 'little man's' trajectory via the mirror stage to the symbolic and subject status; the burning glass and concave mirror that might project a different view. Further, the characterisation of matter as ground (1974: 176) and place (1974: 178) – terms which Irigaray returns to repeatedly throughout *Speculum* to locate the ways in which women are barred access to a subject-space in the specular economy – indicate that there is more at stake here than a reiteration of the Derridean location of the '*féminin*' in language.

As we saw in Chapter 3, some of the strongest resonances between Irigaray and Indian feminisms occur through these evocations of 'woman as ground' and of masculine appropriations of birth and the specifically female in order to produce different collective identities. As I noted above, Butler's project to rethink 'sex', not as a resource but as a site of contestation that needs to be materialised and rematerialised over time, might have offered another route to making the link between female sexed specificity and differences such as race and nation. But this possibility is lost when Butler decides to discount the specifically female, or to see it only as relating to a 'necessarily impossible position in language', so that sexed specificity must be rejected along with that position of the abjected and excluded.

It seems that in tracking the gendered matrix behind and beneath concepts of materiality, Butler concludes that any recourse to sexed specificity will fall into supporting that same matrix, and that the only solution is to problematise both materiality and the sexually specific body. If this exclusionary gendered matrix works by fixing masculine and feminine, and insisting that they remain resolutely distinct from one another, then the transgressive, emancipatory move is to un-fix those distinctions. Any attempt to redefine what might be specific to women can only, in her view, lead back to supporting that matrix.

This is why, in contrast to Irigaray's strategy of redefining the specifically female, Butler's prefers to re-read Plato's receptacle as the prohibited lesbian, as that which defies the attempt to keep masculine and feminine positions stable and distinct from each other in a heterosexual 'compulsory gendered matrix that supports the order of things' (Butler 1993a: 51). The problem, which I think recurs when Butler re-reads Lacan to produce 'The Lesbian Phallus', is that this strategy of undermining the sexually specific body, is just as susceptible to reappropriation within a 'masculine order' as the sexual difference model she rejects here.

Bodies, language and the lesbian phallus

In *Bodies that Matter*, the argumentative trajectory that leads Butler to the 'lesbian phallus' is a complicated, and often confusing one, that takes in readings of Freud and Lacan along the way. It is not my purpose here to rehearse those readings, or to try to impose my own version of clarity and cohesion on a difficult text. Instead, I want to focus only on tracking Butler as she again allows the specifically female to disappear. While in her reading of Irigaray, Butler effects this erasure through restricting her gaze to the 'feminine' in language, here the problem becomes the restrictions of the overall model of language itself which underpins Butler's analysis, and the way sexual difference is 'materialized' through language in this model.

In the chapter of *Bodies that Matter* entitled 'The Lesbian Phallus and the Morphological Imaginary', one of Butler's aims is to destabilise sexual difference by dislodging the phallus from its central and non-transferable place as transcendental signifier in Lacan's symbolic order. She starts from the premise that, in a Lacanian framework, 'having the phallus' is to assume the 'masculine' position, both within a heterosexual matrix and within language. Conversely, 'being the phallus' equates with the 'feminine' position. Butler then moves on to suggest that destabilising the one distinction ('having the phallus'/'being the phallus') is also to destabilise the other distinction ('masculine'/'feminine'). Thus, Butler's provocative celebration of the lesbian phallus is a way of insisting on the phallus's transferability and of undermining the 'logic of non-contradiction' that appears to hold the two binaries in place (Butler 1993a: 62–3).

Again, for Butler, the privileged move in terms of social change is the one that destabilises, rather than redefines, sexual difference. However, we might respond to Butler by asking: is the link between sexual difference and phallocentrism a necessary one? That is, do we have to reject sexed specificity when we reject the model that organises sexual difference around the central signifier of the phallus? And is the move to blur these distinctions any more immune to reappropriation when we still live in societies where the dominant power-knowledge regimes still take the male/masculine as norm?

Of course, Butler does not deny that bodies can be 'materialized' in sexually specific ways. But, for her, what allows these bodies to persist over time in their specificity is '*a demand in and for language*' (emphasis in the original); what is needed is 'to cast the notion of "bodies" as a matter of signification' (1993a: 67). With this move, Butler takes us away from the female in two ways. First, she draws us away from ontological considerations of the female, the female body and its possible relations to models of the self, towards epistemological questions of what can be represented about the body. Second, the model of language she draws on can only represent the feminine position in language within a logic of exclusion and differentiation, where securing the distinctness of masculine and feminine requires purifying each of all traces of the other. The transgressive move, therefore, is to destabilise those distinctions, rather than attempt to redefine them. Any attempt to redefine would be doomed to failure because of the overriding logic of language itself.

There are, of course, feminist theorists who have tried to combine a Lacanian view of language with a focus on the specifically female, most notably Luce Irigaray. But as we have seen, Butler's reading of Irigaray closes off this aspect of her work altogether; nor is she convinced by Kristeva's attempts to find a role for the maternal body in signification (1993a: 69–71). For Butler, any attempt to 'recover' the repudiated 'maternal' remains locked into the logic of the system that repudiated it in the first place (Butler 1993b: 164–5). The only available strategy, then, is to destabilise the central location of the phallus in Lacan's symbolic, and with it, the distinctions between masculine and feminine subject-positions. While Butler recognises that the Lacanian privileging of the phallus is underpinned by a masculine-marked morphology and an 'androcentric epistemological imperialism' (Butler 1993a: 73), rethinking the female body, or a feminine morphology, is never an option.

But this strategy only holds if we accept its underlying model of language, in which coherence is always purchased at the price of abjection, so that the distinctness of 'masculine' and 'feminine' requires purifying each of all traces of the other (1993a: 87). But is this the only way to proceed? Does language always only work in this way? Feminist theorists who are less committed to a poststructuralist language model have suggested a more complex situation. For example, Christine Battersby has argued that the 'feminine' can be appropriated, absorbed and managed by the male genius of Romanticism; her work suggests that blurring the boundaries between 'masculine' and 'feminine' can be perfectly compatible with discursive systems that subordinate women (see Battersby 1989, 1995).

Furthermore, as we saw in Chapter 1, destabilising the distinction between masculine and feminine through such figurations as the 'virile Mother-India' can be an enabling option for the male national subject, without seriously destabilising gender hierarchies. Is opening up sexual difference 'as a site of proliferative resignifications' (Butler 1993a: 89) such a *necessarily* enabling move? Is it possible to contest the still dominant regimes of power-knowledge that allow for any 'unmarked' resignifications to be 'always appropriated by the "masculine"' (Irigaray 1974: 133), if there is not also a parallel move to valorise and redefine the specifically female? Conversely, if language does not only work through the exclusion of all traces of the other, then it should be possible to approach the project of redefining the female/feminine without taking the relation to the phallus as constitutive, as Butler claims.

By de-authorising a focus on the female through her reliance on this kind of language model, Butler also limits the potential impact of a number of important insights that she brings to feminist theorisations of identity. For example, as we saw at the beginning of this chapter, she wants to problematise the way that identity categories are designated as *origins*, when for her they are in fact the *effects* of multiple discourses, institutions and practices (Butler 1990: xi). Yet by turning attention away from the specifically female body and from birth, she closes down a space in which she might have thought about women's specific relationship to the question of origins, and how this relationship figures in the emergence of a variety of identity categories.

Furthermore, in developing the concept of performativity, Butler points to the ways in which authority is constituted through an infinite deferral to an irrecoverable past, which becomes 'authority's groundless ground' (Butler 1993a: 108). Again, this might have been a space in which to consider 'Woman's' and 'women's' specific relationship to time, tradition and an 'irrecoverable past' in many models of race, nation and community identities. By discounting the female, Butler undermines her own project of bringing a greater complexity to feminism's understanding of women's identity and the apparent coherence of identity categories such as sex/gender and race.

In this chapter I have identified a number of ways in which Judith Butler's problematisation of identity can be enabling for feminist attempts to keep a theoretical space open for the differences between women. First, her genealogical critiques of sex, gender and, to a lesser extent, race, point to the instabilities behind these apparently coherent identity categories. Second, she contests the primacy of sexual difference in identity constitution, and works to destabilise the Lacanian model of the symbolic both by dislodging sexual difference from its location as sole centre of that model, and by arguing that the symbolic's inherent instabilities can be a source of social change. Third, her problematisation of identity leads her to rethink 'women' as a political signifier in ways that provide some important insights for feminist politics. The point is not to give up on the category 'women' but to recognise that it is always a field of political contestations. Parodic 'repetitions which fail to repeat loyally' can mean that 'women' are evoked in radically democratising ways that destabilise the apparent coherence of dominant social systems.

Nevertheless, there remains an unresolved tension between incompatible models of power and language in Butler's work. As we have seen, these limit the extent to which Butler can follow through with these insights to consider women's specific relationship to identity constitution. At times, she is working with a Lacanian/Derridean model of power that focuses on the necessary exclusion of the 'abject' and the 'unrepresentable' that provides the ground upon which the subject stands. At other times, she adopts a Foucauldian view of power as productive, that enables subjects as it constrains them. As we have also seen, the Derridean focus on signification alone and on what can be represented within a unitary symbolic system sits uneasily with the Foucauldian view of multiple discursive systems that cannot be looked at apart from material practices, institutions and social relations.

I have argued that, repeatedly, Butler's arguments move towards a privileged focus on language as a system, and on language working primarily through exclusion. In so doing, she both closes down the possibility of feminist redefinitions of the specifically female, and understates the complexity of women's specific location in the multiple networks of power relations through which particular community identities emerge. This limits both the extent to which Butler sustains a focus on 'women' and the space in which she can consider specific differences between them. Her strategic focus on destabilising sex and gender is meant to bring greater complexity into feminist understandings of women's identity. But this strategy derives from a model that reduces the complexities of both language and power by focusing on the single move of exclusion. The result is that Butler's intended focus on the complexities of 'women', identity constitution, and the relationship between them, is also undermined.

In Chapter 3 I argued that a sexual difference model of identity such as Irigaray's, causes serious problems for considering women's complex location across a multiplicity of identity categories, but that Irigaray's focus on the specifically female also produces some unexpected openings to that complexity. In this chapter, I have suggested that a strategy of destabilising sex/gender, whilst producing important insights for complicating identity, can also create its own difficulties for capturing women's specific relation-ship to that complexity. Is it possible to hold together a focus on women's specificity with an attention to multiplicity? In the next two chapters, I look at the different ways in which Rosi Braidotti and Donna Haraway have attempted to address this double focus.

Chapter 5

'All that counts is the going'

Rosi Braidotti's nomadic subject

In many ways, Rosi Braidotti's project to 'develop and evoke a vision of female feminist subjectivity in a nomadic mode' (Braidotti 1994a: 1) promises to address at least some of the difficulties identified in the work of Irigaray and Butler. She wants to open up Irigaray's feminism of sexual difference to consider other differences between women, to capture the simultaneity of 'axes of differentiation such as class, race, ethnicity, gender, age and others' (1994a: 4). Like Butler, she wants to unsettle models of identity that are grounded in a desire for fixity, but unlike Butler, she thinks that a redefinition of the specifically female can offer a way towards an alternative model of the self.

Her engagement with Foucault and Deleuze promises an attention to the relationship between identity and power relations, and to the tensions between power's productive and exclusionary aspects. Following Foucault, she speaks of the 'set of interdictions and permissions which inscribe one's subjectivity in a bedrock of power' (1994a: 12). Following Deleuze and Guattari, she seems attentive to the potential dangers of reproducing hegemonic power relations in the name of resistance (1994a: 5). She refers to both Butler's treatment of performative parody and Irigaray's use of strategic mimesis, not just as ways of troubling the system of Language itself, but within a framework of radical political contestation, as 'spaces where alternative forms of agency can be engendered' (1994a: 7). She wants to think about difference outside binary paradigms (1994a: 78) and insists on the importance of not losing a focus on 'women' while problematising our concepts of the 'subject' (1994a: 77). Braidotti's work repeatedly turns attention to the political implications of different theoretical approaches and to the need for feminism to succeed as a radical theoretical *and* political project.

Nevertheless, I will argue in this chapter that Braidotti's nomadic trajectory fails to follow through completely on these promising beginnings and in fact takes a number of problematic turnings which subtly reintroduce sameness in the name of difference, and hierarchy in the name of multiplicity. A number of small but significant theoretical moves undermine Braidotti's undoubted sensitivity to questions of difference and to the problem of racism in European thought and politics, and result in an unintended re-centring of her theoretical project around the white Western woman. If this chapter appears to focus unfairly on the problems in Braidotti's approach, it is because I think they provide important lessons for white Western feminists about both the difficulty of sustaining a double focus on 'women' and their differences, and about how theoretical models of power, language and identity impinge on our ability to sustain that double focus.

I develop this argument through six sections. I begin by introducing Braidotti's concept of the nomad. In the second section, I discuss the problems created by Braidotti's failure to consider adequately the question of location in her version of nomadism. In the third and fourth sections, I question Braidotti's methodology and speaking-position for the way they fail to think through thoroughly her own location as a white Western feminist, and will show how she de-authorises many of the insights that emerge from postcolonial locations. In the fifth and sixth sections, I discuss how Braidotti's underlying models of identity and language contribute to the reintroduction of a hierarchy of differences in her project.

Nomadic subjects

In her collection of essays written between 1980 and 1993 entitled *Nomadic Subjects*, Rosi Braidotti offers the model of the nomad as a way of rethinking 'female feminist subjectivity'. The 'female feminist' is a phrase Braidotti first used in *Patterns of Dissonance* (1991). She uses it to refer to the type of project, initiated by Irigaray, that takes sexual difference as the starting point for developing new modes of thought to counter the specular feminine of the phallocentric order, and thus to counter a notion of Woman as 'other of the same'. For Braidotti, the female feminist subject is a 'new epistemological and political entity to be defined and affirmed by women in the confrontation of their multiple differences, of class, race, sexual preference' (Braidotti 1994a: 30).

Braidotti uses this formulation to add to the Irigarayan project an attention to the multiplicity of differences between women:

> In feminist theory one *speaks* as a woman, although the subject 'woman' is not a monolithic essence defined once and for all, but rather the site of multiple, complex, and potentially contradictory sets of experience, defined by overlapping variables such as class, race, age, lifestyle, sexual preference and others.
>
> (1994a: 4, emphasis in the original)

Braidotti recognises that the question of differences between women, 'especially on the ground of culture and ethnic identity', is not a strong point in Irigaray's work (1994a: 170), and she wants to give this question a more central place within sexual difference feminism.

It is largely through the figuration of the nomad, adapted from Deleuze and Guattari, that Braidotti hopes to achieve this double focus. A 'figuration' is Braidotti's term for 'a style of thought that evokes or expresses ways out of the phallocentric vision of the subject. A figuration is a politically informed account of an alternative subjectivity' (1994a: 1). Figurations are the necessary political fictions, new frameworks and images that suggest ways out of predominant paradigms and modes of thought (1994a: 3).

Braidotti evokes the nomad to tackle questions of subjectivity and identity at a number of levels. Here, I want to look at three of these: first, the model of the self, and self–other relations implied by Braidotti's appropriation of the figuration of nomad; second, how the nomad is evoked to suggest the constituent elements of a sense of self, in particular the intersections of sex, gender, race, ethnicity, etc.; and third, what Braidotti's use of the nomad suggests in terms of the nature and possibilities of agency.

At the level of models of the self, Braidotti finds the figuration of the nomad empowering because it expresses:

> the kind of subject who has relinquished all idea, desire, or nostalgia for fixity. This figuration expresses the desire for an identity made of transitions, successive shifts, and coordinated changes, without and against an essential unity.
>
> (1994a: 22)

The nomadic subject has not abandoned unity altogether, but its cohesion derives from movement rather than from fixity:

> It is a cohesion engendered by repetitions, cyclical moves, rhythmical displacement. [...] [T]he point of being an intellectual nomad is about crossing boundaries, about the act of going, regardless of the destination.
>
> (1994a: 22–3)

The nomadic self draws its sense of coherence from its mobility, and thus 'aims to rethink the unity of the subject, without reference to humanistic beliefs, without dualistic oppositions, linking instead body and mind in a new set of intensive and often intransitive transitions' (1994a: 31).

Braidotti's view of the nomadic self has its origins in Deleuze and Guattari's project in *A Thousand Plateaus* to rethink multiplicity outside the constraints of systems of binary logic (Deleuze and Guattari 1988: 4–5). Binary logic, they argue, takes its models from the linearity of trees and roots, plotting points, fixing order, locating origins (1988: 7). Deleuze and Guattari's counter-model is the rhizome, in which connection exists only in the context of heterogeneity and multiplicity: 'any point of a rhizome can be connected to anything other, and must be' (1988: 7). 'Tree logic' makes its links through subject/object binaries (1988: 8), through plotting the place of each unit in relation to a universal 'One' (1988: 21). It is a logic of tracing and reproduction (1988: 12). Rhizomatic connections, by contrast, are like a map which is open, susceptible to constant modification, and which has multiple entry ways (1988: 13). The rhizome is acentred, nonhierarchical, without an organising memory (1988: 21).

Tree logic leads to molar models of identity that privilege being – stable, defined, distinct. The molar subject is fixed in position on the grids of sedentary, striated space. The logic of the rhizome privileges instead molecular models of becoming, and the smooth space that resists hierarchies, enclosure and symmetry. The space inhabited by the nomad is a type of smooth space, which is characterised by relationships of deterritorialisation, rather than reterritorialisation. In terms of thinking about the differences between women, then, a nomadic model of the self can be seen as a way of respecting multiplicity in its own terms, without folding it back into the constraints of a logic of the same.

At the level of the constituent elements of a sense of self, Braidotti evokes the nomad as a way of capturing the simultaneity of a variety of 'axes of differentiation such as class, race, ethnicity, gender, age and others' in the constitution of subjectivity (Braidotti 1994a: 4). For her, therefore, it is an important way of imagining a female feminist subject while respecting the space for ethnic and racial differences between women. She also evokes the nomadic mode as a feminist method of practice that will allow for united action across those differences, while respecting racial, ethnic or cultural specificities.

Here again, Braidotti evokes Deleuze's concepts of nomadic becoming and deterritorialising 'lines of flight'. A Deleuzian approach, she argues, stresses emphatic proximity and intensive interconnectedness, while resisting any notion of a centre, originary site or authentic identity, notions that can lead to movements of imitation, reproduction and appropriation. 'Some states or experiences can merge simply because they share certain attributes' (1994a: 5–6). For Braidotti, one of the historical tasks of the feminist as nomad is to 'restore a sense of intersubjectivity that would allow for the recognition of differences to create a new kind of bonding, in an inclusive (i.e. nonexclusionary) manner' (1994a: 36).

Braidotti calls this process a collective 'becoming polyglot' in which feminists can:

> become fluent in a variety of styles and disciplinary angles and in many different dialects, jargons, languages, thereby relinquishing the image of sisterhood in the sense of a global similarity of all women *qua* second sex in favor of the recognition of the complexity of the semiotic and material conditions in which women operate.
>
> (1994a: 36)

In linking the figuration of nomad to the multiplicity of languages, and to the complex interrelations between the discursive and the material, Braidotti again echoes a Deleuzian move that contests a unitary focus on Language as a system:

> there is no language in itself, nor are there any linguistic universals, only a throng of dialects, patois, slangs and specialized languages. [...] There is no mother tongue, only a power takeover by a dominant language within a political multiplicity.
>
> (Deleuze and Guattari 1988: 7)

At the level of questions of agency, Braidotti argues for a nomadic style because for her it captures the need to recognise the distinctions between conscious and unconscious processes and the interconnections between both of these and power (Braidotti 1994a: 31). It is important at this point to clarify how Braidotti uses the terms 'subjectivity' and 'identity', since her usage is rather atypical of feminist theorists. Throughout *Nomadic Subjects*, Braidotti returns to the point that it is important to distinguish between 'subjectivity in the sense of historical agency, and political and social entitlement' (1994a: 163), and identity, which, for her, is linked to desire, the politics of the personal and which, especially, 'bears a privileged bond to unconscious processes' (1994a: 166). For Braidotti, the nomadic mode expresses the need to respect both levels, as well as the need to develop points of transition and overlapping between them, to 'negotiate between unconscious structures of desire and conscious political choices' (1994a: 31).

Braidotti makes strong claims for the nomad to both embrace the transformative possibilities and correct the perceived shortcomings of other feminist alternative figurations. She claims that her nomad is like Haraway's cyborg, but equipped with an unconscious and a psychoanalytic pedigree which Haraway resists. She is also Irigaray's 'mucous', or 'divine', but 'endowed with a multicultural perspective' (1994a: 36). The nomad's route is indeed far-ranging, enlisting under her banner a variety of projects, from de Lauretis' 'eccentric subjects', to Laurie Anderson's performance art, to the cockroach-eating G.H. of Clarice Lispector's novels.

Yet I find Braidotti's figuration of the nomad, who 'has no passport – or has too many of them' (1994a: 33), disturbing, particularly when looked at closely in terms of the space it leaves for differences between women. I want to examine the problems in this respect from two angles: first, in terms of the status of the nomad herself, as described by Braidotti; and second, in terms of Braidotti's methodology in privileging the nomad. On both levels, I want to argue that Braidotti's nomad fails to think through thoroughly the differences that race, nation and other community identities might make to her model.

The nomad and a politics of location

As we have seen, one of Braidotti's reasons for privileging the nomad is to capture the complexity of the many differences between women. But the figuration of nomad, as Braidotti has drawn it, begins to cause problems as soon as we start thinking about the specificities of those differences. Braidotti's nomad is all about mobility:

> All that counts is the going, the process, the passing.
>
> (1994a: 170)

> The nomad is only passing through: s/he makes those necessarily situated connections that can help her/him to survive, but s/he never takes on fully the limits of one national, fixed identity. The nomad has no passport – or has too many of them.
>
> (1994a: 33)

> Nomadism [...] is [...] an acute awareness of the nonfixity of boundaries. It is the intense desire to go on trespassing, transgressing.
>
> (1994a: 36)

But to put all the emphasis on the going, on the transgressing of boundaries, is to sidestep, or at least downplay, the question of place in the construction of a sense of self. And to downplay the question of place makes it particularly difficult to engage seriously with the kinds of differences that race, nation and ethnicity can make for women. To be marked by one's race or ethnicity, as are women of colour and 'postcolonial' women in a world which takes whiteness and Western-ness as the invisible, unmarked norms, is to be 'placed' in ways that Braidotti's nomad never is. Also, as we saw in Part I, women's particular relationship to place can be key to the emergence of specific raced and national identities. One can work to complicate that placing, to undermine the apparent unity and fixity of that location, to explore what Paul Gilroy has called the creative tension between 'roots and routes' (Gilroy 1993: 133), but one cannot simply forget about 'roots' and take to the road. That Braidotti is aware of this problem with her paradigm is indicated by her attempt to graft a 'politics of location' and a notion of 'situatedness' – which she recognises is not in itself a nomadic concept (Braidotti 1994a: 32) – onto the nomadic framework. Indeed, each of the three passages quoted above is either preceded or followed by mediating or qualifying statements that attempt to bridge the gap between what Donna Haraway calls 'views from somewhere' and the nomad's delight in her permanent dislocation on the road. But these always remain general statements, and Braidotti never follows through on her commitment to a politics of location that involves a specific 'attention to and accountability for differences among women' (1994a: 21) by actually engaging in any detail with, for example, the ways in which black or postcolonial feminists work with notions of place in the construction of gendered-raced-national identities.

This omission is surprising in a theorist who is clearly aware that location can inform the kinds of choices made in theory. We see this, for example, in Braidotti's analysis of the relationship between Deleuze's treatment of 'becoming woman' and his gendered location (1994a: 123), and in her genuine concern, throughout *Nomadic Subjects*, to point out the connections between her own theoretical choices and the specific locations that have made up her own life trajectory to date. A more detailed engagement with postcolonial considerations of place in relation to different identity categories might have significantly altered the content of Braidotti's concept of nomad. Without it, her version of a politics of location remains a general appeal to recognise differences; however, those differences rarely seem to trouble the patterns of her wanderings.

And it is hard not to see those wanderings as just a bit too comfortable. I understand that for Braidotti the nomad is a fiction that allows us to think a politics of 'as if', to begin to break away from the actual constraints of predominant theoretical paradigms and power relations, and is not a description of the way we can simply be by choice. But to speak of having 'no passport, or too many', of being able to pick and choose the connections one finds most useful, of never taking on 'fully the limits of one national, fixed identity' (1994a: 33) strikes me as a fiction that can only emerge from a position of considerable privilege at a number of levels. There is, of course, the suggestion of class privilege that allows for the purely joyful and voluntary mobility of the nomad as high-flying academic, which has little in common with the forced, or at least more uncomfortable and complicated, trajectories of migrants, exiles and others who travel without tenure. But I would also argue that Braidotti's figuration emerges from an unexamined race- and nation-inflected privilege as well. Put simply, it is so much easier for white Westerners to refuse the limits of fixed racial or national identities, when 'whiteness' and 'Western-ness' continue to function as the invisible, unmarked norms that don't seem to fix identity at all. There is a crucial difference between Braidotti's nomad who is 'only passing through' (1994a: 33) the various locations on her itinerary, and a theoretical approach which begins by rigorously examining its own location in terms of gender, race, nation and other community identities, and then works to undermine the apparent unity and fixity of that location. Much of the work discussed in Part I, I would argue, follows this second strategy: both in considering women's symbolic and strategic connection to concepts of 'place', 'home' and 'inner-ness' in the production of different community identities (Sarkar 1987; Loomba 1993; Sen 1993; Niranjana 1994a); and in arguing for models of identity that both recognise women's location within specific community categories and that resist reducing women's identity to static symbols of those communities (Rao 1990; Sangari 1993; Butalia 1993; Hasan 1994b; Kannabiran and Kannabiran 1995).

Maria Lugones identifies two different approaches to what she calls 'world' travelling, by which she means the acquired flexibility of shifting between different constructions of life in which the self may feel more or less at home (Lugones 1990: 390). For Lugones, 'world' travelling is a necessary skill for the outsider, but it is also something that those at ease in the mainstream can exercise. The outsider is often compelled to travel to hostile 'worlds', but this should not obscure the enabling possibilities that the skill to 'play' across worlds can embody. What is important for Lugones, however, is what kind of play is at stake.

Lugones distinguishes between agonistic and loving playfulness. Agonistic play is all about competence: it takes pleasure from knowing the rules and from feeling at ease to compete and to overcome the uncertainty of different worlds (1990: 399). Loving playfulness across worlds takes a different kind of risk: it involves sustaining an openness to being changed by the worlds one travels to, and to changing the ways in which one understands those who live there (1990: 401–2).

In Deleuzian terms, competence is part of the tree logic of reproduction and tracing (Deleuze and Guattari 1988: 12–13), of travelling in order to reterritorialise. As Caren Kaplan has remarked in a different context, those from the mainstream who play across worlds without recognising that they travel with 'all [their] cultural baggage intact' or that there is no pure deterritorialisation, run the risk of engaging in theoretical tourism (Kaplan 1987: 191). In stressing that 'all that counts is the going', Braidotti runs the risk of revelling in her nomad's competence to travel across worlds, without sufficiently attending to how and why she travels, where she comes from and what she takes with her.

Indeed, if Braidotti had taken this question of location more seriously, another version of the nomad might have been privileged. As Eleanor Porter has argued:

> the nomad survives, not through 'transitory attachment' to the land, as Braidotti suggests, but on the contrary through intimacy with it. Rather than flying endlessly over undifferentiated space the nomad travels with specific needs across landscapes she or he can know and use. [...] The nomad must be aware of herself as a being that dwells in space, that is dependent upon that space, whose sense of self is built through interaction with a highly differentiated and storied environment. Narratives of identity then grow out of this engagement with local space.
>
> (Porter 1995: 9)

Indeed, Deleuze and Guattari argue that '[i]t is [...] false to define the nomad by movement' (Deleuze and Guattari 1988: 381). Rather, 'the nomad distributes himself in a smooth space; he occupies, inhabits, holds that space' (1988: 381).

What is important then, even within the terms of a Deleuzian project, is *not* 'the going', but a different kind of relationship with the space one inhabits, that resists the striations of binary logic. Other appropriations of the nomadic subject have placed more emphasis than Braidotti on the necessary tension between a located identity and the openness to movement and change. In Lawrence Grossberg's version, for example:

> The nomadic subject is amoeba-like, struggling to win some space for itself in its local context. While its shape is always determined by its nomadic articulations, it always has a shape which is itself effective.
>
> (Grossberg 1988, cited in Woolf 1995: 119)

This kind of evocation of the nomad resonates much more clearly with the kind of model of location and movement that emerges from Vidya Rao's treatment of *thumri* and the 'feminine voice', discussed in Chapter 2. Like Grossberg's nomad, Rao's *thumri* both adheres to and transgresses the shape and space available to it (Rao

1990: WS37); rather than jettisoning the limitations and rules of musical form and 'taking to the road', it works to mine the impurities inherent in the form, creating a new relationship with the structures it inhabits (1990: WS32).

A second way in which the dislocation of Braidotti's nomad suggests an unexamined privilege is in her relation to the *polis*. Recalling the etymological origins of the term 'nomad', Braidotti argues that:

> *noumos* [plot of land] is a principle of distribution of the land and as such it came to represent the opposition of the power of the *polis* because it was a space without enclosures or borders. [...] Metropolitan space versus nomadic trajectories.
>
> (Braidotti 1994a: 27)

Adopting Deleuze's opposition of the smooth space of nomadism to the stratified civil space of the state (Deleuze and Guattari 1988: 351–423), Braidotti suggests a possible privileged position for the nomad outside the structures and constraints of power relations. Deleuze and Guattari's warning, 'Never believe that a smooth space will suffice to save us' (1988: 500), seems to have been forgotten as Braidotti instead presents the smooth space of the nomad as just such an unproblematised site of salvation.

So, for example, Braidotti criticises Seyla Benhabib for her figuration of the critical feminist intellectual as the exile camping outside the city gates. For Braidotti, the temporary exile who seeks eventual readmission to the city/*polis* on new terms suggests a 'diaspora of the chosen few'; she counterposes it to her image of 'active nomadism' as 'a massive abandonment of the logocentric *polis*, the alleged "center" of the empire, on the part of critical and resisting thinking beings' (Braidotti 1994a: 32). But whatever the problems with Benhabib's project to reform the project of modernity and its moral and political universalisms (Benhabib 1992: 2), which cannot be discussed here, her emphasis on 'situatedness' within specific power relations and social systems is something that Braidotti's nomad allows to slip away. There is a difference between asserting one's 'nonconfidence in the capacity of the *polis* to undo the power foundations on which it rests' (Braidotti 1994a: 32), with which I would sympathise, and thinking that it is ever possible to 'abandon' the *polis* strategically or symbolically, to find an unsullied space that already functions 'according to different rules and designs' (1994a: 32). Braidotti makes the *noumos/polis* opposition too absolute, and the claim for a massive nomadic abandonment of the *polis* is simply too strong. Are the 'masses' really outside the *polis* and can the nomads so easily get them there, especially if they never go inside the city gates to find them?

In celebrating the nomad's location outside the city gates, Braidotti's model also contrasts sharply with those Indian feminist reflections, discussed in Chapter 2, on the need to rethink and perhaps reappropriate the concept of citizen as enabling for women. Rethinking women as citizens involves working with the possibilities of resistance and change that exist precisely within the impure space of the *polis* and civil society, rather than locating those sources of change elsewhere. I will return to this point in more detail in Chapter 8.

Privileging the nomad: Braidotti's methodology

As we saw earlier, Braidotti privileges the Deleuzian style of 'nomadic becoming' as one of her ways into the question of respecting the differences between women, of identifying those experiences that 'merge simply because they share certain attributes' (1994a: 5–6) while resisting acts of reterritorialisation or appropriation. But knowing when attributes are 'simply shared' is not simple: it requires an attentiveness to the specificity and complexity of each difference. To do this it is not enough, as Braidotti suggests, to be clear and explicit about one's own location, one's own experiences of deterritorialisation and reterritorialisation (1994a: 6), although, as we shall see in the next section, we can also question the degree to which Braidotti is explicit about her own location. While Braidotti states that she wants to avoid romanticising or appropriating the exotic, or the other, I do not think she has given herself the tools to do it.

Precisely because of the ever-present multiplicity and interconnectedness she celebrates, each particular 'embodied genealogy' (1994a: 6) includes its connectedness to practices and discourses that are contested from other subject-positions. This is important when feminists seek to establish 'rhizomatic connections' with anti-racist and postcolonial theorists in refiguring the place of gender, race and national differences in new models of the self or alternative subjectivities. We need to know enough about those other locations so that we do not come up with new figurations that simply appropriate or reterritorialise in new ways. Equally, in foregrounding a particular figuration, such as the nomad, it is important not to do so in ways that de-authorise other figurations that, from other subject-positions, are seen as productive ways into theorising questions of the self, identity and agency. I think there are a number of occasions when Braidotti does precisely this.

An example of this appears in her book's introductory essay, 'By Way of Nomadism'. Braidotti begins by stressing the importance of developing relations between women based on respect and understanding of differences, using the example of white intellectuals (like herself) and the 'domestic foreigners' in Europe who are either migrants or exiles (1994a: 21–2). But her text then shifts into a celebration of the nomad, a celebration that is in part achieved through pointing out the limitations of the 'exile' and the 'migrant' as alternative liberatory figurations. Of course there is a shift in register at work here. To begin with, Braidotti is describing the actual material and discursive positions of 'real-life' women migrants and exiles, something she does with great sensitivity and sympathy. She then moves to a conceptual register, where she is exploring the transgressive potential of different theoretical models. But it is hard for the reader *not* to make some connections between the two discussions, coming so close together as they do. Since Braidotti is the only nomad in the text at this point, it is very difficult not to read this as reinforcing a hierarchy in which the white Western feminist stands above those Third World women and women of colour who are migrants and exiles.

Braidotti also reveals here her lack of attention to the ways that terms might be contested in a postcolonial mode. Her dismissal of the image of the traveller as 'banal and hegemonic' (1994a: 24) jars with the work of Paul Gilroy who argues against 'the folly of assigning uncoerced or recreational travel experiences only to whites while viewing black people's experiences of displacement and relocation exclusively through the very different types of travelling undergone by refugees, migrants and slaves' (Gilroy 1993: 133). For Gilroy, the history of what he has termed the 'black Atlantic' includes an important tradition of writers and thinkers who associate questions of self-exploration with the exploration of new territories, and who ground their theory in the fruitful tensions between 'roots and routes' (1993: 133).

Similarly, Braidotti oversimplifies the complex concept of the diaspora which has proved so important to many black and postcolonial theorists when she reductively locates 'diasporic' thinking within a simple framework of nostalgia for a lost origin (Braidotti 1994a: 24). In contrast, Gilroy privileges the idea of diaspora, as an intermediate concept that helps to 'break the dogmatic focus on discrete *national* dynamics which has character-ised so much modern Euro-American cultural thought' (Gilroy 1993: 6). Analogously, Avtar Brah uses the concepts of diaspora and 'diaspora space', precisely in order to critique the kinds of discourse of fixed origins that Braidotti claims are part of 'diasporic thinking' (Brah 1996: 180). For Brah, the concept of diaspora takes 'account of a homing desire which is not the same thing as desire for a "homeland" ' (1996: 180); it thus holds together questions of location and dislocation. The concept of diaspora space, in which both 'native' and 'migrant' are implicated, also problematises the question of origins, by stressing the 'entanglement of genealogies of dispersion with those of "staying put" ' (1996: 181).

Gilroy's and Brah's projects are as much about unsettling and dispensing with dualisms as Braidotti's nomadism is. However, because these two theorists of the diaspora are working from different specific subject-positions, in which race and national differences cannot ever be set aside, they privilege a concept that Braidotti dismisses. There is a certain irony in a self-proclaimed polyglot nomad, who relishes her position between several languages (Braidotti 1994a: 12) not recognising sufficiently that feminists, anti-racists and postcolonial theorists may not all speak the same language, and may contest meanings among themselves.

In her reading of exiles and migrants, Braidotti makes an excep-tion for the 'postcolonial position'; but this also is based on a too-simple reading of a highly contested and complex figuration. Braidotti says that both the exile and the migrant are caught in nostalgic and debilitating relationships with time. In contrast, because the postcolonial condition is linked to movements of political resistance:

> time is not frozen for the postcolonial subject, and the memory of the past is not a stumbling block that hinders access to a changed present. Quite the contrary, the ethical impulse that

sustains the postcolonial mode makes the original culture into a living experience, one that functions as a standard of reference.

(1994a: 25)

Braidotti's only reference for this sweeping statement is an article by Gayatri Spivak on *The Satanic Verses* (Spivak 1990). But the relationship between time and the 'postcolonial mode' is a point of great contestation within postcolonial theory. As we saw in Part I, for many postcolonial theorists, it is precisely the problematising of questions of time, origin, pre-colonial culture or tradition, rather than their certainty as reference point, that is emblematic of the postcolonial condition.[1]

Thus, whilst appearing to embrace the insights of postcolonial theory in her project, Braidotti has in fact oversimplified those insights to the point of misreading them. This oversimplification, like the de-authorising of important concepts discussed earlier, suggests that Braidotti has not sufficiently armed herself against the dangers of reterritorialisation that she identifies. These problems in methodology can, I believe, be linked both to her speaking/writing position, and to the theoretical assumptions underpinning her brand of sexual difference feminism. In both cases, I will argue, Braidotti closes down the open-ended possibilities of her nomadism by failing to take issues of race and nation differences between women sufficiently into account.

The speaking/writing subject of *Nomadic Subjects*

Braidotti introduces her book, and her concept of nomadism, through her own autobiographical experience as structurally displaced. She says that her multi-lingual experience has left her in no stable relationship to language, evoking Kristeva's view that the state of translation is the common condition of all thinking beings. Her own nomadism between a number of countries and cultures has also, she says, left her with no stable relationship to a fixed identity (Braidotti 1994a: 12). But Braidotti's lack of fixity in linguistic and cultural terms is still always from a position of relative privilege – her whiteness, her Europeanness – however careful she may be at times to deconstruct the apparent unity of these terms (1994a: 9). What concerns me is a tendency to elide all displacements, deterritorialisations and nomadisms together, without giving them the benefit of their own complexity, and without examining the implications of her own position of privilege.

An example of the ways in which Braidotti's speaking/writing position closes down the question of differences between women can be found in her chapter 'Sexual Difference as a Nomadic Political Project'. This chapter begins badly, as Braidotti first lists over a dozen US-based black and postcolonial feminists in three sentences and accompanying footnotes, and then refers to them as 'ethnic and colonial thinkers' (1994a: 155). The latter designation suggests a stunning insensitivity to the meanings these terms bear in anti-racist and anti-imperialist movements, and is another example of the carelessness with terms discussed earlier. We might, perhaps, give Braidotti the benefit of the doubt, and assume that an intended 'postcolonial' was turned into 'colonial' by careless proofreading. But the 'ethnic' designation suggests that Braidotti believes that only non-white and non-Western people have 'ethnicities'.

The undifferentiated listing also repeats a move which occurs all too frequently among white Western feminists approaching questions of race and nation, and that is to lump together widely varying projects under the same rubric. To assume that simply because the feminists concerned are all US-based 'women of colour', they also automatically share theoretical starting points, methodologies or overall approaches is to deny these women the 'privilege of complexity' that white Europeans have denied their 'others' since colonial times (Mani 1992). In producing lists in this way, rather than selectively engaging in some detail with the very different ideas these women are developing, there is no way that uninitiated readers can get any sense of either the richness of debate within black, diasporic and postcolonial feminisms, or of their pertinence to white Western feminists.

Braidotti then moves on to discuss briefly the focus on feminism, race and ethnicity in Europe. She argues that the issue of race and ethnicity has been more difficult to articulate in Europe than in the US, 'partly because national differences in brands and styles of feminist political cultures have always been so great that no one dominant feminist line or standpoint has ever emerged' (Braidotti 1994a: 155). But this apparent explanation, on closer examination, proves to be problematic. Is Braidotti suggesting that it takes some kind of monolithic feminist hegemony to focus the mind enough to produce critiques of racism or ethnocentrism? If so, such a position presumes a level of homogeneity that has never existed within US feminism and, more importantly, erases the significance of anti-racist and anti-colonial/imperialist movements in putting these issues on everyone's agenda, including the agendas of feminism. Or is she implying that feminism needs to sort out 'its' theory and agenda first, before it can deal with these complicating factors of race and ethnicity? If so, this is precisely the type of attitude black and postcolonial feminists around the world have been contesting for at least two decades – that feminism is a white Western project, to which other women will be asked to contribute, but on 'our' terms and at 'our' invitation.

Braidotti's only examples of pre-1990s feminist consideration of issues of race and ethnicity in Europe leave the assumptions of her own brand of feminism unexamined. She speaks of the resistance by southern European feminists to the 'hegemony of English-style feminism' and its focus on 'gender', and argues that it is this resistance which helped put ethnicity and race on the agenda of feminist practice (1994a: 156). Bewilderingly, as an example of this, she cites (American feminist theorist) Elizabeth Spelman's critique of de Beauvoir's treatment of issues of race (see Spelman 1990: Chapter 3). If Braidotti could not find a continental European feminist critique of racism within feminism to cite (and if there are none, she should be asking why), she could at least have turned to the work of black British feminists, or to feminists working within continental Europe's former and neo-colonies.

Braidotti knows that concepts of 'difference' in the history of western European thought have been intimately linked to racism, colonialism and ethnic terror (Braidotti 1994a: 147). Her Women's Studies Department in Utrecht is involved in an inter-European exchange network committed to analysing specifically European issues of race and ethnicity (1994a: 156). Yet in discussing this work she seems reluctant to consider the ways in which racism, (neo-) colonialism and ethnocentrism may have left their traces within European feminism as well. Race and ethnicity are important for analysing the 'out there': 'anti-Semitism, the persecution of gypsies and other nomads, the various forms of economic neo-colonialism and phenomena such as intra-European migration' and their effects on women and their identities (1994a: 156). However, they seem less pertinent categories of analysis for interrogating the assumptions 'in here' that ground feminist theory. The question Braidotti never asks is the self-reflexive one: is there anything about the racial/ethnic positioning of sexual difference theorists that makes it easy for them to presume the primacy of sex and/or gender, as the ontological difference at the heart of signification and subjectivity, and to leave relatively unexplored their own unmarked categories of race and ethnicity?

The place for race and nation within sexual difference feminism

I want to suggest that, ultimately, this gap in Braidotti's project derives from the ways in which other differences are situated in relation to sexual difference in her overall theoretical framework. Braidotti wants to redefine female subjectivity so that it captures 'notions of the self as process, complexity, interrelatedness, *postcolonial simultaneities of oppression* and the multi-layered technology of the self' (1994a: 157, emphasis added). She wants to think about sexual difference as 'the difference that women can make to society – that is, not as a naturally or historically given difference, but as an open-ended project to be constructed' and about how this project can allow 'women to think of all their other differences. Foremost among these differences are race, class, age and sexual lifestyles'(1994a: 105). However, as Braidotti develops her argument, she allows the focus on other differences to slip away. How does this happen?

Braidotti works to insert racial, ethnic and other differences between women into her project by proposing a three-level cartography of sexual difference. For Braidotti these three levels refer to 'different structures of subjectivity, but also different moments in the process of becoming-subject' (1994a: 158). As such they are not necessarily sequential, and may well exist simultaneously. She describes these three levels of sexual difference as: (1) differences between men and women; (2) differences among women; and (3) differences within each woman.

Level one involves exposing the move that links the masculine to the universal and that constructs 'Woman' as devalorised other to that male-identified universal (1994a: 159). The feminist response at this level is to 'assert the specificity of the lived, female bodily experience' (1994a: 160), and to refuse for women the position of 'Woman' as man's other. It also entails a refusal of 'homologation', i.e. emancipation on the model of 'masculine' modes of thought, practice and values (1994a: 160). Level two involves a deepening of the analysis by an insistence that 'Woman-as-other' does not correspond to 'real-life women' who are rather characterised by, among other things, their embodiment, situatedness and a multiplicity of differences. Thus it is at level two that Braidotti first brings questions of race, nation, etc., into her framework (1994a: 163). Level three involves developing a model of the 'female feminist subject' as a multiplicity in herself, in which both conscious subjectivity and unconscious identity interplay, and in which such multiple variables of identity as 'class, race, age, sexual choices' (1994a: 165) are seen as 'successive identifications, that is to say unconscious internalized images that escape rational control' (1994a: 166).

There are at least three problems with this three-level model. The first is the uncritical reliance on a psychoanalytic account of how subjects are constituted, that underpins each level. Nowhere is it recognised that the privilege given to sex/gender in the psychoanalytic account of subject-constitution might be problematic for considering other differences, and that this account is a contested one. I am not saying that the psychoanalytic account can never deal adequately with other differences. We have already seen how many of Irigaray's guerrilla forays into the Lacanian model can produce resonances with postcolonial feminisms, and how Butler works to insert race into the centre of the Lacanian symbolic.[2] But it seems to me that anyone working within this framework, and aware of the criticisms of racism and ethnocentrism within feminism, needs to recognise that such accounts will be contested. Braidotti does not seem to feel this need. I will return to this point later.

The second, related problem is that when Braidotti comes to talk about the differences between women, she has nothing *specific* to say about the difference race or ethnicity may make. In fact, after making some general statements about the need to recognise that women are not all the same, and on the importance of a politics of location (1994a: 163), Braidotti moves back to look at the way in which a few white Western feminists deconstruct and challenge the concept of 'Woman' (1994a: 164). Her examples here are de Lauretis, Butler, Irigaray and Wittig. The absence of any discussion of the differences between women at level one is problematic as well. As I discussed in Part I, many Indian feminists would argue that race and nation do make a difference to the ways in which 'Woman' is posited as 'Man's other', and in which 'Man' hides behind assumptions of the universal. These moves can work through institutions, discourses and practices that are as much structured by the categories of race, religion, caste, class and nation as they are by gender, but this consideration is absent from Braidotti's level one.

It is in her chapter 'The Politics of Ontological Difference' that Braidotti begins to make more explicit why she has little specific to say about other differences. Here she shifts away from thinking about sexual difference as an 'open-ended project to be constructed' (1994a: 105) in which the differences that women can make to society are considered in relation to all the differences between them. Instead her argument moves back towards a hierarchical model in which sexual difference is prior to all other differences, and in which all other differences can be productively subsumed under the umbrella of sexual difference. For Braidotti, sexual difference is ontological: 'For me, "being in the world" means already "being sexed," so that if "I" am not sexed, "I" am not at all' (1994a: 175–6). The question for feminism then becomes 'how to connect the "differences within" each woman to a political practice that requires mediation of the "differences among" women, so as to enact and implement sexual difference' (1994a: 180). Braidotti argues that 'My "being-a-woman" just like my "being-in-language" and "being-mortal" is one of the constitutive elements of my subjectivity' (1994a: 186). And it is only once this is established, that we can take up the question of differences between women:

> The recognition of the sameness of our gender, all other differences taken into account, is a sufficient and necessary condition to make explicit a bond *among* women that is more than the ethics of solidarity and altogether other than the sharing of common interests. Once this bond is established [...] the basis is set for the elaboration of other values, of different representations of our common difference.
>
> (Braidotti 1994a: 186)

The slippage here from 'being *sexed*' as an ontological difference, to 'the sameness of our *gender*', is instructive. It indicates that Braidotti has the same problems with incorporating an attention to race, ethnicity and other differences into a sexual difference framework that I suggested, in Chapter 3, were present in Chanter's and Hodge's discussions of Irigaray. Again, a potentially productive opening in the sexual difference model is closed down. Instead of considering how the specifically female way of 'being sexed' might be simultaneously related to a multiplicity of gendered, racialised, ethnic and other identities, which are mutually constitutive, 'being a woman' is again primarily linked to an economy framed by sex/gender alone. Instead of taking the focus on the specifically female as an opportunity to open out 'being a woman' to these other differences, it becomes a way of subsuming them under the general umbrella of sexual difference. A hierarchy is re-established in which other differences are 'taken into account' only once the bond of common gender is established. This makes sense if one accepts a Lacanian account of the constitution of the subject in language, but not if one questions this account as the only possible description of how we come to be selves in language and in society. This is the great 'unsaid' in Braidotti's project, and yet it seems to me to be vital for any feminist working to open up the space for differences between women.

If we take differences between women seriously, then we need to recognise that, for many women, being-a-woman, being-in-language and being-mortal are not the only constitutive elements of their sense of self, nor are they exclusively related to questions of gender. Being raced, or being marked by both the discursive-symbolic and bodily-material codes of particular national, ethnic or religious communities, may also be fundamentally constitutive of subjectivity. And it is precisely the 'bond of common gender' that is blocked until these 'other differences' are 'taken into account'. While Braidotti has recognised that black and postcolonial feminists have problems with the sexual difference approach, 'for its globalizing tendency that cancels out all other differences by submitting them to its overarching importance', she has never done more than 'regret not being able to pursue' this critique in her writing (Braidotti 1994b: 170). But this response itself suggests that Braidotti is still seeing the question of those 'other differences' as something that needs to be added on to a pre-existing theoretical framework, rather than as evidence of a need to move beyond prevailing paradigms.

The third problem with this approach, which I will discuss in the final section, is the underlying model of language that Braidotti turns to, and the way she positions desire, reason, the unconscious and resistance in relation to this model of language.

The univocal polyglot?

As we saw in the first section, Braidotti's evocation of the nomad as polyglot seems to agree with a Deleuzian focus on a multiplicity of languages rather than a universal system of Language, and on the ways in which languages intersect with 'diverse modes of coding (biological, political, economic, etc.) that bring into play not only different regimes of signs but also states of things of differing status' (Deleuze and Guattari 1988: 7). This could have been an entry point to redressing some of the difficulties that occur when feminist theorists work with a singular model of language that focuses primarily on exclusion.

Thinking about the feminist as polyglot could also have offered a site from which Braidotti might move away from the Lacanian model of entry into language and subjectivity, which, as we saw above, leads to a privileging of sexual difference over all other differences. Instead, Braidotti takes the figuration of the nomad as polyglot in quite a different direction, one which reinstates a univocal model of language that in turn closes down the space in which to consider both women's complexity and their possibilities of resistance. One way that Braidotti does this is by linking her own experience as polyglot to the arbitrariness of language. She begins by charting her own multilingual trajectory from Italy, through Australia and France to the Netherlands (Braidotti 1994a: 8–12). However, the important point for her about living between a number of languages becomes, not the specificities of different languages, but rather the way they are all the same in their arbitrariness (1994a: 14–15). She holds to the Lacanian view that 'all tongues carry the name of the father and are stamped by its register' (1994a: 11). It is this kind of univocal 'being-in-language' that Braidotti evokes in her problematic privileging of sexual difference discussed above. If 'being-a-woman' always means 'being-in-language' in this way, then where is multiplicity to be found?

For Braidotti, the 'key notion to understanding multiple identity is desire, that is to say unconscious processes' (1994a: 14). Language and the 'imperialism of rational thought' (1994a: 198) need to cover over the excess that is pre-discursive, pre-conscious affectivity and desire, and what Braidotti refers to as the non-thought at the heart of thinking (1994a: 14). It is these 'unconscious internalized images that escape rational control' (1994a: 166) which can point to the 'steps, the shifts, and the points of exit that would make it possible for women to move beyond the phallogocentric gender dualism' (1994a: 170). Following this language model, then, means that both multiplicity and resistance are to be found in some space at the edge of language, consciousness and reason.

On one level, Braidotti recognises the difficulty of change at the level of our unconscious structures, identifications and desires (1994a: 31). She is trying to find ways of initiating what can only be a slow and complex process for feminism of negotiating between 'unconscious structures of desire and conscious political choices' (1994a: 31). But, as in her unproblematised celebration of the nomad space as a kind of power-free zone, Braidotti tends to undermine this attention to complexity by celebrating unconscious desire as the pre-discursive foundation for a new model of the subject that takes multiplicity as its starting point (1994a: 198). But this brings us back to that binary logic in which language only works through excluding multiplicity and indeterminacy, and which posits an 'outside' as the only possible space of resistance. As a feminist project for rethinking identity, this can turn attention away from the differences between women in two ways. First, by positing some pure space of unproblematic multiplicity that is 'outside' language and the *polis*, it turns attention away from the complex intersections of discourses, material practices and social institutions in which specific differences emerge. Second, it can disarm feminists into thinking that their resistance is safe from the dangers of re-importing those power relations into their projects. In Braidotti's project, we see both of these dangers materialised; she neither has anything very specific to say about differences of race, nation and other community identities, nor does she remain attentive to the ways in which she re-centres the white Western feminist subject in the name of nomadism.

In this chapter I have argued that Rosi Braidotti's project to rethink identity through the figuration of the nomad ultimately fails to follow through on its promise to maintain a double focus on women and their differences. Braidotti's difficulties emerge from her failure to take the question of location adequately into account, on a number of levels. First, while the Deleuzian image of the nomad might have led her to rethink the terms within which location and dislocation are related, Braidotti opts instead for a pure celebration of dislocation. This closes down her project from engaging with some of the most important insights of postcolonial feminisms. Second, Braidotti's own locatedness is not taken sufficiently into account, both in terms of the ways her celebration of the nomad re-centres the experiences of white Western women, and in terms of the ways in which her sexual difference framework ultimately privileges sex/gender over other differences. Third, her tendency to locate resistance in a space outside language and power relations undermines her objective of breaking out of the inclusion/exclusion paradigm of a logic of dualisms to a more complex model of identity and difference.

One of the feminist theorists Braidotti claims to draw inspiration from in her development of 'sexual difference as a nomadic political project' (1994a: 146) is Donna Haraway. Haraway too begins from a desire for a feminist theory of difference that breaks out of a logic of binaries in order to hold sex, gender, race and other differences analytically together. In the next chapter, I discuss how her approach to this challenge differs significantly from Braidotti's and opens up possibilities that Braidotti closes off.

Chapter 6

Donna Haraway's promising monsters

At the start of this book I quoted Donna Haraway as she argued that feminist theory and politics will always have trouble holding together sex/gender, race and other identity categories without 'a theory of "difference" whose geometries, paradigms, and logics break out of binaries, dialectics and nature/culture models of any kind' (Haraway 1991: 129). Haraway's arithmetical challenge to feminism – that it learn to 'count to four' – is a call to think about paradigm shifts that would problematise many of the assumptions about ontology, power and language that much of feminist theory still takes as its starting points.

Thus, while her work has many points of convergence with that of Irigaray, Butler and Braidotti, I will argue in this chapter that Haraway's project is also a highly distinctive one within white Western feminist theory. Where Irigaray, Butler and Braidotti, in different ways, work to unsettle the stability of dualistic systems of thought, Haraway works to elaborate an alternative system that embodies a different logic altogether. Where Irigaray aims to locate the transgressive excess that can jam the theoretical machinery of Language as a system, Haraway argues that a more complex and unstable field already exists in which languages, codes and 'cyborg noise' intertwine. Where Butler discounts any move to ontology as reinstating a logic of pure origins and stable, pre-discursive identities, Haraway argues for a redefined ontology of *im*purity, based on 'mutation, metamorphosis and diaspora' (Haraway 1992a: 378), in which it is possible to acknowledge that all stories begin, not at a site of pure origin, but 'in the middle' (1992a: 280). Furthermore, where Braidotti celebrates a dislocated 'line of escape' from a logic of dualisms that has the unintended effect of leaving that logic intact, Haraway works with a more complicated model that redefines situatedness within impure spaces.

I argued in Part I that one of the key insights to emerge from a reading of Indian feminisms is that women's location within and across identity categories such as gender, race and nation cannot be easily contained within binary models. In this context, Haraway's attempt to elaborate a different model of difference, and her insistence that evidence of such a model already exists, takes on particular significance. Whilst not always completely successful, Haraway's project to think multiplicity outside a logic of binaries allows her to address many of the complications to feminist theoretical approaches to identity and differences between women that emerge from my reading of Indian feminisms.

In this chapter, I discuss four aspects of Haraway's work. I begin by looking at the alternative model of the self that emerges from Haraway's efforts to rethink multiplicity outside a geometrics of dualisms. In the second section, I discuss Haraway's approach to the questions of location and dispersal, and the underlying model of power that shapes her insistence on situating both knowledges and selves in impure spaces. I then consider the implications of her model of situatedness for feminist politics. The third section looks at the ways in which Haraway challenges many of the assumptions about language as a system that are predominant within Western feminist theory. In the final section, I evaluate the degree to which these problematisations in terms of ontology, epistemology and politics enable a double focus on 'women' and their differences.

Counting to four – thinking multiplicity outside a geometrics of binaries

Writing from the intersecting space of the history of science, political economy and feminist theory, Donna Haraway argues that fundamental paradigm shifts are already under way in the late twentieth century that provide the possibility of different ways of conceptualising the self and difference. These emerging paradigm shifts might allow us to rethink the self outside the self/other, part/whole framework that has hitherto dominated Western thought. Haraway identifies these break-points in current discourses and practices across a wide field: in science and technology; in science fiction literature; in the reorganisation of capitalism in the late twentieth century; and in a variety of political resistance movements, including feminist politics.

Haraway brings these disparate elements together in a writing style that is notoriously complex and multi-layered, but which also engages the reader by its rich use of irony and playfulness. All this makes Haraway's work particularly difficult to summarise, without oversimplifying it in ways that suggest a homogeneity across the different fields she incorporates into her work. At the same time, there is a tendency in Haraway's work that does lend itself to such totalising readings. For example, when she presents wide-ranging lists and tables of the varied human activities that converge to produce a single 'informatics of domination' or which locate 'women in the integrated circuit', it is tempting to conclude that she is arguing that the world always works in one way (Haraway 1991: 161–2, 170–2). The repeated use of terminology drawn from militarised communications technology, such as C3I – command-control-communications-intelligence – can suggest that there is a single, monolithic grid on which we are all positioned as 'code problems' (1991: 175). There is also at times a slippage from considering the globalising effects of technological change (which may be highly specific and varied in different places) to suggesting a single view of the globe. These elements of a grand narrative, with its totalising claims, actually work against Haraway's project for acknowledging complexity by freeing difference from the constraints of a logic of dualisms.

Rather than focus on the Haraway who perhaps tries to make too many connections in order to tell us how things are, I find it more useful to look at the Haraway who tells us how things might be. The specific paradigm shifts that she identifies in her travels across disciplinary boundaries remain contested and contestable models. However, by challenging the logic of the self/other, part/whole paradigms from which they emerge, these shifts offer possible ways out of those paradigms. Haraway argues that the world has moved beyond the 'organic, hierarchical dualisms ordering discourse in "the West" since Aristotle still ruled' (Haraway 1991: 163) and that our models need to keep pace. In a world in which the codes and standards that process information are in a perpetual state of reconstruction, and where, consequently, any component can be interfaced with any other, there are no sacred bodies, spaces, or objects anymore (1991: 163). The self that emerges from these paradigm shifts is both 'disassembled and reassembled' and 'collective and personal'. Feminists need to learn to code this self outside the familiar frame of dichotomies between mind and body, public and private, organism and machine, men and women, etc. (1991: 163).

Two key aspects of these alternative models of the self are a problematising of origins, and also of distinctions between inside and outside. As we saw in Part I, these are also crucial factors to developing a more complicated understanding of women's location within and across identity categories such as race and nation. In particular, we have seen that women are positioned in highly problematic ways in narratives of national or community identities when they have to stand for the pure space of origin and home, the authentic, unchanging tradition through which contemporary identities are linked to a glorious past. The models that interest Haraway in her search for multiplicity outside a frame of dualisms give up the desire for stories about a 'pure' origin, and work instead with noise and pollution (1991: 175–6). They are illegitimate couplings that subvert 'the structure and modes of reproduction of "Western" identity, of nature and culture, of mirror and eye, slave and master, body and mind' (1991: 176).

In a telling contrast to Braidotti's engagement at the level of generalities, Haraway repeatedly engages in detail with the ideas of black and postcolonial feminists to suggest who these 'illegitimate' selves might be. She often evokes Trinh T. Minh-ha's notion of 'inappropriate/d others', who are inappropriate within prevailing paradigms and so, perhaps, never fully appropriated. Haraway also draws on Chicana feminist retellings of the story of Malinche, the indigenous South American woman who was Cortez' first interpreter, and who was, as his mistress, 'mother of the mestizo "bastard" race of the new world' (1991: 175). Reviled within male-centred Chicano nationalist discourse as the whore who bears the shame of conquest and national impurity, from a feminist perspective, Malinche can be refigured as a different kind of model of the self and of identity that does not depend on access to an original language and the right to 'natural' names, father's or mother's. Malinche's mastery of the conqueror's language is seen as an illegitimate production that ensures a survival of the self, based not on innocence, but on the ability to live without a founding myth of original wholeness (see Moraga 1986; Alarcon 1994). Amrita Chhachhi has argued that women need not only to challenge predominant models of national and other community identities, but also to actively participate in redefining the content of these identities (Chhachhi 1991: 148). The re-reading of Malinche can be seen as just such an effort to develop alternative narratives of community identity that don't start from assumptions of purity.

Haraway also returns often in her writing to the work of black American science fiction author Octavia Butler. Butler's work is concerned with disturbing the boundaries between self and other as they are worked through categories of gender, race, species and kind. Haraway is interested in its 'resistance to the imperative to recreate the sacred image of the same' (Haraway 1992a: 378), in its promise of 'an ontology based on mutation, metamorphosis and diaspora' where there is no simple access to origins (1992a: 378). In Butler's *Xenogenesis* trilogy of novels, the interactions between humans and gene-trading aliens result in hybrid communities in which none of the players has a pure origin story to tell and none of their bodies can be thought of as stable, unchanging containers for a fixed identity. None of their origin stories begin in a 'Garden' of pure beginnings (Haraway 1991: 151) but rather always somewhere 'in the middle'. Nevertheless, these troubled and troublesome communities persist, and their messy origin stories continue to be told to and by the strange metamorphosing selves that emerge through the three novels of Butler's narrative. Identity categories do not disappear, but both the self and the unity of community identity persist without dependence on a 'myth of original unity out of which difference must be produced' and dominated (1991: 151).

Similarly, Haraway looks to new formulations in areas such as immunology, computer communications and the foetal economy to contest the power to define of traditional inner/outer, self/other paradigms. In immunology, traditional paradigms of the external invader assailing the body's internal defence mechanisms are being challenged; instead it is suggested that the molecules of the immune system work by mirroring and rehearsing responses to possible interactions with other molecules. In such a system, inner/outer distinctions lose their power to define (Haraway 1991: 218–19), and a 'radical conception of *connection* emerges unexpectedly at the core of the defended self' (Haraway 1992b: 323).

Computer communications 'breakdown' can be reconceptualised, not as a purely negative situation where boundaries break down, but rather as a productive moment in which the different components in a network of relationships become more visible

(Haraway 1991: 214–15). Haraway also uses the example of the foetal economy which only functions because the immune system works to mask rather than expose the foreignness of foetal tissue, so that it is accepted by the maternal body (1991: 253 fn 8). These new formulations in scientific discourse suggest ways of holding on to a notion of self by shifting the terms within which it is understood. The fiction of an economy of the same, in which contained selves only reach truth by excluding the other, gives way to a semi-permeable, but still finite, self:

> Immunity can also be conceived in terms of shared specificities; of the semi-permeable self able to engage with others (human and non-human, inner and outer), but always with finite consequences; of situated possibilities and impossibilities of individuation and identification; and of partial fusions and dangers.
>
> (1991: 225)

Haraway's best-known counter-model of the semi-permeable self is, of course, the cyborg, which has attained a certain cult status both within and beyond feminist theory, and which has helped to inspire a variety of brands of 'cyberfeminism' (Marsden 1996). For Haraway, the figure of the cyborg emerges at the breakdown of boundaries between human and animal, organism and machine, physical and non-physical, nature and culture (Haraway 1991: 150–3). Like Haraway's other counter-models, it both rejects recourse to pure unified origins and confounds categorical distinctions. But with the figure of the cyborg Haraway also introduces a third challenge to a logic of dualisms. She challenges binaries by refusing to assign one term with the status of 'resource for appropriation or incorporation' for the other (1991: 151):

> It is not clear who makes and who is made in the relation between human and machine. It is not clear what is mind and what is body in machines that resolve into coding practices.
>
> (1991: 177)

Haraway's cyborg is a model that refuses the binary separation into object and subject. In dualistic paradigms, the machine might be viewed as the 'object' upon which the human 'subject' acts. For

Haraway, that 'object' is rather always 'an actor and agent, not a screen, or a ground or a resource' (1991: 198).

For Haraway, the cyborg is a protean monster that can break through 'the maze of dualisms' (1991: 181) by not foreclosing on the possible connections that might be made between 'problematic selves and unexpected others' (Haraway 1992b: 300). But protean monsters will, by their nature, have unintended manifestations, and the cyborg has taken on a number of different shapes within feminist theory, not all of which are equally amenable to the reading of Haraway I am proposing in this chapter. This shape-shifting of the cyborg is, to some extent at least, a product of Haraway's style and determinedly eclectic theoretical approach. In making her enthusiastic and wide-ranging connections to articulate a cyborg-self, she often puts together terminology from a variety of theoretical approaches, including deconstruction and psychoanalysis. This has led some feminists to engage with the cyborg as operating either within a deconstructive or psychoanalytic frame, usually to conclude that it does not fully succeed within these terms.

For example, Mary Ann Doane has characterised the cyborg in deconstructive terms as 'a performative utterance – a staging of an uninhabitable feminist position' (Doane 1989: 209). Analogously, Christina Crosby criticises Haraway for not fully following through on what she identifies as a deconstructive desire to 'open a text beyond any thematic coherence' (Crosby 1989: 208). I agree with Crosby when she questions the ways in which Haraway sometimes juxtaposes theories that don't fit together (1989: 207), but disagree with her conclusion that Haraway is trying, and failing, to work within an overall deconstructive approach.

To be more explicit in my criticism of such readings of Haraway: a deconstructive approach argues that the apparently stable and coherent subject depends on the excluded, abjected ground of the object, and that this exclusion needs to be made visible in order to destabilise Language as a system. But what interests Haraway is 'not just literary deconstruction but liminal transformation' (Haraway 1991: 177). For her, the presence of such counter-models as the cyborg demonstrate that it is already possible to move beyond destabilising binary systems to a different paradigm altogether. It is not identifying an 'uninhabitable feminist position' within a single symbolic system that interests Haraway, but rather identifying the *in*habitable 'inappropriate/d' positions that are already emerging from a multiplicity of discursive and material practices.

Moving from deconstructive to psychoanalytic models, Mary Ann Doane also criticises Haraway's cyborg for its rejection of a narrative of origins (Doane 1989: 210). For Doane, this leads Haraway to foreclose on the possibility of a theory of subjectivity. What she means is that Haraway rejects a psychoanalytic theory of subjectivity, which is not necessarily the same thing. For Haraway, it ought to be possible to have a sense of self without reference back to a single, stable origin, and without a binary division between the subject-self that acts and the object of desire and appropriation. Haraway seeks to work with something other than the 'paradigmatic psychoanalytic question' that always views the self in terms of '(always unrealizable) identity; always wobbling, it still pivots on the law of the father, the sacred image of the same' (1992b: 324).

For Haraway, psychoanalytic paradigms still hold on to the subject/object binary she argues is both unnecessary and obsolete. So, when Irigaray asks questions such as 'what if the "object" started to speak?' and 'if the earth turned and more especially turned upon herself?' (Irigaray 1974: 135, 133), Haraway might answer, 'the object' already does. When Braidotti argues for a 'cyborg equipped with an unconscious' (Braidotti 1994a: 36), Haraway would question the need for any such additional baggage.

Rather than limiting feminist theory to destabilising the ways in which nature is positioned as the ground of culture, sex as the resource for gender, woman the specular mirror for man, etc., Haraway argues that we can already revision the world as composed of both human and non-human actors, as a 'coding trickster with whom we must learn to converse' (Haraway 1991: 201). Nature, sex, etc., are not 'natural' but 'artifactual', with their own specific histories. They are not resources but 'an achievement among many actors, not all of them human, not all of them organic' (Haraway 1992b: 297).

Although this insight of Haraway's has often been used to focus on revisioning humans' relationship with nature or with machines (Halberstam 1991; Alaimo 1994), I think it has important implications as well for thinking about women and differences. Such an approach suggests ways of both holding on to and transforming the 'woman-as-ground' formulation that I have discussed in relation to Irigaray and to Lata Mani and other Indian feminists. It allows a double focus that simultaneously recognises that (1) 'Woman' and 'women' can be positioned within prevailing power relations as the ground upon which gendered, raced and national identities are constituted; and that (2) that ground is never fully silent, abjected or objectified, but is rather always a fertile one, with agency and a voice that are always playing their part in its reconstitution. Refiguring the ground as already speaking and acting means that sources of instabilities and resistance are to be found from within prevailing power relations and not from their abjected, excluded outside. For Haraway, what needs 're-coding' is not just the binary logic that locates 'Woman' and 'women' as object, ground or resource, but also the conceptualisation of that ground as inert.

Through counter-models such as the cyborg, Haraway is making the strong claim that it is possible to think multiplicity outside the frame of dualisms. But, as the above discussion suggests, this is not an unproblematised flight into an 'elsewhere' such as is offered at times by Braidotti's nomadic trajectory. Haraway avoids many of the pitfalls I identified in Braidotti's nomadic project through her very different approach to the question of location, and through the model of power which underpins her work. I turn to these points in the next section.

Promises and risks, pleasures and responsibilities

Haraway calls her counter-models of the self 'promising monsters' (Haraway 1992b); they are the misfits that reside within and potentially work against currently dominant paradigms. But precisely because these alternatives emerge from within prevailing paradigms, and from within power relations as structured by those paradigms, they are never secure from the destructive monsters those same paradigms produce (Haraway 1991: 190). A careful reading of Haraway shows that each of her alternative figurations is always contested and contestable. They are possible but dangerous articulations of an alternative world that emerge from within a complex network of power relations; they are the unintended, but never innocent, results of productive power that enables as it constrains.

Haraway's cyborg is often enlisted in projects that aim for a more contingent, relational and shifting view of the subject.

Ironically, this paradigm of undecidability, of category confusion, is evoked at times in decidedly, categorically unproblematised ways, including by Braidotti (Braidotti 1994a: 102–10). But this is to read a one-dimensional character onto the cyborg that Haraway herself consistently resists:

> From one perspective, a cyborg world is about the final imposition of a grid of control on the planet [...]. From another perspective, a cyborg world might be about lived social and bodily realities in which people are [...] not afraid of permanently partial identities and contradictory standpoints. The political struggle is to *see from both perspectives at once because each reveals both dominations and possibilities unimaginable from the other vantage point.*
>
> (Haraway 1991: 154, emphasis added)

Thus, one of the strengths of Haraway's approach is that, whilst making a passionate and committed argument for alternative feminist visions, she works hard to sustain an awareness that the constructs she evokes remain contested and heterogeneous (1991: 212), promising and risky, possible and dangerous.

This underlying model of power, which recognises both that there are no pure power-free zones, and that power is productive of the means of contestation, is important to understanding Haraway's approach to questions of location. If Braidotti's nomadic self takes pleasure in transgressing boundaries, Haraway's cyborg adds to that pleasure the complicating factor of accountability for their construction (1991: 150). This means that Haraway's project of envisioning an alternative model of the self always holds questions of location and dispersal in productive tension. For Haraway:

> boundaries materialize in social interaction. Boundaries are drawn by mapping practices; 'objects' do not pre-exist as such. [...] But boundaries shift from within; boundaries are very tricky. What boundaries provisionally contain remains generative, productive of meanings and bodies. Siting (sighting) boundaries is a risky business.
>
> (1991: 201)

There are four interconnected moves involved here. First of all, boundaries do not simply exist, they emerge via social interactions and relationships. Second, then, boundaries are contestable, shifting and permeable. Third, however, we can't do without boundaries. Fourth, then, we need to be accountable for how we construct those boundaries. By 'counting to four' in this way, Haraway reclaims a more complicated sense of locatedness that derives from a recognition of the impurity of all spaces.

The need to draw contestable borders and to be accountable for how we draw them, is also central to Haraway's concept of 'situated knowledges'. This has implications for the way she views differences between women within a feminist politics:

> The knowing self is partial in all its guises, never finished, whole, simply there and original; it is always constructed and stitched together imperfectly, and *therefore* able to join with another, to see together without claiming to be another.
>
> (Haraway 1991: 193)

The feminist subject-position sought by Haraway is not one that claims a unified identity for all women, but rather one that starts from recognising situatedness and partiality. It is our inevitable incompleteness that makes partial connection possible, not our ability to represent the complete range of women's experiences and identities. There is no single privileged standpoint, since there is no way to be simultaneously and fully in all positions structured by gender, race, nation and class. The search for such a position is 'the search for the fetishized perfect subject of oppositional history' (1991: 193). Being everywhere is just the flip side of being nowhere, the disembodied Eye-I, the 'god-trick' of infinite vision. Feminists need to counterpose this either/or model with one that privileges 'the joining of partial views and halting voices into a collective subject position that promises a vision of the means of ongoing finite embodiment, of living within limits and contradictions, i.e. of views from somewhere' (1991: 196). This is quite different from Braidotti's nomad, who is in a sense claiming to be nowhere in particular, and therefore everywhere.

Recognising that feminists need to be accountable for the borders they necessarily draw in developing their 'views from somewhere' means that Haraway is also consistently more attentive to the dangers of 'multilingualism' than is Braidotti's polyglot nomad. Whilst Haraway's 'situated knowledges' have become common currency for many feminist theorists, including Braidotti, few present the concept with as much attention to the difficulty of the process as she does. Nor do all appropriations of Haraway share her insistence that 'views from somewhere' involve political and ethical choices: 'politics and ethics ground struggles over knowledge projects' (1991: 193), including within feminist theory.

In terms of a possible feminist politics that combines pleasure in transgressing boundaries with responsibility for their construction, Haraway privileges the idea of coalitions, based on affinities, rather than any model of identity politics. For Haraway, 'affinity groups' recognise that negotiating differences will be an intrinsic part of their politics (Haraway 1992b: 318). They come together, not because of an assumed, pre-existent and 'natural' identity, but because they are 'imperfectly stitched together' as partial, differently situated selves. They are 'wary of holism but needy for connection', looking for 'united front politics without the vanguard party' (Haraway 1991: 151). Affinity groups thus involve an acknowledgement of difference – that no one individual or collective political position can ever be fully representative of all those it claims to 'speak for' – rather than an assumption of a representable identity of interests as the basis of their politics (Haraway 1992b: 311–13).

Haraway has defined affinities as 'related not by blood but by choice' (Haraway 1991: 155), although we need to be careful in how we read her use of the term 'choice' here. While Marsden (1996: 14) has accused Haraway of allowing a 'decisionist vocabulary' and a concept of 'transcendent agency' to creep back into her project through her use of terms like 'choice' and 'responsibility', I think it would be wrong to conclude that Haraway is working with an unproblematised understanding of these terms. She clearly rejects definitions of 'choice' framed in terms of a 'liberal epistemology and politics' that posits an autonomous human agency which pre-exists its social and discursive locatedness (Haraway 1991: 176). Elsewhere, she describes possible feminist coalitions based on affinity as 'adopted families and imperfect intentional communities, based not so much on "choice" as on hope and memory of the always already fallen apart structure of the world' (1991: 121). I will return to Marsden's critique of Haraway at the end of this section, but first, I want to pursue a bit further the distinction Haraway makes between 'identity' and 'affinity politics'.

My understanding is that Haraway distinguishes between identity 'by blood' and affinity 'by choice', in order to stress that feminist political unity needs to be achieved rather than presumed. The category 'women', as the subject of/for feminist theory and politics, is not something that is 'natural', 'organic' or 'in the blood'; it is rather a difficult achievement, which involves making many non-innocent choices. For Haraway, feminists:

> must negotiate the very fine line between appropriation of another's (never innocent) experience and the delicate construction of the just-barely-possible affinities, the just-barely-possible connections that might actually make a difference in local and global histories.
>
> (Haraway 1991: 113)

The never innocent 'intentional imperfect communities' that emerge in the impure space of an 'already fallen apart structure of the world', need to replace those apparently more 'natural' unities of 'mothers and daughters, co-wives, sisters, or lesbian lovers' (1991: 121) that presume unity as a resource, rather than as an achievement. For Haraway, then, feminist politics always needs to be ready to ask 'Who are "we"?' This is, for her, an inherently open question: 'one always ready for contingent, friction-generating articulations' (Haraway 1992b: 324). These articulations involve making 'terms of agreement', putting 'things together, scary things, risky things, contingent things' (1992b: 324). Here, Haraway can be heard to be speaking to the insights from Indian feminisms discussed in Part I in two different ways. First, her problematising of the collective subject of feminism speaks to the concerns of Ania Loomba (1993), Flavia Agnes (1995) and others who have pointed to the dangers inherent when women's movements take for granted their right to speak for a 'we', particularly in the context of racial, ethnic and other communal conflicts. Second, her definition of communities as never innocent, and as always needing to be achieved, works as a challenge to those narratives of fixed community identity that depend on an active management of women and on constituting 'woman' as their site of pure origin.

Haraway's version of feminist politics has been criticised from two quite different directions from within white Western feminist theory. On the one hand, some read the cyborg who is 'needy for connection' as a possible route to relativism. Thus, Christina Crosby has argued that Haraway's cyborg may not know how to say 'no' to some of its possible and more problematic connections.

Since Crosby wants a feminist politics of exclusion as well as inclusion, she questions whether Haraway really provides a basis on which to 'make the right connections and block the wrong ones' (Crosby 1989: 208). But this is to read only one half of the double move I have argued Haraway sustains throughout her work. The cyborg who is 'needy of connection' is also 'wary of holism'; she/it is a promising *and* dangerous monster who both takes pleasure in transgressing boundaries *and* is accountable for constructing them.

Similarly, Stacy Alaimo wonders about feminists' ability to separate from what she calls 'phallotechnology' if they embrace the cyborg (Alaimo 1994: 149). Alaimo argues for a reversal of Haraway's affinity formulation: 'Instead of grounding politics in affinity (which often slides into essentialist definitions) [...] feminism could ground affinity in politics' (1994: 149–50). But this is to mis-read affinity as something easy to establish – as something 'in the blood' – rather than as the difficult and ongoing achievement that Haraway describes.

On the other hand, others have accused Haraway of falling back into a 'security system of humanist values' by holding on to such concepts as responsibility, choice and progressive politics (Marsden 1996: 14). In particular, Jill Marsden argues that Haraway's cyborg feminism can only defend itself against accusations of technological determinism by allowing appeals to 'political accountability', 'transcendent agency' and a 'decisionist vocabulary' to sneak in by the back door (1996: 14). But is responsibility inevitably linked to a concept of transcendent agency? Is agency only and always transcendent? Why does holding on to some concept of responsibility have to lead to taking on the whole package of 'humanist values'? Indeed, it seems to me that, in Haraway's usage, responsibility for constructing boundaries is a way of working against transcendence. It is about recognising that things never free-float forever; that they do, if only contingently and impermanently, coalesce in a kind of stability; that there is no transcendent outside to these bounded times and spaces from which to act politically; and that therefore we need to be vigilant about what political effects these borders will have, so that, when necessary, they can be re-drawn.

Marsden also criticises Haraway for failing to note the contradiction between her rejection of 'the tradition of progress, the tradition of the appropriation of nature as resource for the productions of culture' (Haraway 1991: 150) and her continuing to advocate 'effective progressive politics' (1991: 165, cited in Marsden 1996: 16 fn 63). But Marsden is conflating two different things here. One is the contesting of a particular definition of progress, one that posits a teleology and a single agent of progress. The other is judging some actions progressive, because they give those who are subordinated greater space in which to speak and act. To unapologetically call such actions progressive (as Haraway does) is not necessarily to accept the teleological narrative of progress as the triumph of human culture over nature.

Marsden simply asserts that agency is necessarily 'transcendent'; she never engages directly with the ways in which Haraway problematises agency in terms of her model of the self or her model of power. Marsden never discusses Haraway's attempts to de-link agency from the model of the 'humanist subject' in its binary relation with an acted-upon object. Haraway's use of concepts such as 'agency' and 'responsibility' needs to be placed in the context of her alternative model of a 'semi-permeable' and situated self, and of her view of power as a 'field of enabling constraints' (Haraway 1991: 135). It is only on the basis of re-working the relationship between self, other and power that Haraway can speak of the possibility of 'agency – or agencies – without defended subjects' (1991: 3).

Language, languages, codes and noise

As I have already argued, although Haraway uses some poststructuralist terminology throughout her work, it would be wrong to conclude that her overall project depends either on a Lacanian or a Derridean-inspired focus on Language as a system. Like many feminists, Haraway is highly critical of the tendency to organise thought around binary categories. But while most feminist appropriations of poststructuralist theories focus on the inevitability of the binary within Language as a system (even when there is a move 'beyond' the binary), Haraway is more interested in the political and social history of particular binary categories in specific languages. And this is an approach which leaves more space open for the susceptibility of linguistic categories to variation and to change.

Haraway's essay 'Gender for a Marxist Dictionary' is a good example of this approach. Beginning from a reflection on the difficulties involved in comprehensively defining any term within a single language, let alone trying to find its 'match' in any other language, Haraway's focus is on specific languages as sites of political contestation (Haraway 1991: 128–48). She explores the different meanings of gender within and between languages. She notes that the sex/gender distinction that English-speaking feminists often now take as a given, has its own unruly history, and is also difficult to sustain in other languages. She looks at how the work of black American feminists and other women of colour unsettles the sex/gender binary by insisting on adding race to the equation. What emerges from these historically specific discussions is a view of languages as unstable, as directly related to power relations and as polyvocal.

Whilst moving from a focus on Language to languages, Haraway's engagement with changes in technology and their social and economic impact suggests that we need to work with a still broader field of meaning and communication. Both communications science and modern biologies view the world as a problem of *coding* (Haraway 1991: 164). Furthermore, codes do not work in the same way that it is generally assumed natural languages do. As we saw in the consideration of Butler's work in Chapter 4, theorists who take Language as the model on which identity is constituted and power is exercised tend to privilege differentiation and exclusion. In Butler's view, the logic of Language still rests on binaries, so that coherence and control are always purchased at the price of abjection, and asserting an identity always entails a loss of connection and complexity.

But, within informatics and biology, codes do not function according to a logic of exclusion, and this model of coding has also had an impact on current paradigms of knowledge. Here, codes work through connection, not exclusion, and control is gained, not through fixing boundaries, but by finding codes that open up transitions between apparently separate and bounded components (Haraway 1991: 164–5). For Haraway, in a world increasingly fashioned through microelectronics and biotechnology, the logic of control through connection needs to be taken into account, at least as much as the logic of differentiation drawn from language models.

In this more complex field of mechanisms of control and of meaning, resistance has to come from more than one direction. One of those directions is the cyborg's:

> struggle against perfect communication, against the one code
> that translates all meaning perfectly [...]. That is why cyborg
> politics insist on noise and advocate pollution, rejoicing in the
> illegitimate fusions of animal and machine. These are the cou-
> plings which make Man and Woman so problematic, subvert-
> ing the structure of desire, the force imagined to generate
> language and gender.
>
> (Haraway 1991: 176)

If we think of noise as undifferentiated sound, as sound which
has not yet been fitted in to the recognisable patterns of either
language or codes, then it suggests a field rich in possibilities for the
self to draw from, pattern and re-pattern. Noise can be thought of
as an 'infinite and continuously evolving flow ... an impermanent
and continuously changing plane of sound' in which the self
constitutes itself through an 'openness to difference, the indefinite
and the indistinct' (Battersby 1998: 180). In Haraway's model,
'noise' is the field, rich in information and possibilities, through
which the cyborg self moves. Cyborg 'noise' contests both the code
model logic that locks all connection into controlled patterns, and
the Language model logic that locks meaning only into processes of
exclusion and differentiation. Cyborg noise challenges coding
attempts at perfect communication, but it also resists those clear
binary distinctions of self and other, of a self separated from and
desiring the other, that are 'imagined to generate language and
gender'.

Yet at the same time Haraway also claims that cyborg politics 'is
the struggle *for* language' (Haraway 1991: 176, emphasis added). I
read this in the context of Haraway's view of languages as a site of
political contestation, discussed above, but also in the context of
her alternate model of 'illegitimate' or impure selves who give up on
the search for original languages and 'natural names, mother's or
father's' (1991: 175). Against the dream of a common language,
Haraway privileges 'a powerful infidel heteroglossia [...] an
imagination of a feminist speaking in tongues' (1991: 181). The
cyborg struggle *for* language can also be read as part of Haraway's
project to revision the 'natural', the 'object', and all that which is
conventionally considered 'other' within binary paradigms, as a
coyote 'trickster with whom we must learn to converse' (1991: 201).
In this typically rich and multi-layered image, Haraway suggests a
number of points at once: the ever-presence of power relations

(since 'trickster' moves to control through both exclusion and connection persist); the multiple nature of power and resistance (the coyote is known for its shape-changing abilities and its many different manifestations); but also the possibilities for new ways of 'conversing', of thinking identity and negotiating power relations.

The trickster figure at the heart of Haraway's complex field of languages, codes and noise also invites a link between her work and that of Vidya Rao, discussed in Chapter 2, which also draws on the complexities of sound to rethink identity. Rao compares the Indian musical form of *thumri* to the fairy tale figures of the 'foolish third child' or the 'trickster' who laugh ironically at the pedantic differences set up between different *ragas* or forms of music. What might at first appear, within conventional paradigms, to be a closed and tightly patterned field of sound, in which a logic of differentiation and exclusion operates, is opened up to reveal the many other possible patterns that are there to be picked out (Rao 1990: WS35–6). Like Rao, Haraway wants to open up an apparently closed and tightly patterned field to its inherent complexities and instabilities. For Haraway, the binary logic of Language as a single symbolic system needs to be peeled back to reveal the complex networks of languages, codes and cyborg noise that constitute the field within which identities and selves are constituted. In the final section of this chapter, I discuss how Haraway locates 'women' in this more complex field.

Women in the integrated circuit

In my discussion of debates within Indian feminisms in Part I, I suggested that one recurring underlying issue was the way in which different theoretical approaches to power and identity position women. Is women's subordination always achieved through their exclusion, marginalisation or displacement, or do we need to look also at how they are made central to processes of identity-constitution and to specific networks of power relations? Of the four Western feminists examined in this book, Donna Haraway is most explicit in her insistence that women's positioning cannot be adequately expressed in terms of exclusion models alone. For Haraway:

> The marked bodies of race, class and sex have been at the center, not the margins of knowledge in modern conditions.

These bodies are made to speak because a great deal depends upon their active management.

(Haraway 1992a: 289)

If a great deal depends upon the active management of the marked female body in modern conditions of power and knowledge, then feminists must begin by recognising that women are 'fully implicated in the world' (Haraway 1991: 176); feminist theory needs to give up on the illusion that it can speak from the comfort of the margins as a space of 'moral superiority, innocence or greater closeness to nature' (1991: 176).

While I have already criticised some of the totalising tendencies of Haraway's description of 'Women in the Integrated Circuit' in the first section of this chapter, Haraway also evokes this image in more promising ways. Technological and economic changes in the age of globalisation restructure women's locations as they disassemble and reassemble traditional boundaries between home and work, public and private, etc. In these emerging 'social relations of the new technologies' (1991: 169), there is no one, easily discernible 'place' for women, 'only geometrics of difference and contradiction [...]. The issue is dispersion. The task is to survive in the diaspora' (1991: 170).

Haraway's image of 'Women in the Integrated Circuit' thus repositions women in two ways that resonate with the work of Indian feminists discussed in Part I. First, women's activities are seen as crucial to reconfigurations of social relations. Second, it is women's *dispersal* across a multiplicity of fields of social relations, their hyper-visibility across a 'profusion of spaces and identities' (1991: 170), that needs to be taken into account, not their marginalisation or invisibility. In this view, women's social location is complex and, as such, is not easily contained within an inclusion/exclusion binary.

Because it is women's dispersal across a profusion of spaces and identities that needs to be taken into account, Haraway also resists focusing only or even primarily on dualisms structured around gender or sexual difference. As I read her, it is the more general tendency to structure thought around 'endless socially enforced dualisms' (Haraway 1992a: 3) that she identifies as the problem. Haraway therefore turns her attention to a multiplicity of relationships that re-work the self/other binary. As a biologist and historian of science, she is also very attentive to the ways in which the nature/culture binary is at work in delineating differences of gender, race, class and ethnicity.

Haraway's principal strategy, then, is neither, like Braidotti's, to open up sexual difference so that other differences can be contained within it, nor, like Butler's, to destabilise sex and gender. It is, rather, to take a step back from sex/gender altogether. As a feminist, she is interested in seeing how 'Woman' and 'women' function as both sign and 'material-semiotic actor' across all the differences that evoke, or are worked through, the self/other divide, including sex, race, ethnicity, class, but she never makes a claim for the primacy of, or a privileged place for, sexual difference. Rather, she looks for 'Woman' and 'women' in more than one place at once.

The danger in Haraway's approach is that in making connections between a multiplicity of dualisms she might collapse the differences between them and erase their specificities. The lists and tables of dualisms that Haraway sometimes produces can have the same totalising effect discussed in section one above (see for example 1992a: 11–12). For feminists, this could mean that women's specific strategic and discursive location gets lost in the process. The promise of her approach is that, by trying to keep more than one set of differences in play at once, she can produce a richer, more complicated picture of how these differences interact with each other. This is where Haraway's attentiveness to the contestability of the constructs she uses becomes so crucial, in order to see both the dangers and promises simultaneously.

For Haraway, the danger of *not* looking in more than one direction at once, in privileging sexual difference above all other differences, is to risk being insufficiently attentive to the other relations of power and domination at work that relate to differences between women. It makes it too easy, for example, to unproblematically celebrate female sexuality, or *jouissance*, without recognising how the history of racism can make this a contestable concept for black women. Given the history and continued impact of racist characterisations of black women as highly sexualised and as, therefore, closer to an animal state, 'universalizing discourses about sexual pleasure as a sign of female agency' reinscribe feminism 'within one of the fundamental technologies for enforcing gendered racial inequality' (Haraway 1992a: 355).

For Haraway, sexual difference, even understood as a complex cultural construct, is not a sufficient starting point for feminist theory. Drawing on the work of black feminists such as Hazel Carby (1987) and Hortense Spillers (1987), Haraway suggests that bringing in questions of race doesn't just complicate the Lacanian symbolic, as Butler would propose. Given the context of slavery, for example, it becomes questionable whether a single symbolic can be said to apply when some females become 'women' and others become property:

> free men and women inherited their *name* from the father [...]. Unfree men and women inherited their *condition* from their mother [...]. They had no *name* in the sense theorized by Lévi-Strauss and Lacan. [...] In these discursive frames, white women were not legally or symbolically *fully* human; slaves were not legally or symbolically human *at all*.
>
> (Haraway 1992c: 94, emphasis in the original)

In Haraway's terms, 'each condition of oppression requires specific analysis that refuses the separations but insists on the non-identities of race, sex, sexuality and class' (1992c: 95). This means that race can neither be subsumed within a sexual difference framework, nor viewed as a distinct category. Instead, what is required is a simultaneous focus on 'racial and sexual difference in specific historical conditions of production and reproduction' (1992c: 95).

As I argued in Chapter 3, Irigaray's feminism of sexual difference produces some unexpected resonances with postcolonial feminist explorations of women's positioning in relation to national and raced identities. One of the sites of this convergence is Irigaray's focus on how the specifically female capacity for birth becomes appropriated in origin narratives that privilege the male/masculine subject. But feminisms of sexual difference seem to have great difficulty taking seriously the difference that race and nation can make, as we have seen in both Irigaray's and Braidotti's projects. On the other hand, Butler's project of destabilising sexual difference can, as we saw in Chapter 4, lead to losing any focus on the specifically female. Haraway's work is important in this regard, because she seems to be able to find a place for the question of appropriation of birth and origins, without insisting on the privileged focus on sexual difference.

For example, a recurring theme in *Primate Visions*, Haraway's most extensive and least discussed work, is the constitution of self through modern myths of male birth (Haraway 1992a: 117, 232, 280). Here, Haraway takes a step back from gender or sexual difference to look at how questions of origins are played out through the nature/culture divide. Nature – as fixed, certain origin – becomes the stable ground on which white European man can construct a sense of truth about the self. Haraway tracks the recurring fascination with communication across the nature/culture divide within modern primatology: the gesture of trust from animal to human 'in the field'; cyborg apes in space communicating with their human controllers on the ground; bringing gorillas 'into culture' by teaching them sign language. Each of these 'dramas of touch' (1992a: 149) is, for Haraway, a working through of a framing myth about contact with, and control over, the origins of the human self.

In these narratives of origin, gendered, racial and ethnic specificities all come into play. It is white Western man who secures his sense of self through the fiction of controlling his own origin. White women are often positioned as intermediaries between man and nature, but '[w]oman in these narratives fulfills her communicating, mediating function because of a triple code, only one part of which is gender' (1992a: 149). Haraway looks simultaneously at how race and class also work through the bodies of women (1992a: 149–56).

From the history of primatology, Haraway draws very similar insights to those of Irigaray: '[i]n the major western narrative for generating self and other, one is always too few and two are always too many' (1992a: 352). And it is women, and the female capacity for birth, which is most troubling to the modern Western conception of the unencumbered self:

> Ontologically always potentially pregnant, women are both more limited in themselves, with a body that betrays their individuality, and limiting to men's fantastic self-reproductive projects. To achieve themselves, even if the achievement is a history-making fantasy, men must appropriate women. Women are the limiting resource, but not the actors.
>
> (1992a: 353)

The difference is that, by approaching the question of origins through the nature/culture divide, Haraway works with a more complex field which includes gender, race, nation and other community identities. In her view, 'Woman' is defined as closer to nature, as origin, and is thus positioned as the 'limiting resource' for a variety of origin narratives about identity. Feminists need to attend to a multiplicity of processes of differentiation so that 'women's part in the building of persons, families and communities cannot be fixed in any of the names of Woman and her functions' (Haraway 1991: 123).

For Haraway, one of the ways of doing this is to give back to nature its unruly history, as she does, for the particular field of primatology, in *Primate Visions*. This relates back to Haraway's strategy, discussed in the first section of this chapter, of dispensing with dualisms by refusing the subject/object divide, by insisting on seeing the 'object' as 'actor'. In terms of the nature/culture divide, bringing back into view nature's 'artifactuality', its historical genealogy, is important because it is precisely by covering over this history that nature – as fixed, certain origin – becomes the stable ground for identity narratives. Within these narratives, getting back in touch with the self's origins 'is about boundary crossing, about the drama of touch across Difference, but not about the finite, difference-laden worlds of history' (Haraway 1992a: 149).

Haraway's move places the contentious 'difference-laden worlds of history' right at the centre of her project. Rather than trying to open up a single symbolic system to contestation and resistance, Haraway begins from the polyvocal, noisy and always uncertain spaces in which specific differences are constituted. Her strategy then is to track the sometimes conflicting, sometimes mutually constitutive ways in which 'Woman' is evoked, and 'women' are located, across the historical categories of sex/gender, race, nation, and class. In this way, she argues, feminists might begin to be able to 'count to four'.

In my reading of her, then, Haraway seems to offer a way of sustaining a simultaneous focus on 'women', the specifically female, and the differences between women. Nevertheless, it needs to be recognised that Haraway is not always completely successful in keeping all these aspects in view. Whilst I have privileged those moments in her work where 'women' are seen as 'promising monsters', Haraway is not always consistent in her approach. As I argued in the first section of this chapter, her enthusiasm for making cyborg connections sometimes puts together theoretical approaches that work against each other, and this creates a certain ambivalence in Haraway's approach to 'women' and the specifically female.

For example, in both 'A Manifesto for Cyborgs' (in Haraway 1991) and 'The Promises of Monsters', Haraway argues for a shift from paradigms of birth and reproduction to models of regeneration. Traditional narratives of identity use concepts of birth and reproduction to support models of pure origins, of 'the sacred image of the same, of the one true copy' (Haraway 1992b: 299). Haraway suggests that 'cyborgs have more to do with regeneration and are suspicious of the reproductive matrix and of most birthing' (Haraway 1991: 181). The concept of regeneration, for Haraway, suggests possibilities of change, difference and the 'interpenetration of boundaries between problematic selves and unexpected others' (1992b: 300) that the concept of rebirthing cannot. For Haraway:

> We require regeneration, not rebirth, and the possibilities of our reconstitution include the utopian dream of the hope for a monstrous world without gender.
>
> (1991: 181)

If we read these moves on their own, it could be concluded that, for Haraway, the specifically female capacity for birth has been so tainted by its appropriations within prevailing identity narratives that feminists cannot ever hope to redefine it. This reading of Haraway would put her quite close to Butler's view that any feminist redefinition of the specifically female is bound to reintroduce the abjection it seeks to resist. The similarities with a deconstructive position like Butler's are also suggested when Haraway argues that 'destabilizing the positions in a discursive field and disrupting categories for identification might be a more powerful feminist strategy than "speaking as a woman" ' (Haraway 1992a: 310).

On the other hand, as we have seen above, Haraway also argues that reproduction and birth don't actually fit into prevailing self/other paradigms, however hard 'masculine myths of self-birth' try to contain them. 'The issue from the self is always (an)other' (1992a: 352), never a sacred image of the same. The female body's 'troubling talent for making other bodies' and the confounding of clear inner/outer distinctions of the foetal immune system (1991: 253 fn 8) are part of Haraway's evidence for her alternative model of the 'semi-permeable self'.

Reading this Haraway, it would seem clear that she makes a distinction between the ways in which the specifically female has been appropriated to produce the various 'names of Woman', and the 'women' who resist those names in order to remain promising monsters. This distinction seems to hold when she argues, towards the end of the Cyborg Manifesto, that:

> there is another route to having less at stake in masculine autonomy, a route that does not pass through Woman, Primitive, Zero, the Mirror Stage and its imaginary. It passes through *women and other present-tense, illegitimate cyborgs*, not of Woman born. [...] These cyborgs are the people who refuse to disappear on cue.
>
> (Haraway 1991: 177, emphasis added)

It is when we remember that Haraway includes women in her list of 'illegitimate cyborgs' that her work can be most productively used to sustain a simultaneous focus on women and their differences.

Throughout this chapter I have concentrated on Donna Haraway's attempts to rethink identity outside a logic of dualisms at the levels of ontology, epistemology and politics. While not always completely successful, Haraway's alternative approach to models of the self, location, politics and language produces some 'promising monsters' for feminist attempts to keep a space open for multiplicity and difference. Through counter-models like the cyborg, she redefines the self within an ontology of impurity, change and diaspora. In calling for feminist politics to combine the pleasure of transgressing boundaries with the responsibility for constructing them, she offers a more complicated sense of locatedness that recognises the impurity of all spaces. She resists the constraints of working with a model of a single symbolic system of Language, to focus on a more complicated field of contested and contestable meanings which includes languages, codes and 'cyborg noise'.

In resisting the limitations of a 'logic of dualisms' at all these levels, Haraway's project repositions women in two ways. First, she looks for 'Woman' and 'women' not only at the margins of identity categories and power relations, in those spaces where they are made invisible, but also at their highly visible centres. Second, she positions 'Woman' and 'women', not within a single symbolic system, but across a multiplicity of historically specific and variable categories of identity. This offers the possibility of a simultaneous focus on the specifically female and on the differences between women.

Part III

Against purity

Chapter 7

Power, identity and impure spaces

At the end of Part I, I identified four challenges to feminist theories of identity and difference that emerge from a critical reading of Indian feminist scholarship:

- first, feminist theoretical approaches to identity need to focus on the productive but subordinated role that 'Woman' and 'women' play in the simultaneous emergence of multiple categories of social identity, including sex, gender, nation, race and other community identities;
- second, they need to recognise that women's location within this intersecting landscape of social identities is a complex one that is not easily contained within a logic of dualisms;
- third, they need to take into account not only discursive constructs of the feminine, but also the female body and its relation to women's activities;
- fourth, they need to redefine, and not only destabilise or deconstruct, models of the individual self and its relation to collective identities.

Throughout my discussions of the work of Irigaray, Butler, Braidotti and Haraway in Part II, I began to suggest some of the ways in which their theoretical approaches invite and/or resist a productive engagement with these complications. In Part III, I will expand on these initial suggestions to discuss how the insights I have drawn from Indian feminisms can be taken on board within Western feminist theory, in order to develop more complicated models of power, identity and the self. I argue that it will only be possible to sustain a simultaneous focus on women and their differences if feminist theory works against purity on three levels.

First, it requires a model of power that gives up on the search for pure, power-free zones and works instead with the instabilities power produces as it both enables and constrains women. Second, it is necessary to see 'women' as a complex, impure category that bleeds across the borders of apparently discrete identities, such as sex, gender, race and nation. Third, we need to develop alternative models of the self that take these complex, impure spaces as a valid and valorised position from which to speak and act. In this chapter, I will discuss the question of models of power. In Chapter 8, I turn to questions of 'women' as a complex category, and alternative models of the self.

In both chapters, I follow a similar structure in an attempt to keep clear the many different voices of Indian and white Western feminisms that I am working with, and to indicate how I think they might be brought together. I begin by reviewing the main insights to be drawn from the Indian feminist material I have examined; in this chapter I focus on the implications of underlying models of power to explain how 'women' are positioned in the emergence of social identities. In terms of the four challenges delineated above, I look particularly at what it means to say that (1) women's role in constituting these multiple identities is both productive and subordinated, and (2) women's strategic and discursive positioning in the emergence of these identities is a complex one that is not easily contained within a binary logic of exclusion and inclusion. I then look in turn at the models of power at work in the projects of Irigaray, Butler, Braidotti and Haraway to see if they do or do not provide a space in which to accommodate these insights. In the final section of this chapter, I draw from all these sources to outline the key elements of the more complex model of power I believe is necessary, and discuss its implications for feminist politics and resistance. Before turning to these specific points, however, I want to discuss briefly why I believe that feminist attempts to rethink identity cannot proceed without a simultaneous attention to models of power.

Why models of power matter

When feminist theorists confront the difficulties of taking seriously the differences between women, they tend to focus on the problems caused by the concepts 'Woman' or 'women'. Whether the issue is to capture the complexities of the ways in which women are socially subordinated, or to delineate a non-exclusionary but nevertheless effective 'subject of/for feminism', the principal task has tended to be to redefine, problematise or even move beyond, 'Woman' and 'women' as the key category of feminist inquiry. In the next chapter, I will return to this troublesome category, and propose my own reading of what it might mean to theorise women 'in a postcolonial mode'. But first, I want to focus on another concept which is as crucial to feminist efforts to theorise the differences between women, and yet which is much less often interrogated in feminist debates – the models of power that underpin different theoretical approaches to questions of identity, self–other relations and feminist politics.

For example, in one of the most frequently cited examinations of the exclusions at work in Western feminist scholarship, Chandra Mohanty takes issue with the tendency to posit women as a category of analysis in ways that assume that 'all of us of the same gender, across classes and cultures, are somehow socially constituted as a homogeneous group identified prior to the process of analysis' (Mohanty 1991: 56). Within this framework, the focus is on women as an 'always already constituted group', made singular by its 'shared oppression' (1991: 56). Mohanty then goes on to argue:

> This focus is not on uncovering the material and ideological specificities that constitute a particular group of women as 'powerless' in a particular context. It is, rather, on finding a variety of cases of 'powerless' groups of women to prove the general point that women as a group are powerless.
>
> (1991: 57)

Mohanty then moves to explore how Western feminism constructs a paradigmatically powerless 'Third World Woman' as its necessary other, against which it can define a subject of/for feminism, and can assert its authority to speak for all women.

Mohanty's article has been tremendously influential in getting white Western feminists to rethink the 'non-innocence of the category "woman" ' (Haraway 1991: 157). It is one of a handful of key references that recur in footnotes and introductions whenever the subject of differences between women is broached. It has become so familiar, indeed, that a rather general reference by the author, and an equally generalised response from the reader, seem to be all that is required. Citing Mohanty is a useful shorthand for raising the problem of the univocal category 'women' and, in particular, the problem of constructing a 'homogeneous category of Third World women who stand as Other to western feminists, who define Third World women as powerless victims of patriarchy' (Young 1994: 715). What seems to go unnoticed in most of these references, as in Iris Young's cited above, is that there are two issues at play in Mohanty's critique – first, that there is a universal category 'women' being constructed, but second, that it is characterised by powerlessness.

Mohanty herself focuses on the first of these issues, and so it is perhaps not surprising that most of her commentators do the same. But the issue of the model of power at work follows behind the main thread of her argument, like some persistent, troublesome shadow that is caught only out of the corner of the eye. If we turn around and look at it fully, we need to ask, why does feminism need to define women as 'powerless victims of patriarchy'? Why does it need to define itself against these paradigms of powerlessness in order to locate its own agency? Why does it have to presume that if women are oppressed or subordinated, then they must also be powerless? If feminists can only define themselves as agents against a powerless other, are they not complicit in the same kind of hierarchical logic of dualisms as they identify in patriarchy? Mohanty's critique of white Western feminism calls out as much for a rethinking of the models of power at work in the texts she examines as it does the model of 'women' she contests.

Just about any statement regarding 'women' as the subject of/for feminism is also, implicitly, a statement about a model of power. Consider Iris Young's claim:

> The very act of defining a gender identity excludes or devalues some bodies, practices and discourses at the same time that it obscures the constructed, and thus, contestable character of that gender identity. [...] [G]ender discourse tends to reify the fluid and shifting social processes in which people relate, communicate, play, work and struggle with one another over the means of production and interpretation. The insistence on a subject for feminism obscures the social and discursive production of identities.
>
> (Young 1994: 715–16)

Here, the power to define identity is seen only from the point of view of excluding, devaluing, and as something that works by covering over complexity. A model of a subject that flows from this understanding of power *will* obscure the more fluid and shifting social processes through which identities can be constituted, as do models of the subject that claim a pre-existence to, or autonomy from, power relations.

But, as I have argued throughout this book, there is another view available to feminist theory, derived mainly from the work of Michel Foucault, which recognises power as both exclusionary and productive. For Foucault, our understanding of power must be taken out of a logic of repression, exclusion and abjection, and placed instead within a logic of proliferation. Power is productive, continuous, diffuse, unstable and multi-vocal. Perhaps most important to my purpose here is Foucault's concept of 'subjectification', what I have called the double move of productive power, which both enables and constrains as it produces impure subjects. Within a logic of proliferation, power requires not abjected or devalued bodies and impassive objects, but knowable, useful bodies and subjects. Within a logic of proliferation, power is not viewed as a 'great absolute Subject which pronounces the interdict' (Foucault 1977b: 140); viewing power as diffuse and multi-vocal multiplies the possibilities of instabilities and resistance emerging from within power relations. When feminist theorists work with this more complex model of power, a different under-standing of 'gender identity' and of the kinds of subjects produced in power relations can emerge.

Each of the four theorists discussed in Part II argues, in different ways, that the linguistic and conceptual tendency to construct systems of dualisms needs to be challenged by feminism. There is a broad consensus in contemporary feminist theory that the linking of 'woman' with body, object, other, etc., in binary systems has deep-seated philosophical and political effects (see also Gatens 1996). But the dualisms such as mind/body, subject/object, self/other that have proved so inimical to acknowledging women's status as full subject in both philosophy and the body politic, are also underpinned by a model of power that focuses on the power to control through exclusion. The mind controls and excludes the body, just as the self is established by excluding and controlling the other. Viewing power as something that some people have and some people do not is to stay within a logic of dualisms; subjects exercise power and objects have power exercised upon them. Foucault's model of power, in which all are fully implicated, through which all are simultaneously made subjects and subjected, confounds this kind of easy binary division. Changing the model of power we work with, therefore, is a crucial part of destabilising the mind/body, self/other divides, of thinking beyond dualisms.

Power's double move

The first insight I want to draw from my reading of Indian feminist scholarship is the double focus on women's productive and subordinated role in constituting social identities informed by differences of gender, race, nation and other marked community categories. Much of the work that I discuss in Part I simply cannot be made sense of within a purely negative model of power that looks only at how women are controlled, excluded or abjected in specific relations of power. While few of the Indian feminists I have engaged with in this project refer directly to the work of Foucault, or make specific the model of power they are working with, I read much of their work as supportive of a Foucauldian feminist approach. The 'women' that emerge from this work are simultaneously enabled and constrained.

On the one hand, women are not a completely silenced, abject 'ground' upon which a masculine subject stands, or upon which national, racial and other community identities are constituted. Women's material practices are actively productive of those social identities, as are the competing discursive norms of 'Woman', of the feminine and of the female body that produce women as subjects of a particular kind. On the other hand, the social identities that women help to produce continue to constrain them within asymmetrical relations of sexed/gendered power. The specific ways in which they become 'knowable', 'visible' and 'useful' tend to reconstitute systems of power and knowledge which privilege both the masculine, and particular groups of men.

Foucault's notion of power that works by making bodies 'useful' is particularly relevant to much of the feminist scholarship emerging from India. Of course, we need to distinguish between the specific ways in which bodies are made useful within power relations that continue to subordinate women, and some unproblematised celebration of the female body. As I discussed in Chapter 2, the work of a number of Indian feminists suggests that the specifically female body is viewed as a problem to be overcome for many models of national or racial identity and of the subject-agent (e.g. Chakravarti 1989; Basu 1995). But this is not the only aspect to be considered. If the female body remains highly unsuitable for housing a subject-agent that continues to be modelled on masculine lines, it is not something that is simply excluded or abjected. It remains rather a focus of intense interest and importance in terms of securing the borders of identity categories.

Tanika Sarkar's work suggests that, in both the nationalist movement of pre-independence India and in the current communalist movement of the Hindu right, women's activities and the symbolic meanings invested in the female body are a crucial focus for the construction of a pure space of national and communal identities (Sarkar 1987: 2011; 1995: 186). Urvashi Butalia's work on both the 1947 India–Pakistan partition crisis and on current Hindu–Muslim communal violence within India also suggests that concepts of purity and impurity of national and racial identities are defined via the female body (Butalia 1993: WS14–15; 1995: 59).

Amrita Chhachhi argues that the concept of the boundaries of community identities, and hence of what is inside and outside the community, works through a feminised language of 'kinship' and 'home', and through a focus on the activities of women (Chhacchi 1991: 163–7). Mrinalini Sinha looks at how, in the colonial period, defining the norms of the female body became a way of constituting norms of both masculine and national identities (Sinha 1987: 224). Male appropriations of the language of motherhood and maternal power become important ways of legitimating nationalist authority (Sarkar 1987; Alexander 1989; Ganesh 1990; Loomba 1993). Lata Mani, looking at competing discourses on *sati* during the colonial period, suggests that norms of womanhood, inscribed on women's bodies, constitute the ground upon which norms of nationhood are constituted (Mani 1990).

As I suggested in Part I, Mani's characterisation of the female body as the ground of national identities might be seen as support for a model of power that focuses only on abjection or exclusion. But, as I also argued in Part I, Mani resists such a reading herself. More importantly, when her work is placed in the context of the other examples given here, it suggests not an abjected or silenced ground, but rather a highly fertile, if still subordinated, one. I will return to this point in the next section, and in the next chapter I will also discuss how and why it is the specifically *female* body that is made useful for national and raced identities. But the first point to note here is that it is as a *useful*, and not only as an abjected or excluded, body that 'women' are put into play in these power relations.

Power's productive double move is at work through the law as well. The debates on personal laws and a Uniform Civil Code currently under way within India (and within Indian feminisms), that I discussed in Chapter 2, are a good example of this. Zoya Hasan argues that the personal laws produce an authorised version of communal identity, and do so primarily through defining appropriate behaviour for women (Hasan 1994b: 61). Of course these laws work in part by excluding and constraining women. Thus, women are denied full participation in devising the laws and, according to Hasan, the laws also constrain women by denying them the right to a distinct gendered identity that is not reduced to the homogenised interests of 'the community' (Hasan 1994b).

To speak only of exclusion in this context is, however, to tell only part of the story. These laws, and the power relations of which they are a part, *produce* women as subjects of a particular kind, and these women's activities in turn *enable* the production of particular community identities. Contesting these legal productions which identify 'women' solely with their religious communities, while at the same time respecting the very real differences in identities between Hindu and Muslim women that these discourses have produced, is a major challenge for the Indian women's movement (Menon, Butalia and Chakravatri, personal interviews 1995). A model of power which focuses only on the ways in which women have been excluded from the legislative process 'as women', and on how their interests now need to be included, cannot address the ways in which power relations help to produce women and their specific differences.

Nor is it enough to say that the identities so produced are simply manifestations of 'false consciousness', or that they represent an ideological burden for women. These are the impure resources with which women must and do resist, mining the discordances between their simultaneous centrality and marginality, their visibility and invisibility within relations of power that continue to subordinate them. The specific ways in which power's double move works need to be explored by feminist theory if it is to address the persistent complaint raised against feminism's portrayal of women as powerless. How often do we hear women who are not feminists, in both Western and postcolonial settings, object that women are valued in their culture; that motherhood is valorised; that women hold a powerful place in the family; that women are at the centre of daily life?

In part, women's rejection of feminism on this basis derives from hegemonic caricatures of feminist goals and discourse. In part it is because feminism asks women to give up the security of whatever authority they do derive from their position within the family, and within existing cultural traditions, to destabilise the status quo without any guarantee of what might replace it (Sarkar and Butalia 1995: 7). But in large part it is also due to feminism's failure to adopt a model of power that takes these productive moves seriously. Since such lines of resistance to feminism often come from outside white Western settings, from women in 'Third World' countries, and from black and other diasporic communities in the West, it is even more important that white Western feminist theory take this question on board when it wants to consider the space it creates for differences between women.

Margins and centres, and dispensing with binaries

The second, related insight about models of power that emerges from debates within Indian feminisms is the need to dispense with a logic of dualisms that characterises women's social and discursive positioning in binary terms of margins and centres. These debates suggest that to locate 'Woman' and 'women' only at the margins is to capture only one part of the way in which identity is secured and power is exercised.

Tanika Sarkar's work on the pre-independence nationalist movement, discussed in Chapter 1, problematises the man/woman, public/private, world/home binaries that have become so familiar to feminism (Sarkar 1987). In her discussions of the ways in which the nationalist movement mobilised women and appropriated 'feminised' imagery and actions as part of its political iconography and tactics, a complex sense of women's location emerges that is not easily contained within these binaries. 'Woman' and women's activities may often figure as the 'home' men can retreat to, but women's presence in the 'world' of public politics is also necessary. By bringing the pure space of the 'private', the 'home' into the public field of political contestation, women's presence reinforces the nationalist movement's claims for authenticity of identity and representativity.

More generally, Kumkum Roy argues that feminists need to take account of women's 'curious visibility' in both colonial and postcolonial discourses and practices (Roy 1995: 10). In the context of contemporary Indian politics, Zoya Hasan places legal and discursive constructs of 'the Muslim woman', as well as Muslim women's activities, at the *centre* of the communal political imagination and of redefinitions of 'authentic' community identities (Hasan 1994b: 61). The foregrounding of women militants in the Hindu communalist movement involves a similar mobilisation of 'authenticity' of racialised identities through the presence of women (Sarkar 1991, 1995; Basu 1995; Roy 1995).

As I discussed in Chapter 2, the foregrounding of women as militants and leaders in the right-wing Hindu communalist movement has sparked some interesting debates within Indian feminisms. For some, like Susie Tharu and Tejaswini Niranjana, the foregrounding of women in political projects that reinforce gendered, racialised, class and caste hierarchies represents an indictment of feminism itself (Tharu and Niranjana 1994). For others, it presents feminism with the challenge to rethink positively its concepts of agency, consent and women's positioning within complex power relations (Sangari 1993; Sarkar 1995).

I would argue that, at heart, these debates are about the different models of power that feminists work with. Whilst there seems to be a broad consensus among Indian feminists that women can't be fruitfully discussed without mapping their relation to a complex network of identity categories, there is less consensus about how to characterise that relationship and, perhaps more basically, where to look for it. By this I mean, are women always to be found on the margins, as the displaced, repressed or excluded ground upon which these identities are consolidated? Or is their location more complex, one that cannot be easily plotted along a binary exclusion/inclusion divide? Are women only made invisible in processes that allow a male, national or raced subject to emerge, or is their problematic visibility also a crucial element in these processes?

When framed in this way, these specific Indian debates are part of the same problematic facing feminist theory in the West, and they suggest a further complication which white Western feminist theory needs to take on board. Whilst the consensus many Indian feminists have reached on the intersectionality of gender with race, nation and community identities is one that is still to be reached within white feminisms, this consensus remains only one part of the problem. Even when feminists agree to look for intersectionality, the models of power they are working with will impinge on where they find that intersectionality, and how they place women within it. And this has consequences for the extent to which those models are able to keep a space open for complexity and for the specific differences between women, without folding difference back into some version of sameness. As I discussed in Chapter 2, at least some Indian feminists who work with poststructuralist theoretical models start from the assumption that women are subordinated primarily through a process of marginalisation. For example, Tharu and Niranjana take as their starting point, the now-familiar poststructuralist narrative that the 'subject of modernity', or of 'Western humanism', is produced through exclusion (Tharu and Niranjana 1994). Underpinning this narrative is a view that power also works primarily through exclusion, and through making those who are excluded invisible and marginal. If power works in this way, then feminism's project must be to make women visible and central. If women are made visible and central in problematic circumstances, as in the right-wing Hindu communal movement, and the examples of caste, class and nationalist politics that Tharu and Niranjana examine, then feminism must be at fault.

In contrast, a Foucauldian model of power as productive complicates the binary logic behind this conclusion. Foregrounding women, making them 'visible, useful and knowable', can be one way of constraining them within power relations that continue to be informed by gender hierarchies. Women's subordination will not always proceed through their objectification, silencing or abjection. The simultaneous foregrounding and limiting/containing of women as 'communal subjects' (Sarkar 1991) points to the need for a model of power that holds these two processes together. Without such a model, the 'positive' or 'productive' can be conflated with the unproblematically 'good', with serious consequences for feminism.

If Tharu and Niranjana have so much difficulty dealing with the hyper-visibility of women within projects like that of the Hindu right, is it perhaps because they begin with a theoretical assumption that women's 'proper' place within this kind of project should be limited to one of exclusion or, at best, displacement? As in the West, both Lacanian and Derridean language models have gained a certain currency within Indian academia, including among some feminist academics. Without wanting to over-generalise a complicated, heterogeneous and rapidly growing body of literature, I do want to suggest that part of the baggage that comes with these language models is an over-emphasis on power as exclusion and an over-estimation of the degree to which women are marginalised, silenced and made to disappear.

But women don't simply disappear – they are produced in highly visible ways. It is this production of women as (impure) subjects – managed, contained, but also valorised, enabled and empowered – that helps to make their subordination so persistent. This is power in its capillary mode, at its most insidious. The complexity of this kind of process cannot be captured with a model of power that focuses on exclusion alone.

I do not want to suggest that it is not useful to recognise the ways in which particular groups of women constitute an excluded or marginalised ground upon which social identities and models of the (male) subject might stand. But I do want to suggest that focusing only on this aspect carries with it the danger of closing off from view other aspects of women's complex social and symbolic locations, and that this both closes down the space in which difference can be considered, and covers over the instabilities that can generate resistance. The Indian feminist material that I find most productive combines an attention to women's exclusion with an acknowledgement of the ways in which they are also enabled, foregrounded and made central to processes of identity-constitution. In the following section, I turn to the models of power underpinning the work of Irigaray, Butler, Braidotti and Haraway, and discuss the degree to which this double focus is sustained in each of their projects.

Western feminisms and models of power

Luce Irigaray: what if the object began to speak?

In my discussion of Irigaray's work, I argued that her locating of 'women' as the 'still silent ground' of a male-centred economy of the same, is both a productive and problematic insight for feminism. On one level, of course, Irigaray is working with a model of power that stresses the negative – the power to exclude. Hers is a model in which Language as a system, the social order built with/through language, and the sanctioned route to subject-status within that symbolic order, all require the gesture of exclusion in order to proceed. Of all the theorists examined in this study, she might be thought furthest from a Foucauldian model of power. When readings of Irigaray focus only on the exclusion of the feminine, on an image of woman only as passive ground, as that which cannot speak or be spoken, then she might seem to be working with a system which is ultimately closed and stable. If we see 'Woman' only as passive ground, we fail to capture the dynamic complexity of the multiple networks of power and women's place in them, and the possibilities of discordance between those multiple networks.

However, I would argue that Irigaray complicates her reading of 'Woman-as-ground' in two important ways. First, in her analysis of the prevailing symbolic order, she locates 'Woman'-Mother-Matter as simultaneously necessary and excluded. When taken outside Irigaray's exclusive landscape of sexual difference, this insight is enriched by postcolonial feminists like Lata Mani who locates 'women' as the excluded but necessary ground upon which what might be called competing national economies of the same are constructed.

In looking at how the economy of the same is built upon masculine appropriations of birth and access to origins, Irigaray defines the maternal, not merely as abject and excluded, but rather as simultaneously potent and constrained within a regime of sameness (Whitford 1991a: 55). The power of the maternal is both mobilised and contained in order to serve as the place in which, and out of which, the masculine subject defines his 'truths'. Woman-as-place is 'experienced as all powerful where "she" is most radically powerless in her indifferentiation' (1991a: 53). By holding together a sense of female potency with a sense that it is confined within an economy of the same, Irigaray can be said to share some aspects of a Foucauldian model of power that both enables and constrains. When Irigaray asks, 'what if the object started to speak', or 'if the earth turned, and turned upon herself', she could be said to be working with a model of power that locates sources of resistance from within this field of enabling constraints.

Second, Irigaray further complicates the 'Woman-as-ground' formulation by arguing for a different symbolic order based on the specifically female. Thus, women are not trapped within a single symbolic, nor are they always limited to disrupting a unified system from its margins, or from the weak side of the binary. As I discussed in Chapter 3, Irigaray privileges the interval, or the space between, as a site that confounds the dualistic logic of a specular economy. It is this in-between space that she works for its possibilities of heterogeneity and fluidity, as a space from which women might speak (as) woman now, and from which a different economy might eventually emerge. The in-between suggests, not a margin, but a new mode of relationality; thus, in this aspect of her work, Irigaray again seems to privilege a more complex model of power than those based on exclusion/inclusion paradigms.

In my reading, there are two models of power at work in Irigaray's project. She remains indebted to the Lacanian model Foucault criticises, of a symbolic order that works by saying 'No', yet in moving away from that model, she also brings in elements of power as productive. Because Irigaray does not stay within the terms of the Woman-as-Other model that informs both the Lacanian project and much of feminism, because she tries to think through a model of Woman as Other-of-the-Same, I would argue that she is also opening up a space in which to consider power's more productive aspects.

'Saming' does not work only through exclusion, but through actively producing norms of Woman that conform to the needs of a specular economy. And while in Irigaray's terms that specular economy needs a 'Woman' who is signified as 'nothing [...] a lack, an absence' (Irigaray 1974: 50), she also sustains a sense that this 'nothing' continues to bear within it the potency to disrupt that economy, and to provide the basis of a new economy.

Even though Irigaray works with a model of Language as functioning primarily through exclusion, she is also arguing for a fundamental instability of that system, and for the possibility of overturning its reliance on a logic of dualisms. I would argue that it is not coincidental that it is in those spaces where Irigaray allows a more complex model of power to emerge that her resonances with Indian feminisms are at their strongest. These occur when she explores the ways in which an economy of the same both acknowledges and appropriates the potency of the female capacity for birth and access to origins. They also occur when she explores the possibilities of resistance that emerge between and across binaries, a point I will return to in the next chapter.

Judith Butler: do bodies matter?

As I discussed in Chapter 4, Judith Butler engages extensively with Foucault's model of productive power. Butler recognises that, if subjects are always both regulated and produced by and through workings of power relations, then their agency cannot derive from some pure space, defined by primary identities, but only from the possibilities that emerge from within those power relations (Butler 1993a: 12–15). These emerge from the instabilities of normative power, whose results are not always predictable or containable, and from the fact that power can only regulate those subjects that it enables, that it makes useful and knowable. Thus resistance is never a pure opposition, but 'a difficult labour of forging a future from resources inevitably impure' (1993a: 241).

Butler's title, *Bodies that Matter*, is rich in resonances with a Foucauldian model of power. It suggests that bodies are made to matter within relations of power, that they are made useful and knowable. Butler's use of the concept of 'materialization' also promises to hold together an attention to both discursive and material processes, through which embodied subjects 'materialize' or emerge. But from a promising focus on 'bodies that matter', Butler's project moves increasingly to focus on the bodies that are made *not* to matter. As I argued in Chapter 4, Butler's engagement with Lacanian psychoanalysis and Derridean deconstruction leads her to over-emphasise the 'gesture of constitutive exclusion' that she identifies at the heart of processes of signification and identity-constitution. Her attempts to hold Foucault, Lacan and Derrida together can lead her to a position where power remains productive only to the extent that what is produced is 'foreclosure [...] a set of constitutive exclusions' (Butler 1993a: 207).

Her focus repeatedly shifts between a model of power working in a complex field of 'institutions, practices, discourses with multiple and diffuse points of origin' (Butler 1990: xi) and what she defines as the imperatives of exclusion and abjection at work in an overarching system of signification. That system's instabilities and sources of resistance seem to come primarily, not from the specific ways in which particular bodies and subjects are made to matter, but from those 'bodies' which have been abjected and marginalised.

Butler's privileging of parody, and of 'the repetition that fails to repeat loyally', do suggest a model in which new possibilities of resistance emerge from the workings of productive power. However, she focuses primarily on those parodic speech acts which destabilise identities produced through abjection, through the 'logic of non-contradiction by which one identification is always and only purchased at the expense of the other' (Butler 1993a: 118–19). This can turn attention away from those identities that are produced in other ways, most notably through a logic of proliferation, in which 'positive' redefinitions of 'Woman' and 'women' are put into play to produce national, raced and other community identities.

Another example of this turn to exclusion models occurs when Butler discusses how authority is constituted through 'perpetual deferral', through an 'infinite deferral of authority to an irrecoverable past' (1993a: 107–8). Indian feminists such as Chakravarti (1990), Sunder Rajan (1993) and Mani (1990) have also argued that national identities are legitimated through reference to an 'irrecoverable past'. And yet, to speak only of deferral in this context is not to capture the complexity of these authority-constituting moments. While the power to define national identities may be legitimated by referral/deferral to a lost past, there is also a productive move involved. As Chakravarti, Mani and others have shown, there is an ongoing active production and reproduction of that past, through constructing norms of purity and authenticity, which include, importantly, the norms of pure, authentic womanhood. In turning to exclusion models, Butler turns away from considering how specific female bodies are made to matter in legitimating both identity categories and relations of power.

Rosi Braidotti: smooth space and the nomad

As we saw in Chapter 5, Braidotti refers more often to the work of Deleuze and Guattari than to Foucault for her model of power. Nevertheless, Deleuze and Guattari's elaboration of the necessary and inescapable tension between the molar and the molecular, between striated and smooth spaces, shares many of the same concerns as Foucault's model of power. First, it too is an attempt to think about power beyond a binary logic of inclusion and exclusion. Second, it also locates resistance within, rather than outside of, power relations. However, Braidotti herself seems to slide into a model of power that reads positive-productive as good, and that locates the positive and negative workings of power in two, relatively separate spaces, the molecular and the molar. It might be argued that Deleuze and Guattari's model, with its proliferation of sets of two (molar/molecular, rhizome/tree, striated/smooth, *polis/nomos*, etc.) does lend itself more easily to this kind of division than does a Foucauldian model where productive power enables as it constrains. Yet Deleuze and Guattari are, it seems to me, very careful not to make this kind of division themselves and to keep their twos in interdependent tension.

In contrast, Braidotti's unproblematised privileging of the nomad as a counter-force to molar identities and oppressive forms of power forgets a key part of both the Foucauldian and Deleuzian models of power that she claims to be working with: that there is no pure space that can be relied on, that can't be 're-territorialized' or 're-striated'. Deleuze and Guattari's warning, 'Never believe that a smooth space can save us' (Deleuze and Guattari 1988: 500), in this sense echoes Foucault's 'There are no margins to gambol in' (Foucault 1977b: 141). Every move to redefine identity is caught up in power relations. Braidotti insists that the nomad is not a new model of a 'humanist' subject, another attempt to fix a molar identity, to provide a centre, and is instead a 'way of becoming' (Braidotti 1994a: 111–13). But even so, it is never immune from the impure field of enabling constraints from which it emerges. Braidotti forgets this, and this, in part, is what allows her not to see the ways in which the space she has delineated for the feminist-as-nomad is itself striated: by the hierarchical gradations of difference that result from her prioritisation of sexual difference; and by the ways in which she de-authorises 'ways of becoming' that have been privileged within postcolonial theory. Both these moves retract the space in which differences between women can be taken into account, and both derive from a failure to sustain an understanding of power's double move.

Further difficulties are produced by Braidotti's uncomfortable combination of a psychoanalytic model of subjectivity and the unconscious, drawn from Irigaray and Lacan, and Deleuze's anti-psychoanalytic account of desire. Thus, Braidotti locates many of the 'lines of escape' of feminist resistance at the level of unconscious desire (Braidotti 1994a: 166–70). This re-imports a logic of dualisms to considerations of power, by locating resistance in some space outside consciousness and language.

Donna Haraway: promises and risks

Of the four white Western feminists examined in this book, Donna Haraway most consistently applies what I have identified as a Foucauldian feminist model of power as productive, continuous, multi-vocal and unstable. For Haraway, power is productive because it is through the 'active management' of useful bodies, not through their abjection or marginalisation, that contemporary relations of power and knowledge are deployed. Thus the 'marked bodies of race, class and sex have been at the center, not the margins of knowledge in modern conditions' (Haraway 1992a: 289).

Recognising that power is continuous means that there are no pure power-free zones. Haraway's image of promising and dangerous monsters suggests both that resistance emerges from within power relations and that resistance is never immune from re-appropriation. Thus, she sustains a dual focus on both the dangers and the possibilities that emerge from the specific ways in which power relations produce impure subjects, who are both enabled and constrained.

Power is multi-vocal because it works, not through the exclu-sionary imperatives of a single symbolic system, but through a more complex field which includes languages, codes and 'cyborg noise', as they intersect with and help produce a multiplicity of material practices and institutions. Perhaps most importantly, each of these components carries with it its own 'unruly history' of contestation and change.

If the field of power relations is productive, continuous and multi-vocal, then it is also unstable, producing unintended, if never innocent, means of contestation. For Haraway, contemporary power relations are always producing those 'inappropriate/d others' that defy the constraints of a logic of dualisms, and which can be built upon to produce alternative forms of resistance.

In the final section of this chapter, I look at what this alternative understanding of resistance might mean for feminist politics, and in particular at how a more complex model of power enables a simultaneous attention to 'women' and their differences.

Power, resistance and feminist politics

As I argued in the Introduction to this book, a Foucauldian model of power makes the possibility of social change 'very urgent, very difficult, and quite possible' (Foucault 1981: 155). It requires a shift in perspective in terms of where we look for possibilities of resistance, and how we try to structure that resistance in political movements. In this final section, I want to look at how such a view of resistance can be useful for a feminist politics that aims to keep the space open for differences between women.

In order for feminism to sustain a dual focus on women and their differences, we need a model of power that can do several things at once. First, in analysing the ways in which women are socially and discursively subordinated, it needs to keep a space open for the differences between women. Second, it needs to propose a way out of that subordination, by locating the instabilities and points of resistance within prevailing power relations. But third, it needs to do this in ways that do not simply reproduce, in a slightly different space, the forms of domination it is contesting. In particular, it needs to give us tools to contest the tendency to construct a pure feminist 'I' by excluding such differences as race and ethnicity, by creating our own 'others of the same'. On all these levels, we need a model of power that works from the perspective, not of purity and authenticity, but of *im*purity.

Impurity and resistance

The first insight to be drawn from a Foucauldian model of power is that the field of power relations is an impure space which produces its own instabilities and means of resistance. Feminist theory therefore needs to sustain the double perspective that resistance is both possible within, and can only happen from within, the complex web of existing power relations.

The question of the models of power feminist theory works with is also a question of whether one locates women's subordination within a closed or an open system. There can be many different ways of defining 'the system' one wants to contest: Language as a single symbolic system whose overriding logic structures the social; a more complex network of discourses, practices and institutions that produce hierarchical relations of domination and subordination; a distinct system of patriarchy that works alongside other discrete forms of oppression and exploitation; a composite system of gender-race-class hierarchies that mutually construct and reinforce each other 'materially' and 'ideologically', etc.

My point here is not to choose among the many definitions of the system on offer within feminism, but to argue that naming the system is only one part of the challenge. Just as important, it seems to me, is how we think power is exercised within that system. If power works primarily through excluding that which it wants to subordinate, then the system's instability, and sources of resistance, must come from outside, from the space of exclusion. If, in contrast, we understand power as *producing* that which it subordinates, and as only being able to subordinate that which it has also made useful, then the possibilities for instability, for unexpected sources of resistance from within systems of power relations, are multiplied.

An overarching model of exclusionary power, based on gender or sexual difference as the single, primary difference, backed by a univocal view of language, gives us a closed system which is far more stable than I think we should concede. When, for example, Irigaray works with such a view, it leads her to conclude that we need to construct a whole other economy – a 'female sociality…, a female symbolic, a female social contract' (Whitford 1991b: 78) – and this would represent an enormous restructuring at both conscious and unconscious levels. As I have argued above, and in Chapter 3, Irigaray's work is more nuanced than this. Even when she is focusing on an overarching economy of the same, she does locate instabilities within it, and she also argues for the possibility of a speaking position for women within it. But between the tremendously demanding guerrilla warfare of jamming the theoretical machinery of hom(m)osexuality in Irigaray's philosophical texts, and the rather anodyne, and politically naive, prescriptions for valorising the female in her latest work, there is little middle ground for considering what might constitute effective political resistance for feminists in the impure and complex world of contemporary power relations.

In different ways, both Braidotti and Butler also suffer from the constraints of working with a closed system. If Irigaray makes resistance too difficult, Braidotti makes it too easy, by positing a pure space outside power relations for her nomad. But by siting resistance outside the *polis*, and to a large extent, outside consciousness, Braidotti leaves the 'molar' space of prevailing hierarchies relatively intact. Butler, on the other hand, works hard to destabilise the system of signification she critically adopts from Lacan, by complicating and displacing each of its elements. She also argues that the whole 'system' only emerges gradually over time, and that it is, thus, subject to social change. But her deconstructive moves to destabilise the Lacanian system can only proceed once she has decided to work with its model of an overarching symbolic to begin with, with its overriding logic of exclusion and abjection. In so doing, she turns away from the inherently more open system she takes from Foucault.

Many feminists have, of course, read Foucault's model of productive, disciplinary power as positing an overwhelming, monolithic force that produces completely docile bodies, with no possibilities of effective resistance (e.g. Fraser 1989; Singer 1989; Hartsock 1990; McNay 1992). These readings fail to follow through on the full implications of Foucault's move from power as repressive to power as productive. It is only when power is understood within a logic of exclusion, repression and abjection that it can be thought to result in fully docile bodies. It is only when power is understood to have one single, overriding logic – as the Subject who says 'No' – that it can be thought of as an overwhelming and monolithic force.

As I read it, a Foucauldian model of power resists both these moves. By shifting from a logic of repression to one of proliferation, Foucault is working with an inherently unstable and open-ended model. Within this model, there is, of course, a proliferation of discourses and practices that sustain prevailing hierarchies and structures of domination. But there is also a proliferation of possibilities – of knowledges, of subjects and of 'useful bodies' that are 'inappropriate/d' to the relations of power from which they emerge.

I understand Haraway to be working with this kind of model of power when she insists that 'The System is not closed; the sacred image of the same is not coming. The world is not full' (Haraway 1992b: 327). It is, in part, because she starts from the assumption of an open system that Haraway looks for, and finds, a proliferation of promising, if always dangerous, monsters, emerging from the instabilities of late-twentieth-century scientific and political culture.

Impure subjects or abjected others

This is closely related to the second insight I think needs to be drawn from a Foucauldian model of power: that is, that sites of resistance come not just from where women have been excluded but also from where they have been made central, where they have been, in Haraway's terms, 'actively managed'. Models of power that position women primarily as abjected others create a number of problems for feminism. First, they overstate the degree to which women disappear, are made invisible or marginal within power relations. Second, they make it difficult to distinguish between moves that foreground women in order to actively manage them, and women-centred contestations of that management. Third, if women are always positioned as abjected others, then the question of their agency is always seen as a problem. How and why does the 'object' begin to speak? Does it speak with a purer voice because it is untainted in its powerlessness? When it speaks in ways that seem to legitimate its object status is this a 'false' voice that covers over its 'true' interests? Both these options have proved very problematic for feminism because they continue to lock questions of agency and resistance into narratives of purity.

In contrast, working with a model of power that positions women as impure subjects complicates the ways in which women are subordinated, but also multiplies the possible sites of resistance. It recognises that women's subordination does not always work in one way, that women are not always objectified and abjected and therefore that different ways of subordinating women can have different effects. Some of those effects can be partially enabling for women, and these can be worked for their destabilising potential. Women's agency, then, is never a pure space immune from the workings of power, but it also does not need to derive from some pure and difficult-to-attain space outside those workings of power.

Purity and identity politics

The third level at which feminist models of power need to contest purity is in terms of the 'we' of feminist politics. Speaking of the questions 'we' expect politics to address, Foucault argued:

> the problem is [...] to decide if it is actually suitable to place oneself within a 'we' in order to assert the principles one recognizes and the values one accepts; or if it is not, rather, necessary, to make the future formation of a 'we' possible by elaborating the question. Because it seems to me that the 'we' must not be previous to the question; it can only be the result –

the necessarily temporary result – of the question as it is posed in the new terms in which one formulates it.

(Foucault 1984: 385)

When feminism follows the model of identity politics, that presumes a stable and unified identity for women as the basis on which to organise, it makes the 'we' previous to the political questions it aims to resolve.

Butler echoes Foucault's problematising of the 'we' of identity politics, when those politics are based on fixing a pure space of identity as the pre-condition for political action; within Western feminism, she argues, each attempt to fix the identity of feminism's constituency in advance produces the very factionalisation it is supposed to overcome (Butler 1992: 14). Donna Haraway also points to the dangers for feminism of imagining women's unity as something 'in the blood', to be presumed, rather than as a difficult and ongoing achievement.

I would argue that most versions of feminist politics as identity politics rely on a narrative of purity in two interrelated ways. First, they cover over both power differentials between women and the inevitable, necessary contestations over what constitutes women's identity and interests in particular conditions. Second, they claim a fixed, coherent and discrete space for women as a category of gender, or sexual difference, separated out from that category's intersection with race, nation, class, etc.

The problems posed by viewing feminist politics as identity politics can perhaps be best illustrated through a specific example. Flavia Agnes' discussion of the difficulties faced by the Bombay women's movement during and after communal riots in the 1990s shows a number of the dangers of purity models. Agnes explains that before the riots, women's groups had identified violence against women as a gender issue uniting all women. After the riots, when Muslim women had seen the men of their community attacked indiscriminately as rapists, a strategy based purely on gender identity or on women's unity could not have the same impact (Agnes 1995: 149–51). Insisting on a pure gender unity outside the context of differences, or taking gender outside the frame of the multiple and intersecting networks of power within which it operates, would simply have reinforced communal differences between women.

In addition, even if the women's movement imagined itself in some pure space where gender unity overrode the workings of multiple networks of power relations, those power relations continue to have an impact within the movement. For example, over the years women's organisations had sought to prove their populism and 'Indian-ness' by drawing on traditional images, in the face of criticisms that they represented only middle-class and 'westernised' women. But, given the prevailing hegemony of the majority Hindu culture, many of the images appropriated by the movement relied on that majority hegemony, 'rather than on the history of a pluralistic society that encompassed within its framework the cultural idioms of minority communities' (Agnes 1995: 139). In order to secure their identity, women's movements tapped into the same repertoire of images used to define communal identities. The full and bitter irony of such a move was realised when women militants of the Hindu right re-appropriated feminist slogans and tactics in order to direct attacks against Muslims (1995: 141).

Amrita Chhachhi has called communalism a form of identity politics (Chhachhi 1994). In making a link between communalism and identity politics, she suggests the dangers for feminism, and any movement for social change, in basing a politics on fixed, pure identities. Chhachhi suggests that communalist discourses tend to construct woman as the border of community identities, and argues that women need both to contest this and to insist on their own rights to define those borders and identities (Chhachhi 1991: 168–9). Might we not take her analysis a step further and argue that feminists also need to question the nature of those borders as well, and find different models of identity on which to proceed politically?

This does not mean giving up on the 'we' of effective politics, but shifting the terms within which it is understood. Rather than presuming a 'we' of shared values and experiences, of pre-given identities, in order to resist, the 'we' is fashioned, shifts and comes to know itself in the process of resisting. Haraway's distinction between identity and affinity politics is useful in this context. Where identity politics presumes a sameness as the basis on which to act politically, affinity politics presumes differences, that will need to be negotiated. It is not because 'we' are all the same that we can act politically; it is rather because 'we' are all partial, different and faced with particular political problems that connect us, that 'we' need to act together politically. It is only on this basis that, for Haraway, 'Who are "we"?' can be reformulated as an inherently open question, 'one always ready for contingent, friction generating articulations' (Haraway 1992b: 324). In the impure world of complex power relations, yet another model of purity, identity based in sameness, will not do if future feminist communities of resistance are to produce 'something other than the sacred image of the same, something inappropriate, unfitting and so, maybe, inappropriated' (1992b: 300).

If sustaining a simultaneous focus on women and their differences requires that feminist theory refuse a logic of dualisms, then one crucial area in which this must happen is in the underlying models of power we work with. Conceptualising power in negative terms perpetuates a logic of dualisms by arguing that power requires an abjected other upon which the subject acts. Feminist theory and politics suffer in a number of ways when they rely on this model of power.

Viewing women as only abjected covers over the many ways in which women are actively implicated in the production of social identities and of power relations. It perpetuates the illusion that feminism, 'speaking for' those abjected others, can speak from a pure space of exclusion from power relations. Such a model makes it difficult to remain attentive to the way power differentials work within feminism, and to thereby keep a space open for respecting differences between women.

Such a model also makes it difficult to acknowledge the extent to which women are enabled by the power relations that constrain them. This makes it hard to conceptualise women's agency without recourse to a language of 'false consciousness' that must be overcome, or some notion of authentic gender interests that can be separated from other aspects of women's identities, and from the power relations in which these identities are constituted. Again, this re-imports into feminism a narrative of purity that turns attention away from the differences between women.

Finally, positioning women only on the margins covers over many of the specific ways in which women's activities, and discursive constructs of the female and the feminine, are central to the emergence of gendered, racialised and national identities. If we fail to look at how the 'active management' of women helps to produce these different community identities, then we cannot take women's differences adequately into account. Conversely, if we do view women as impure subjects, fully implicated in the complex and impure spaces of power relations, then our attention is turned both to the differences between women, and to the possibilities of resistance that emerge from those impure spaces. If power produces subjects of a particular kind, how can we think about the particular subjects called women 'in a postcolonial mode'? If possibilities of resistance and change emerge from within complex relations of power, what are the possibilities for alternative ways of conceptualising the self and agency that are emerging as enabling for feminism? These issues will form the focus of my final chapter.

Chapter 8

Theorising 'women' in a postcolonial mode

Feminism as a political movement and feminist theory as a field of intellectual inquiry are supposed to take 'women' as their central focus of attention. Yet women are all different. Can we speak of something like a unified category 'women' when this unity is constantly undermined by divisions of race, nation, ethnicity, class, sexuality, etc., and by differences in the category's social meaning fashioned in specific times and spaces? One of the most common ways of framing this dilemma in contemporary feminist theory is to argue that holding on to some kind of unified category of 'women' is a tactical move that effective politics requires, even while recognising that it is dangerous because of the exclusions that this necessarily entails.

Feminists have come to some variation on this position from different starting points. Gayatri Spivak (1987: 197–221) has suggested that 'strategic essentialism' may be necessary to effective politics, and writers like Diana Fuss have taken up this concept with some reservations and modifications (Fuss 1989: 31–3). Moira Gatens has argued that, in countering the 'implicit and explicit masculinity' of the modern body politic, which serves to deny an autonomous political or ethical representation to female embodiment, feminists may need, initially, to assert 'a certain homogeneity in the specific situations of women' in order to make a political space for themselves (Gatens 1996: 56). Gatens cautions that such an assertion derives more from tactical necessity than from 'an ontological truth about women that is closed to history' (1996: 56), and that feminism also needs to develop a more open-ended ontology that can move beyond such a position. In making the move to questions of ontology, Gatens takes this position further than someone like Judith Butler. As we have seen, for Butler, there is also a tactical need to work with the necessary fiction of 'women' as a 'political signifier', while recognising that 'one is [...] used and positioned by it' at the same time (Butler 1993a: 29). But Butler, unlike Gatens, discounts the move to an alternative ontology that might begin from reconsidering specifically female embodiment. For Butler, 'women' remains a signifier, that is, something that is always already constrained by the system of language and its necessary exclusions. This signifier can be destabilised to some extent and its 'necessary injuries' can be re-worked to subvert dominant social and symbolic systems to some extent. However, the move to redefine 'women' on the basis of an alternative model of the self, self–other relations or a subject, or to reconsider female embodiment or a specifically female subject-position from a different basis, is not a route that Butler chooses to take.

In this final chapter, I want to argue that feminism cannot do the work of sustaining its focus on women, whilst also attending to the differences between women, without addressing questions concerning the models of the self and of identity that underpin our theory and politics. But I also want to argue that it is possible to push Gatens' type of position a little further, so that the sustained focus on women – as a category of analysis and political practice – is more than a concession to the tactical requirements of politics, one that necessarily involves some downplaying of the differences between women.

As I suggested at the beginning of Chapter 7, this requires that we work against purity in a number of ways. Feminism needs to move beyond analytical approaches to social identity that view 'women' only as a category of gender or sexual difference. If 'women' is a category, it is a complex one, that refers to questions of specific community identities like race, nation, ethnicity and class, as well as to gender or sexual difference. This is both because women's identities are constituted as much by race, nation and other categories of identity as they are by sex or gender, and because, both symbolically and strategically, the 'active manage-ment' of Woman/women seems, in turn, to play a key role in determining the 'truths' around which these identities are con-structed.

Here, the impurity we need to draw on is the way 'Woman' and 'women' seem to bleed across the boundaries of these apparently coherent categories of gender, race and nation. The purity we need to contest is the attempt to fix 'Woman' and 'women' as the unchanging ground upon which these apparently discrete categories stand. Additionally we need to underpin this kind of analysis of social identities with alternative theoretical models of the self that take these complex, impure spaces as a valid and valorised position from which to derive a sense of self, and from which to act and to speak.

Recognising that women's identities are constituted as much by race, nation and ethnicity as by sex and gender, or that these categories are mutually constitutive, is not a terribly new insight for feminism, even among white Western feminists, who have been notoriously resistant to taking it on board. But white feminisms in particular still seem to view this insight as a problem to be overcome, rather than a possibility to be explored. They still tend to see women as primarily related to gender, or to sexual difference, and therefore everything else is seen as a complication that needs to be inserted into this frame.

In part, I think this is because feminists have tended to look at only one side of the relationship between women and these categories of identity, that is, what the categories of identity 'do' to women. But the other side is that the active management of 'Woman' and 'women' also helps to construct those categories to begin with. Contestations over what 'Woman' stands for, and what 'women' do, are key to the stability or instability of these categories. Much of the material discussed in Part I suggests a more positive way of looking at the relationship between women and these different identity categories. I want to suggest that the way both the 'female' and the 'feminine' are actively managed across categories of identity might create some points of unity across the differences normally assigned to those categories. These points of unity then become a basis for talking about a category 'women' that 'looks in several directions at once'.

Thinking more positively about the relationship between women and the different categories of social identity involves breaking out of what Donna Haraway has called the geometrics of binaries, and thinking about ways to refigure multiplicity outside the geometry of parts and wholes (Haraway 1991: 3). Much of feminist theory is perhaps still unnecessarily beholden to binary thinking in two ways. First, there is a tendency to think about 'women' as referring primarily or even exclusively to gender or sexual difference, rather than to a more complex economy that cannot be contained within the conventional dualisms that appear to structure categories or concepts like gender, race, nation. It may be necessary to take a step back from gender or sexual difference, in order to focus more clearly on women.

Second, much of contemporary feminist theory tends to rely on language models that describe the system of language as working through exclusion and the fixing of discrete and univocal meanings, without questioning whether these models adequately reflect either language itself or its interplay with material practices in society. In both cases, they give the system (whether it be 'language' itself or a social system built through/in language) credit for more stability and uniformity than should be conceded.

In this chapter I will first review some of the themes which emerge from my examination of Indian feminists, that open up different ways of thinking about women and differences. I will then look at how these themes complicate 'women' as theorised in the projects of Braidotti, Butler, Haraway and Irigaray. I am not suggesting that any kind of easy translation is possible of analyses of the situation of women in India to any other particular context. What I am suggesting is that some of the questions asked of 'women' in a postcolonial context might be profitably asked of 'women' in Western feminist analyses as well, although the answers are likely to be quite different. I will also argue that some theoretical frameworks within Western feminism make these questions easier to ask than others. In the final section, I discuss the elements of an alternative model of the self that can emerge from considering 'women' as a complex category.

'Women' is a complex category

My starting point for much of what I find useful in the work of Indian feminists is the frequent reference to the ways in which either national or racial/religious community identities are constituted on or through the bodies of women. This suggests that women's actions, and discursive constructs of woman, cannot be looked at merely in terms of what they do to produce what might be called gendered or sexed identities, or social relations structured by gender or sexual difference. 'Women' and 'Woman' circulate across the apparently discrete categories of gender, nation, race, religion, caste, etc. In the work of Indian feminists we see women and Woman 'travelling' in this way from anti-colonial contestations of various forces within the nationalist movement (Sarkar 1987; Sinha

1987; Chakravarti 1990; Mani 1990), to contemporary cultural constructs of a unified national identity (Sunder Rajan 1993; Natarajan 1994), to racial/religious identities in both Hindu and Muslim communities (Sarkar 1991, 1995; Butalia 1993, 1995; Hasan 1994b), to the particularities of caste (Geetha and Jayanthi 1995) and even local or regional (Niranjana 1994a) identities. The work that women and women's bodies are expected to do simply cannot be contained within the analytical borders of a category like gender, or sexual difference.

But, at the same time, it seems that in order to legitimate those particular community identities, women's bodies and behaviour need to be controlled and discursive constructs of Woman need to be promoted as a stable, unchanging and pure ground of those identities. Both strategically and symbolically, there is something about the female body that needs to be appropriated for a sense of national, racial or community identity to persist. It seems clear that at least part of what is at stake here is the female capacity for birth, and the access to origins that birth represents. Wherever group or community identities are 'imagined', to be wholly or partly birth-based – and this remains largely the case wherever nations, races, castes and many other forms of community are imagined – then exercising the power to define those identities must, in part at least, pass through both a symbolic and strategic appropriation of birth and the active management of women.

Identity work, women and the female body

We know that, in violent racial and ethnic confrontations, sexual violence is common. Urvashi Butalia's discussions of the rape and sexual mutilation of Hindu and Muslim women during both the partition period of the 1930s and recent communal rioting in India, and of killings and suicides of Hindu and Muslim women in order to 'protect their purity' in the face of actual or perceived attacks, are specific Indian examples of a much broader phenomenon (Butalia 1993, 1995). Raping women and lynching men who are identified as real or potential rapists remain commonplace tools of racial and ethnic terror. What is at stake is the purity of a community, safeguarded or defiled through the female capacity for birth of community members.

Butalia's work is part of a broader theme in Indian feminist scholarship that suggests that racial/ethnic terror exercised on women's bodies, or on men in the name of 'protecting' women's bodies, is only an extreme form of a process that imbues community identity constitution more generally. As long as identities are defined, at least in part, as being dependent on birth into a specific community, then, as Gabriele Dietrich has noted, there will be a sense that if women's sexuality is not controlled, then 'actual identities will change in unimaginable ways' (Dietrich 1994: 44).

The communal controversies over Hindu and Muslim personal laws that I discussed in Part I reflect the kind of identity-work that is involved in control over the female body and over women's conduct – to form the centre of communal political imagination and of redefinitions of national identities (Hasan 1994a: xviii–xix). Strategically, by legislating on marriage, divorce, custody and inheritance, the personal laws aim to control the relationship between women, the issue of their bodies and a community's property. Symbolically, in the context of communal conflict, they bear the weight of representing the unity of a community identity (Hasan 1994b: 61).

Symbolic appropriations of birth in order to define national and racial identities are seen most directly in the mother-goddess/Mother-India iconography and imagery of both the nationalist movement of the anti-colonial period and the contemporary Hindu communalist movement. Some of the Indian feminists I discussed more fully in Chapter 1 interpret this appropriation as providing a passive, nurturing ground for a nationalist movement that is largely defined by and for men (Bagchi 1990; Lakshmi 1990; Sen 1993). Others complicate their analyses by drawing on both notions of purity/passivity and a kind of inciting, mobilising power of the mother (Alexander 1989; Loomba 1993; Sangari 1993; Sarkar 1995). But both approaches suggest that an active discursive management of the maternal is involved in the constitution of national and community identities.

To these direct discursive evocations of the maternal, we need to add the ways in which related concepts of time (origin, tradition) and space (home, private, inside) are linked to the feminine in order to fix identities. The connection of 'Woman' to tradition and the identification of women's activities as the bearers of a timeless tradition also refers back to questions of origin and birth (Chakravarti 1990; Sunder Rajan 1993). Similarly, appropriation of a language and imagery of home as the private and pure space unsullied by colonial, or more recently a generalised 'Western' or 'modern' influence, and the naming of this space as feminine-maternal, mobilises 'Woman' and 'women' as a discursive ground for national and community identities (Loomba 1993; Sarkar 1987; Sen 1993).

But it is not only through their location in discursive systems that Woman/women mark the borders, the place or the ground of these identity categories. It is also women's activities – how they use time, how they occupy space – that are seen as key to constructing community identities and preserving their purity (Geetha and Jayanthi 1995; Niranjana 1994a). It is not just a question of prescribing the times or spaces of 'purity' or 'inner-ness' that are appropriate for women, because what counts as 'inside' is highly variable according to specific social contexts and economic needs. It is also that women's presence in turn lends an 'inner-ness', a sense of belonging and purity to a particular space, and the purity at stake is one of the community group in question (Niranjana 1994a: 14–15).

A similar point emerges from Sarkar's (1995) and Geetha and Jayanthi's (1995) discussion of organisations of the contemporary Hindu right, and of Sarkar's (1987) and Loomba's (1993) discussions of the pre-independence nationalist movement. The ways in which women are mobilised by these movements, and the movements' appropriation of certain traditionally private rituals and activities, mean that a certain 'private' space gets carried out into the public movement with and through women. This is then mobilised by the movements in order to claim a certain purity or authenticity of identity for themselves. One is reminded of Lou Andreas-Salomé's comment, in a completely different context, that women always carry a sense of home around with them, as a snail carries its shell on its back (Martin 1991: 43).

Each of these texts provides a specifically located discussion of ways in which particular groups of Indian women are discursively and strategically positioned in relation to different community identities. But when we put them together, they suggest a more general point that can, I think, be pertinent to feminist theory when it aims to focus simultaneously on 'women' and their differences. What we see across these specific examples is that 'Woman' and 'women' are being pulled in two different directions. On the one hand, we see 'women' circulating across a multiplicity of identity categories, refusing to settle down inside the analytical borders of social relations structured only by gender. But on the other hand, within the fields of individual national, raced, religious or caste communities, discourses and practices of purity repeatedly work to 'fix' women as the ground of those identities, as the stable markers of authenticity and access to pure origins.

Recognising that women are positioned in these complex ways across and within multiple community identities means that in order to focus on 'women' adequately, we need to look at their productive role in the emergence of national, raced and other differences. Focusing on 'women' as a feminist strategy becomes a way of looking simultaneously at a multiplicity of identity categories. Thus, rather than seeing such a focus as a trade-off between feminist 'unity' and attention to differences, it offers a way of thinking outside the geometrics of binaries.

Women as citizens

For a number of Indian feminists, discussion of this issue of recognising women's complex identity has centred around reclaiming and rethinking the concept of citizenship. The impetus for this in the Indian context has been the rise of communalism in recent years. The communal move is a move from plurality to fixity, from negotiating multiple, intersecting categories of social identity (caste, class, religion, gender, nation) that accommodate and confront each other, to a simplifying process, closing communities and individuals around a single religious identity. And much of this rigidifying process has been directed at women, by positing a fixed, birth-based identity for women and by conflating their identities as individuals with that of a monolithic community.

The communal move, however, only exacerbates, and makes more visible, a general tension that exists between the 'closed' space of community and the 'open' space of civil identities. It also makes more visible the crucial role that women are expected to play in preserving the stability of different forms of community upon which the modern 'individual-citizen' still depends for a sense of identity (Kannabiran and Kannabiran 1995; Sinha 1995). This is not something which is unique to India, or to an underdeveloped 'East', although the manner in which this tension is played out will be different in different social conditions. Moira Gatens has argued that the Western tradition of the body politic also constructs women as 'not whole beings'. There is a tendency to limit ethical relations between the sexes to familial and conjugal ethics, in which women are recognised only as wives and mothers, and denied the full range of citizenship status (Gatens 1996: 42, 54–6).

The Indian feminist discussions of citizenship, however, allow us to see more clearly that what is at stake is not just an exclusion of unspecified women by generic men. Women are positioned in complex ways between a multiplicity of 'closed' spaces of community identities such as race, religion or ethnicity on the one hand, and the 'open' space of civil society on the other. Thus the problem of women's access to full citizenship status is not one that can be adequately discussed if we look only at questions of gender or sexual difference.

Nor, as I argued in Chapter 2, is the complexity of their positioning fully captured by framing it in terms of a conflict between gender and community interests, as Zoya Hasan has suggested (Hasan 1994b: 59–68). Such a framework still conceptualises 'gender' and 'community' as two relatively discrete categories. This suggests that women's identity 'as women' is something that can be detached from their location in specific communities. But what emerges most strongly from the analysis of Indian feminists is that women are not only constituted by their communities but that they are quite central to constituting them in turn. We therefore need ways to speak of women's interests 'as women' which take into account the full complexity of their place in identity constitution, a complexity which is not easily contained within the analytical borders of either 'gender' or 'community'.

In this context, Indian feminist discussions of women as citizens could be considered as an example of what Butler would call a radical 'democratizing contestation' of a particular site within the political field (Butler 1993a: 115). It is not that the status of citizen is, in itself, an unproblematic ideal through which women will gain full emancipation. This would be to stay within the limitations of a liberal feminism which seeks only to include women in contemporary social and political structures, and which does not challenge the way these structures depend on women's subordination. It is, rather, a question of exposing women's particular location in relation to the concept of citizen, and of using the discontinuities and tensions of that location for their destabilising potential.

On one level, thinking about women as citizens means insisting that women be given the same 'privilege' of a complex identity as men, of circulating across all the boundaries of national, raced and other community identities that meet in the space of civil society.

As I discussed in Part I, one way some Indian feminists have approached this is in terms of their critical support for a uniform civil code that would take precedence over religion-based personal laws. For these feminists, working to unbind the personal laws via an egalitarian civil code gives women the same recognition of complexity as citizens as men. At the same time, these feminists recognise that women still have to negotiate their way through the various power relations in society, including struggling with men around the traditions encoded in the personal laws (Chakravarti, Menon and Butalia, personal interviews 1995).

This brings us to the second level at which the notion of women-as-citizens needs to be re-worked. Mrinalini Sinha claims that, in India, the concept of citizen depends both on a modern community of identity in the nation-state, and on an accommodation and reconstitution of 'pre-modern', 'organic' communities of identity, which include religion, race and caste (Sinha 1995: 49–50). But, as we have seen, 'Woman' and 'women' are repeatedly called upon to serve as the ground upon which these community identities are defined. If this is so, then we begin to see why it is so difficult for women to be recognised as full citizens within such a set-up. The apparent mobility of the citizen still requires a fixed, pure place of community identities – home, nation, race, religion – to retreat to. If women have to stand in for, and reproduce that place, then they cannot 'travel' as citizens. If women refuse to settle down in/as that place, then the system's stability is threatened. When women insist on their right to travel as citizens, and to redefine both the female/feminine and the community identities constituted through them, on a different basis – one which refuses the discourses of purity and fixity – they challenge one of the bases on which oppressive forms of social cohesion and social identities are wrought.

A third point I want to draw out of this discussion of citizenship is that it situates questions of multiplicity, and of alternative models of the self, social identity and resistance that start from multiplicity, in historically specific social circumstances. Such an approach locates its sources of complexity and multiplicity not on the margins of Language, 'beyond' consciousness, or outside the *polis*, but firmly inside the realm of the social. It also does this, not by moving beyond 'women' as category of identity, but by exploring 'women' as a complex category in its own right. For both these reasons, such an approach challenges and complicates the analysis of 'women' offered by each of the four Western feminist projects I examine in this book, suggesting ways of moving beyond the limitations each of them experiences in focusing on women while keeping a space open for differences. In the next section, I want to look at how each of the four goes some way towards a model that captures this sense of women as a complex category, and where their approaches turn aside from this trajectory.

'Women', complexity and white Western feminisms

Women as nomads

As we have seen, Rosi Braidotti privileges the concept of nomad to express the complexity and multiplicity of women. Immediately, we can note a difference from the approach I have sketched above. The nomad is precisely *not* a citizen – she is quite deliberately outside the *polis*, troubling it from its edges. She derives her radical potential to upset the hegemonic order of things from her outsider status, not from the fact that her activities and the meanings read onto those activities are quite central to maintaining the stability of social identities and structures.

Yet Braidotti starts from a number of points which can be read as speaking to the themes I have identified in the first part of this chapter. She says that in feminist theory one speaks 'as a woman', but that woman is not a monolithic, unchanging essence and is rather the site of multiple, complex and potentially contradictory sets of experience. The nomad as figuration is supposed to capture the ways in which different axes of differentiation work simultaneously in constituting subjectivity (Braidotti 1994a: 4). Women's 'unity' as a category comes, not from an originary site or authentic identity, but from the 'emphatic proximity and intensive interconnectedness' of different states and experiences (1994a: 5–6). Thus, on these points at least, Braidotti can be said to be arguing for an understanding of women as a complex category. In addition, Braidotti's insistence on the nomad as polyglot, 'who has no mother tongue', in the sense of a fixed and steady origin (1994a: 11), could be read as a way to resist attempts to construct the Woman/mother as the fixed, steady origin that stands as boundary for community identities. Against this move, the nomad, like the citizen, insists on her right to travel.

But, as I have already noted, the nomad is not a citizen, and it is their difference in location that becomes significant in turning Braidotti away from a full recognition of women's complexity. Rather than building on her initial attention to multiplicity in specific social circumstances, Braidotti takes this insight about the woman/nomad as polyglot in quite another direction. The problem, she says, is that all tongues carry 'the name of the father' and are stamped by its register (1994a: 11), and this leads to an inevitable imbalance between pre-discursive, pre-conscious desire (the unthought and the non-thought) and the symbolic forms available to express that desire. Moving away from considering the polyglot as historically and socially situated, Braidotti turns to the universalising constraints of language and psychoanalytic models to argue that the 'key notion to understanding multiple identity is desire, that is to say unconscious processes' (1994a: 14).

For Braidotti, multiplicity – both as acknowledgement of the differences between women and as a potential, positive 'line of escape' from women's subordination – is no longer to be found in the specific location of women, but rather in (unconscious) desire, that which language always needs to cover over and can never adequately express. This necessarily turns attention away from the multiplicity that functions at conscious, social levels, and which also needs to be addressed as a possible source of instability and resistance. For Braidotti, then, it is primarily the 'unconscious internalized images that escape rational control' that point the way forward to a new model of identity and resistance (1994a: 166). But this model brings with it its own baggage – its tendency to see power in purely negative terms, its elevation of sexual difference to primary difference – that tends to fold multiplicity back into a univocal sameness.

As if in response to Braidotti's privileging of desire, Donna Haraway calls for more cyborg 'noise' as a way of 'subverting the structure of desire, the force imagined to generate language and gender' (Haraway 1991: 176). I think what this can mean is that recourse to something 'before' or 'outside' thought or language – which is how Braidotti positions desire – is still to stay within a geometrics of binarisms. Braidotti wants to locate some kind of unproblematically good multiplicity somewhere beyond the noise and impurity of the world, instead of dealing with the dangerous multiplicity that refuses to separate out these spaces. In turning to a language model to frame her project, and a pre-linguistic desire as the privileged 'line of escape' for her woman-nomad, Braidotti turns away from women in their specificity. This is why, for all her initial claims to attend to multiplicity, she has so little to say about women's multiple locations and remains so inattentive to the ways in which she folds other differences back into a single frame of sexual difference.

Women as signifiers

Judith Butler's work is informed by the insight that the apparent coherence of categories like sex and gender is a product of power relations (Butler 1990: 136). For Butler, these are regulatory norms that need to be constantly re-materialised, and which are therefore always being contested (or at least the possibility of contestation always exists) (Butler 1993a: 2). She also argues that sex and gender cannot be looked at apart from other norms such as race. With these two moves, Butler provides a theoretical basis on which to discuss both the underlying instability of apparently discrete identity categories, and the ways in which the normalising effects of power attempt to cover over that instability by fixing truths about identity. She also wants to complicate Lacan's notion of the symbolic so that, at both psychic and social levels, we are dealing simultaneously with sex/gender and race (1993a: 181–2).

The category 'women', for Butler, 'marks a dense intersection of social relations that cannot be summarized through the terms of identity' (1993a: 218). I take this to mean that for Butler, 'women' won't or can't settle down into a stable, unified category of sex or gender. The category 'women' is a permanent site of contest; there can be no closure on the category, nor, for compelling political reasons, should there be (1993a: 221). 'Women', for Butler, ought to remain 'a discursive site whose uses are not fully constrained in advance' (1993a: 230) so that this site's 'specific historicity' can be exposed, affirmed and re-worked (1993a: 230).

Thus Butler neither dispenses with the category 'women', nor does she completely disallow attempts to positively re-work it as 'a political signifier'. Nevertheless, as I have argued in Chapter 4, she does close down some avenues for fully exploring 'women', both in terms of the ways in which the category is put into play in relations of power that subordinate women, and in terms of its 'radical democratizing potential' for feminism. In both cases, this limits the extent to which her model is one that enables a simultaneous focus on women and their differences.

I would argue that a large part of Butler's problem in this respect comes from insisting on thinking about 'women' as a signifier, thereby locking it into a language model and thus tending to focus on questions of exclusion and disruption to a unified 'system'. This move constrains her project in two interconnected ways. First, as I argued in the last section of Chapter 4, Butler's engagement with Lacanian and Derridean language models leads her to disqualify any focus on the specifically female, and in particular any positive redefinition of 'women' on the basis of the specifically female. This closes off consideration of the ways in which birth and the female body are put into play in the emergence of race, nation and other community identities. It also closes off consideration of ontological issues such as alternative models of the self that might be based on a reconsideration of female embodiment.

Second, the kinds of resistance strategies that Butler privileges are similarly limited by her reliance on a language model. Butler's privileged forms of resistance – parody, the 'repetition which fails to repeat loyally' – are all aimed at disrupting the apparent stability of a unified system. They are about refusing origins and any notion of an original identity (Butler 1990: 138); they work by marking the 'ground' of identity as 'groundless' (1990: 141). In undermining notions of origins and grounds, Butler goes some way towards addressing the problem of identities which rely on models of pure origins or on an unchanging ground or sense of place. But again, because she has discounted a focus on the specifically female, her model does not go on to consider women's particular and complex positioning in relation to questions of origins. Nor does her model welcome strategies that might move on from disrupting prevailing concepts of origins, ground or place to redefining them on another basis.

Clearly, models of race, nation and other community identities that fix 'Woman' and 'women' as sites of pure origin or unchanging ground need to be challenged, and the parodic exposure of their 'groundless ground' may be one way of doing this. But parody cannot fully address the strategic need for women to also occupy these sites (even if contingently) on a different basis. To adopt Irigaray's terminology, parody cannot enable women to *take* a place and not just *be* the place on which community identities are constituted (Whitford 1991a: 53).

Women as cyborgs

In many ways, Donna Haraway speaks most directly to the 'women' I have drawn out of my engagement with Indian feminisms. As I argued in Chapter 6, Haraway's work has a strong tendency to step back from sex/gender and to focus on women across the multiple manifestations of the self/other, nature/culture divides, including race and national differences. Like the Indian feminists discussed above, Haraway recognises that the appropriation of birth and origin stories is key not only to gender identities, but also to race and imperial narratives. It is from her work that I draw the need to find ways to refigure multiplicity outside the geometry of parts and wholes (Haraway 1991: 3), to dispense with the geometrics of binaries (1991: 129).

Haraway argues that 'each condition of oppression requires specific analysis that refuses the separations but insists on the non-identities of race, sex and class' (1991: 146). I understand this to mean that we need to hold together two moves. The first is that apparently discrete categories of social identity such as sex and race bleed into each other. The second is that these categories are not the same and cannot be reduced to each other. Thus, other differences cannot be subsumed into sexual difference, as can happen in a project like Braidotti's, but women's activities and constructions of 'Woman' need to be seen as productive of more than social relations strictly defined by gender.

Haraway's evocation of 'women in the integrated circuit' (1991: 170) can be read as a way of thinking about how 'women' circulate across categories, disassembling and reassembling the boundaries of categories such as home/work, public/private (1991: 166); through their circulation across categories, women become key to the 'social relations of the new technologies' (1991: 169). For Haraway, then, women are dispersed across multiple networks, and it is in this diaspora that we need to learn to survive (1991: 170). Haraway's linking of women and multiplicity to dispersal and diaspora is significant. Dispersal emphasises the hyper-visibility of women within multiple locations, the multiple levels at which women's activities, women's bodies and discursive constructs of 'Woman' are called upon to work. It also, of course, suggests Haraway's attentiveness to a term which is of central importance in postcolonial theory (Gilroy 1993; Brah 1996).

Haraway recognises that if feminism is to hold on to a category 'women' as a basis of unity, it needs to take account both of that dispersal and of the attempts to lock women into fixed truths through constructs of 'Woman'. For her, this means looking for possible affinities and connections that do not begin from the assumption that there is a closed narrative into which parts need to be fitted (Haraway 1991: 113). If 'women' hold together, it is not as anything unproblematically natural, organic or authentic, but as 'adopted families and imperfect intentional communities' (1991: 121). Part of this process means that 'locally, and globally, women's part in the building of persons, families and communities cannot be fixed in any of the names of Woman and her functions'(1991: 123).

Yet there remains a certain ambivalence in Haraway's approach to women and the specifically female. At times she seems to share Butler's strategy of moving directly to destabilising sexual difference or male/female distinctions, rather than redefining the female. When Haraway argues that 'destabilizing the positions in a discursive field and disrupting categories for identification might be a more powerful feminist strategy than "speaking as a woman" ' (Haraway 1992a: 310), it sometimes seems as if she is adopting a deconstructive strategy rather than any move to redefine the female. There is also Haraway's call for a paradigm shift from reproduction to generation, a move away from narratives based on birth, since it is so implicated in traditional paradigms of pure origins. Her move to the metaphorics of the cyborg is a move away from birth to regeneration as the basis for an alternative narrative of reconstitution, which includes the 'utopian dream of the hope of a monstrous world without gender' (Haraway 1991: 181).

Of course, as I have argued in Chapter 6, there are other places in which Haraway argues that reproduction and birth do not actually fit into prevailing self/other paradigms, despite the recurring attempts to appropriate them. This is both because the issue of the self is always (an)other (Haraway 1992a: 352), never the same, and because women's reproductive bodies and the specifically female nature of birth do not fit with the model of the singular self-contained self. Women's personal bounded individuality is always 'compromised by their bodies' troubling talent for making other bodies' (Haraway 1991: 253 fn 8). Men's dream of self-contained autonomy is always betrayed by their reliance on women's capacity for birth (Haraway 1992a: 353). In this aspect of her work, Haraway seems to be arguing for a revaluing of the specifically female, outside of the prevailing paradigms that tend to reduce it to closed narratives and to the 'sacred image of the same'.

Perhaps this ambivalence is a product of the notorious density of Haraway's work; she looks in so many directions at once, both drawing on and problematising so many different theoretical models in the same text, as well as speaking in more than one voice in each text. In my own appropriations of Haraway, I have tended to focus on her desire to valorise women by breaking them free from the constraints of 'Woman' as variously constructed in multiple narratives, including the psychoanalytic and language models that have become so influential in feminist theory. I have focused on the productive move to link 'women and other present-tense, illegitimate cyborgs, not of Woman born' (1991: 177).

Women as more and less than one

With Irigaray there is no doubt that the category 'women' is a promising source for understanding identity in a radically different way, one that privileges multiplicity, impurity and category confusion. Of course, Irigaray remains indebted to a language model that links women, the feminine and multiplicity together as that which language cannot represent and which language also needs to exclude. As I have argued in Chapters 3 and 7, this can close down Irigaray's project, both in terms of the space available for considering differences between women, and in terms of possible spaces of resistance. Yet, ironically and insistently, Irigaray's 'women' lend themselves to a reading in a postcolonial mode, at least as much as Haraway's, and far more than Butler's and Braidotti's.

Butler cautiously embraces a problematised 'women' while giving up on the specifically female, and Braidotti takes 'women' and the 'female feminine' on a nomadic trajectory outside thought, language and the *polis*. In both cases, this limits the extent to which their projects speak to the 'women' who emerge at the centre of nation, race and community identities in Indian feminist analyses. Haraway, without the constraints of a language model, arrives at many of the same locations occupied by these 'women'. But her work can sometimes seem to leap beyond women to a post-human landscape, without passing through the still-to-be-fought struggles to recognise women as fully, if differently human.

Irigaray, beginning in almost the opposite space from Haraway and committed to sexual difference as the fundamental difference, nevertheless also arrives at many of these same locations. With

Irigaray, the commitment to 'women' and valorising the female on a different basis remains intact; what is missing is the recognition that the locations she visits cannot be contained within a landscape of sexual difference alone. To read Irigaray's 'women' in a postcolonial mode is to open up that landscape.

To illustrate this point, I want to return to two moments in the section entitled 'Volume without Contours' in Irigaray's *Speculum of the Other Woman*, first discussed in Chapter 3, to suggest how her position takes on an added complexity when considered in the light of the themes that emerge from Indian feminisms. First, in the opening paragraphs of the section, Irigaray looks at how 'Woman', within an economy of the same, serves as the fixed ground or place for the masculine subject while being dispersed into multiple places that are never gathered together into a space that she defines on her own terms (Whitford 1991a: 53).

Irigaray writes of 'woman' functioning 'everywhere elsewhere', of being 'dispersed into x places which do not gather together in anything which she can recognise as herself and which remain the support for reproduction – especially of discourse – in all its forms' (1991a: 53). Read in the light of the themes that emerge from Indian feminisms, Irigaray's words take on the added complexity of 'woman' functioning across the categories of social identity to produce truths which privilege a male subject, not just in his masculinity, but also in terms of all the communities he constructs as grounds for his identity.

Irigaray captures the duality of Woman/women both functioning as stable place within the terms of individual community identity discourses, while being dispersed across categories. She argues that women still need to 'take (a) place', to re-work their relationship to place on a different basis. She also captures something of the duality of being 'all-powerful' and 'powerless' at the same time. On the one hand, the maternal-feminine is invested with certain 'truths' about access to origin, to timeless tradition or to a purity that sustains community identity. On the other hand, men appropriate the right to define those truths, and control that access to origin through controlling the activities of women.

Second, it is also possible to read in a postcolonial mode Irigaray's evocation of a 'non-specular' female/feminine/woman who can neither be reduced to nor universalised into a 'One'. This analysis of 'woman' as 'more-than-One' speaks to Indian feminist accounts of the management of women across unequal power relations informed by sex/gender, race, nation and community. Her evocation of 'woman' as 'less-than-One' is also relevant to the kinds of models of the subject and agency feminism relies on to speak 'as women'.

In 'Volume without Contours' Irigaray evokes women as '*in-fini*' (1991a: 59), both infinite and unfinished. Women are more than One: they can never be 'closed/shut up in one volume' (1991a: 65), or subsumed 'under one term, generic or specific'(1991a: 59). For Irigaray there is a 'plurality of the female commodity' that the (male) subject is always trying to gather up and regroup into a Same-One (1991a: 60). But in Irigaray's terms, women also are, and should be, less than the universal, generic One: 'one woman + one woman + one woman never will have added up to some generic: woman' (1991a: 55–6). Here the '*in-fini*' functions as the refusal to be finished, to be a complete, closed subject along male/masculine lines.

But what if we take both these moves outside the frame of an unspecified male/female or masculine/feminine and think about the interconnection of notions of sex/gender with race, nation, etc.? In this case, women's multiplicity is referred back not only to a morphology of the female body, but also/rather to the ways the female, the feminine, 'Woman' and 'women' circulate across and between the discourses, practices and institutions that produce gender, race, nation and community. The refusal of 'women' to settle down into a One is then seen within a more complex context of interconnected power relations that sustain and influence each other, but which also produce discontinuities and points of tension. Feminist evocations of the category 'women' need to sustain and valorise that refusal to settle down as the 'still silent ground' that hom(m)osexual economies require to produce gendered, raced and national identities. Irigaray's insistence that 'woman' remains 'more and less than One' also challenges the notion that there might be a new universalising 'generic woman' who provides a univocal feminist response to that economy, a most important insight for theorising in a postcolonial mode.

Alternative models of the self

To say that feminism can claim a speaking position for 'women' while refusing to settle down into a One is to suggest that a different model of the individual self is at work. In the final section of this chapter I want to look at how certain elements of this different model of a situated and embodied self might emerge from theorising 'women' in a postcolonial mode.

Place, location and dislocation

Questions of place or location have been an important focus of feminist debates about theorising difference. Notions of located-ness, in the sense of accountability for one's speaking position, have been tremendously important in contesting universalising claims that result in exclusions of women, both outside and within feminism. Concepts like Adrienne Rich's 'politics of location' (Rich 1986), or Donna Haraway's 'situated knowledges' (Haraway 1991) contest the model of a knowing self that transcends its particular location and gains access to an objective truth through the workings of a disembodied or universal reason.

For Haraway, the self is always partial, located and incomplete. Because it is partial and incomplete, it both needs to and can connect to others. Because it is located, because it can never be everywhere, because we cannot do without drawing borders around the self, we need to be accountable for the ways in which we draw those borders. Locatedness – acknowledging and being accountable for one's place – should form an important part of feminist alternative models of the self which aim to keep a space open for differences between women.

But another important theme in feminist theories of difference focuses on dislocation as a source of radical potential. If women are positioned as the 'still silent ground' upon which community identities are constituted, then insisting on women's 'right to travel' can be transgressive. This privileging of dislocation is seen in Irigaray's evocation of 'woman, the fluent'. We also see it in Indian feminist discussions of women as citizens, 'travelling' across the complex spaces of civil society. We see it as well, if less successfully, in Braidotti's celebration of the feminist as nomad.

However, as Irigaray suggests, women must not only refuse to 'be (the) place' upon which identities are constituted; they also ought to *take* (a) place of their own, to define their own relationship to place on a different basis. Thus feminist alternative models of the self need to hold together the transformative possibilities of both locatedness and dislocation. The preceding discussion of 'women' as a complex category suggests that one way of doing this is to recast locatedness in terms of the impurity of all spaces. My readings of Indian and Western feminisms suggest that it is not so much the association of 'women' with 'place' that is problematic, but rather the overarching framework of purity and authenticity within which predominant notions of 'place' are constrained. What can make a difference to prevailing paradigms of social identity, and the place of the self within them, is insisting on the right to define 'place' in terms that don't rely on purity.

Vidya Rao's treatment of *thumri* is evocative of this kind of reworked, valorised impure location. She begins from the place conventionally assigned to women (small, confined) and re-works it from within, drawing on its impurity (the lack of clear dividing lines between *ragas*) to expand the space available to the women performers of *thumri* (Rao 1990). We can add to this Amrita Chhachhi's more directly political suggestion that women of particular racial, religious or national communities need to claim their place within those communities while also insisting on their right to contest monolithic definitions of those communities (Chhachhi 1991: 168–9). Such strategies can also be seen as a way of redefining place outside a framework of purity.

A similar model of the relationship of the self to location can be found in Haraway's privileging of those 'illegitimate selves' whose locatedness is defined, not by access to pure origins, to 'natural and proper names', but by 'mutation, metamorphosis and diaspora'. Haraway's promising monsters – which include women – offer the possibility of a self that survives and acts by coming to terms with, and working the possibilities available in particular impure spaces.

Embodiment

A similar turn to the possibilities of impurity might also be productive for considering women and the embodied self. As I have argued in the first part of this chapter, the work that women and women's bodies are expected to do in constituting social identities within present systems of power relations cannot be easily contained within the analytical borders of such categories as gender or sexual difference. Nor do women's hyper-visibility and multiplicity fit easily within the symbolic role assigned them in so many discourses of national, racial or other community identities, in which 'women' serve as the fixed, passive and pure ground upon which these identities are to be constructed. If women are called upon to do the 'body work' within these community identities, as so much of the work I have examined has suggested, then the body in question is one that seems deeply at odds, both with women's activities and with the particularities of the female body.

It is a highly contestable 'imagined body' that is pressed into service to sustain a variety of 'imagined communities' (Anderson 1991). The material effects of such imagined bodies and communities are not to be denied, nor are the constraints they create in terms of possibilities of resistance and change. Nevertheless, their dissonance with significant aspects of women's activities and women's bodies do make these imagined bodies contestable. This dissonance opens a space for other views of the embodied self, because what gets covered over in terms of women's activities is also related to what is problematic about women's bodies. 'Women' don't settle down as the borders of separate and stable community identities. Like the leaky female body 'women' bleed across those borders. Like the productive female body, 'women' give birth to all sorts of new identities. Like the female body's 'troubling talent for making other bodies' (Haraway 1991: 253 fn 8), 'women' cannot be easily contained within a closed frame.

I am not arguing here that it is possible to get in touch with some unproblematic core of the 'real' female body as the basis of a different model of the embodied self. Feminist re-workings of female morphology and of embodiment are as partial and situated as the models they seek to contest. These new feminist ontologies remain, at best, promising monsters that suggest alternative ways of thinking about the self, but which are never immune from the dangers of re-appropriation within predominant relations of power. The challenge is to remain attentive to the risks while exploring the potential of these alternatives to undo prevailing paradigms.

Reading Irigaray through the refracting prism of the postcolonial mode, we can argue that female embodiment, and particularly birth, need to be taken out of the context of an economy of the same, which links it to multiple discourses and practices of rigid community identities. Drawing on the break-points and dissonances in dominant models of identity, we can argue with Haraway that birth is always the birth of (an)other, and not the reproduction of the same. A differently imagined body and birth might provide a different basis on which the birth-based identities of communities are imagined, one which places change and fluidity-fluency at its centre.

It might also suggest different ways of conceptualising the relation between individual selves. If the dualistic or dialectical models of the excluding self/other relation find their reflection in an imaginary model of the self-contained, bounded body, what can be made of the leaky female body and its troubling talent for making other bodies? Irigaray suggests, for example, that the placental relation between mother and foetus offers the possibility of conceptualising identity as a continuous negotiation between self and other, through which both are actively modified, while still remaining distinct (Irigaray 1990: 39–41).

Vidya Rao draws on the dual nature of the female body as open body – both open to pollution and therefore the source of life and continuity – to imagine an alternative model of the self. This self takes its impurity as a positive basis on which to act, as a source of possibility for expanding the space available to it through unexpected connections, and not just of dangers that need to be guarded against (Rao 1990: 37). Haraway too discusses the female body and the relationship between foetus and mother, in terms of rethinking the immune system and its implications for self–other paradigms and for what counts as an individual self (Haraway 1991: 203–30). Her alternative model is of the 'semi-permeable self able to engage with others [...] but always with finite consequences; of situated possibilities and impossibilities of individuation and identification, and of partial fusions and dangers' (1991: 225). All these relocated bodies suggest a self which persists yet which is not constrained or defined by pure distinctions between 'inner' and 'outer', 'self' and 'not-self', 'community' and 'outsider'.

This double move – of holding on to a notion of the individual self while taking it out of a framework of pure inside/outside delineation – has important political consequences. It has consequences both for the ways power relations are played out within feminism, and for the ways Woman/women are mobilised in the constitution of community identities that are defined by just such inner/outer distinctions, with potentially violent and violating consequences.

In Chapter 7, I discussed the problems that emerge when feminism takes on an unproblematised 'we' of identity politics in order to fix a pure space of identity as the pre-condition for political action. As Butler has argued, each attempt to fix the identity of feminism's constituency in advance produces the very factionalisation it is supposed to overcome (Butler 1992: 14–15). Presuming a collective subject of feminism as a point of departure tends to cover over the power differentials between women and also tends to conceal the necessary contestations over what constitutes women's identity and interests in particular conditions.

While feminism makes no sense as either a theoretical or a political project if it problematises a collective 'women' out of existence, it also needs to be attentive to the dangers of subsuming the individual self within a collective identity. As I argued in Chapter 2, submerging the individual self within a pure and stable collective identity is very much the project of communalism, fundamentalism and fascism. Even in its less extreme forms, we have seen that the constitution of fixed collective identities mobilises women in ways that perpetuate their subordination.

Many of the feminists I have discussed in this project argue for the need to rethink the nature of collective identity outside of paradigms of exclusion in order to leave a space open for the differences between women. In this chapter I have argued that it is possible to rethink the 'we' of feminism while holding on to a collective category 'women' precisely because of the discontinuities between those paradigms and women's complex place in contemporary power relations. Those discontinuities also make possible alternative models of a self, without which any project for a collective 'we' runs the risk of folding difference back into sameness.

Conclusion

One of the questions asked in the Introduction to this book is what is lost by relying on purity models in theorising identity. Throughout these chapters I have identified a number of ways in which feminist theory has a stake in rejecting purity if it is to sustain a simultaneous focus on women and their differences. In concluding, I want to review the problems with purity models that I have argued become more visible when the complications that emerge from my reading of Indian feminisms are placed together with white Western feminist theoretical approaches to identity. But I also want to reflect on what difference it can make to think about identity, the self, agency and feminist politics from the starting point of impurity.

In terms of the ways in which women are socially and discursively positioned, I have argued that the fixing of 'Woman' and 'women' as the pure and stable markers of community identities emerges as one of the key ways in which women are made central to identity-constituting processes that continue to subordinate them. Feminist theory needs to contest this purity model for two interrelated reasons. First, as we have seen in relation to debates within Indian feminisms, as long as women and women's bodies are required to stand for the pure space of fixed community identities, their 'right to travel' as complex subject-agents and as citizens is severely compromised. Second, the community identities constituted through these discursive and strategic positionings of 'Woman' and 'women' remain the fertile ground for the development of racism, 'ethnic absolutism' and fundamentalisms of all kinds.

In the relatively peaceful and stable polities of the West, we tend to think of these threats as something that happen somewhere else or that may once have happened here, but in the distant past. But even if we feel secure from the worst excesses of racial and ethnic terror (a security which is more apparent than real), we need to recognise that racism and narrow nationalism remain persistently part of our political reality. So, for example, when political discourses and strategies gesture towards the familiar calls for 'family values' or 'back to basics', we need to recognise that 'Woman' and 'women' are being positioned by these calls in ways that not only promote a particular version of gender relations, but also particular versions of fixed community identities and of 'nation-ness'. In the 'diaspora space' of modern Western societies such as the UK or the US, these versions of community or of nation reproduce and refigure racial and ethnic difference within nations at least in part through the ways that they position 'Woman' and 'women'. *Some* basics, and *some* family values are privileged, as the pure, immutable 'truths' that are to define the community or the nation, while others are disqualified, thus marking off, hardening and hierarchising categories of racial, ethnic and class difference.

Women have a personal stake in rejecting these versions of social identity, since racism and fundamentalism have never been particularly kind to most women. But, as I have argued throughout this book, we need to look not only at what these identity categories 'do to' women, but also at how women are central to their emergence. If women are central to their emergence, then they can also be central to destabilising and redefining them, and in ways that break down the assumptions of purity and fixed identities on which racism and fundamentalism depend. I will return to this point later.

In this book, I have also identified a number of ways in which feminist theorising remains unnecessarily and dangerously dependent on purity models. Perhaps most obviously, there is the tendency to view gender, or sexual difference, as an identity category that can be isolated from other categories such as race and nation, or that is prior to, or more fundamental than, other forms of difference. In quite different ways, both Irigaray's and Braidotti's projects suffer from constraints imposed by trying to clear a pure analytical space in which to consider sexual difference as 'the issue of our age'. As we saw most strikingly in the case of Braidotti, models which begin from the assumption that sexual difference is *the* ontological difference, within which other differences are to be subsumed or accommodated, result in a re-centring of white Western women and a failure to take differences such as race and nation adequately into account. Despite the unexpected resonances I have identified between Irigaray's focus on the specifically female and many concerns of the Indian feminists discussed in Part I, Irigaray's starting assumption, that the landscape of an 'economy of the same' can be delineated purely through a focus on sexual difference, remains an obstruction to hearing those resonances more clearly.

But I have also argued that there are less obvious, and perhaps therefore more insidious, ways in which feminist theory remains indebted to purity models. Running throughout this project has been an argument against underlying models of power and language that focus primarily on a logic of exclusion, abjection and objectification. I call these purity models because they have a tendency to solidify pure distinctions between inside and outside, centre and margins, inclusion and exclusion, subjects with agency and abjected others. Such models might also lead us to locate 'Woman' and 'women' in a space outside, or on the edges of power relations and language, a space which may be characterised as abjected, but which also dangerously promises some kind of purity in its disconnection from power.

My reading of Indian feminisms through a Foucauldian model of power as productive, and as simultaneously enabling and constraining for women, suggests that a focus on pure exclusion/inclusion paradigms covers over many important ways in which women are socially and discursively positioned, and in which different raced, national and community identities emerge. I also have argued that, when feminists work with models of power and language that privilege exclusion and that position women as abjected others, then there is a danger of returning to a language of 'false consciousness' when theorising agency and resistance, or to locating some space of pure 'gender interests' from which to speak and act. At the same time, feminist characterisations of women as powerless, abjected others fail to convince large numbers of women who see their social positioning as more complex than this model of power allows.

As I argued in my reading of Butler, the turn to exclusion paradigms through poststructuralist language models can also lead to a turn away from the possibility of positively redefining the specifically female. If identity is secured only, or even primarily, by what it excludes, then the best we can hope for is a perpetual destabilising of the always unsatisfactory versions of 'women' that language and power produce. But if, as I have argued, power and language do not only work through excluding indeterminacy and multiplicity, but can also work through producing them, then the destabilising strategy is no guarantee against re-appropriation. At the same time, it surrenders the terrain of positively redefining 'women' and the specifically female to those who want to preserve both women's subordination, and asymmetrical raced, ethnic and national relations of power.

The four key complications I drew out of my reading of Indian feminisms in Part I all suggest that feminist theory needs to dispense with a logic of dualisms, to work from an impure space which is not adequately contained within the familiar binaries. These complications emerge from reading Indian feminist attempts to make sense of specific political issues – in particular the place of women in India's anti-colonial struggles and in the recent rise of communalism. They suggest (1) that women play a simultaneously productive and subordinated role in the emergence of multiple categories of social identity, including sex, gender, race and nation; (2) that women's location within this intersecting landscape of community identities is a complex one, that cannot be contained within an exclusion/inclusion binary; (3) that both the feminine and the female are crucial to the emergence of these identities; and (4) that alternative feminist models of agency and resistance need to redefine, and not only destabilise models of the self and its relation to collective identity.

I have argued that these insights, which emerge from the complex, messy space of specifically located struggles, have a more general theoretical importance, and that feminist theoretical approaches to identity need to be able to accommodate their complexities. In Part II, my close readings of the work of Irigaray, Butler, Braidotti and Haraway brought these specifically located insights into the more general field of theory, to gauge the extent to which these four influential theoretical projects succeed in making space for this complexity. By submitting these theoretical approaches to a close scrutiny on the basis of questions emerging from 'a postcolonial mode', I have identified both unexpected resonances with and resistances to the kind of complexity required if feminists are to sustain a simultaneous focus on 'women' and their differences.

In Part III, I proposed my own synthesis of these insights with theoretical models of power and identity. I argued that, by attending to women's complex location within intersecting landscapes of sex/gender, race, nation and other community identities, feminist models of identity can resist a logic of dualisms in order to redefine, and not only destabilise, 'women' as the subject of/for feminism. This requires working against purity at three levels. First, it requires a model of power that gives up on the search for pure, power-free zones, and works instead with the instabilities power produces as it both enables and constrains women. Second, it requires seeing 'women' as a complex, impure category that bleeds across the borders of apparently discrete identity categories such as sex/gender, race and nation. Third, it requires the development of alternative models of the self that take these complex, impure spaces as a valid and valorised position from which to act and to speak.

The next step would be to move back from the field of feminist theory to the specific political issues that white Western feminists face, to see how starting from theoretical models of impurity can make a difference to feminist politics, and specifically to see how we sustain a simultaneous political focus on women and their differences. This kind of detailed, specifically located inquiry is beyond the confines of this project. However, I want to conclude by suggesting some of the ways in which the questions we ask of feminist theory and politics change when we begin from a framework of impurity. As Foucault argued, changing the terms within which one poses the questions we expect politics to answer is a necessary first step to making possible the future formation of a different kind of political 'we' (Foucault 1984: 385). If a future 'we' of feminist politics is to neither theorise women out of existence nor perpetuate the exclusions of difference by which it has too often proceeded, then complicating the questions we ask may be a crucial starting point.

Starting from a framework of impurity means, first, looking for women in more than one place. It means asking how 'Woman' and 'women' emerge and are put into play across a variety of identity categories, and not just in relation to gender or sexual difference. It also means looking for women not as abjected others, but as impure subjects; we need to look, not only at how women are strategically and discursively marginalised or excluded, but also at how they are made central to identity-constituting processes, at how they are 'actively managed' and how their active management helps to produce specific political, cultural, and economic realities across multiple networks of power relations.

It also means identifying the ways in which women's social and discursive positioning defies the neat separation between private and public, margin and centre, self and other which has become a rather stale analytical grid into which women are inserted. It means acknowledging that women are enabled by the same relations of power that constrain them, and that their resistance is, in Butler's terms, never 'a "pure" opposition, a "transcendence" of contemporary relations of power, but a difficult labour of forging a future from resources inevitably impure' (Butler 1993a: 241).

But, against Butler, it also means thinking about how models of the self and of community identities might be positively redefined. Predominant paradigms of identity appropriate the specifically female body and its capacity for birth as a pure, silent, stable ground of racial, ethnic and national identities. Rather than conceding this terrain, beginning from a framework of impurity offers the possibility of working towards a re-imagined model of the individual self and its connection to community, that starts from redefinitions of the female body. Despite her own ambivalence on this question, Haraway's alternative ontology of 'mutation, metamorphosis and diaspora' can find a site for its emergence in an inappropriate/d female body – a body that is productive, semi-permeable and leaky, a body that doesn't settle down easily into the fixed space of purity assigned to it in prevailing narratives of identity.

Of course there are, as Butler argues, dangers in this attempt to positively redefine 'women'. This is where Haraway's insistence that feminists combine the pleasure of trangressing boundaries with the responsibility for constructing them becomes so crucial. Accountability for the borders drawn by redefining 'women' requires a simultaneous attention to the promises and dangers involved, and a resistance to seeing any border as permanently fixed and impermeable. But, as I suggested above, the danger in conceding this terrain is greater because, ultimately, this leaves untroubled the ground in which racism, communalism and fascism persistently take root.

As the reflections of some Indian feminists, faced with the imminent danger of racialised social divisions and communal violence have suggested, contesting these threats requires both a redefined individual self and a redefined narrative of community. I have argued that what is required is a model of the self which resists submersion within the collective, but which also does not depend on a rigid differentiation of the subject-with-agency from an abjected object. Such a re-imagined self should provide a basis for the emergence of radically different models of collective or community identities. One area for future research might be to explore the underlying models of the individual self and collective identity at work in different forms of feminist politics, and how these impinge on the success that political movements have in sustaining a simultaneous focus on women and their differences.

Discussions of women's agency and the possibilities of feminist politics have often focused on the questions, 'Do women resist?', or 'How and why do women resist?' Exploring the creative possibilities of impurity might add some new questions that seem crucial to addressing the persistence of racism and ethnocentrism within feminist theory and politics. Are there any new ways of resisting? What changes occur when political movements start from the assumption that, in addition to the specific issues that connect them, they are united by the need to negotiate differences, rather than to assert their sameness? What difference does it make to politics when the 'we' is seen, to borrow Haraway's terms, not as a taken-for-granted ground or resource, but as an ongoing, difficult, and possible achievement?

Notes

Introduction

1   See, for example, Frankenberg and Mani (1993), Loomba (1991), Mishra and Hodge (1993), McClintock (1993) and Parry (1997), as well as Williams and Chrisman's (1993) summary of debates over the term in their Introduction. Among the many unresolved issues is whether the term should be hyphenated. I take no position on this question; having started with de Lauretis' unhyphened version, I continue this usage for the sake of consistency only.

2   On the family see Phoenix (1987). On sexual violence and reproductive rights see, among many others, the work of Hill Collins (1990), hooks (1982, 1984) and Williams (1991). On models of femininity see for example Hill Collins (1990) and hooks (1992b).

3   See for example Gatens (1996: Ch. 1), Haraway (1991: Ch. 7) and Battersby (1998: esp. 18–23).

4   See, among many others, Bartky (1990), Bordo (1989), Fraser (1989), Hartsock (1990), McNay (1992), Ramazanoglu (1993), Sawicki (1991), Singer (1989) and Smart (1989).

1 Women and community identities in Indian feminisms

1   The term communalism is used commonly in India to refer to 'partisanship or chauvinism deriving from religious identity; communal conflict occurs between members of different religious communities, most often Hindus and Muslims' (Basu 1995: 180 fn 1).

2   See also Sunder Rajan and Pathak (1992) for another account of the Shah Bano case.

3   My thanks to Tanika Sarkar for clarifying this danger for me.

4   For evidence that such temptations still exist, see Clément (1994) who, in her exploration of the concept of syncope as an alternative to the 'classic Western concept of the Subject' (Clément 1994: 156), constructs a univocal India as a privileged site where this suspension of time and the individuated self enjoys free play. In the process, Clément also

asserts that India is a site where the feminine is unproblematically valorised, and where the transgressive blurring of boundaries between masculine and feminine is more possible than in the West (see, for example, pp.138, 143, and 243). Clément reaches her conclusions without any reference to the work of Indian feminists. For more detail, see Gedalof (1996).

5   Chakravarti argues that the only prominent example of mother–child relations in the classical literature is that between Krishna and his mother Yashoda, and that, 'even here the focus is primarily on Krishna rather than on the mother' (1983: 68).

6   See also Sen (1993), Lakshmi (1990), and Natarajan (1994) for further examples of use of the mother-figure within nationalist discourses.

2 Agency, the self and the collective in Indian feminisms

1   Chakravarti's examination of these four *bhakti* women poets is not meant to be an exhaustive evaluation of the role of women in the *bhakti* movement. For other views on this question, see Sangari (1990) and Mukta (1994). For example, Mukta's discussion of the life and poetry of Mirabai contrasts with Chakravarti's account of these four *bhaktins* in southern India. In Mirabai's poetry, the female body and sexuality remain a strong presence; Mukta argues that in Mirabai's case the problem was the way in which the male priests interpreted her poetry to transform the body into soul, and sexual love into the kind of spiritual devotion they deemed appropriate.

2   In this light she cites Mary Douglas' insight that 'the structure of [pollution's] symbolism uses comparison and double meaning like the structure of a joke' (Douglas 1966: 122–3).

3 Luce/loose connections: Luce Irigaray, sexual difference, race and nation

1   For a reading that links the challenges posed to Western philosophy by the work of Bernal, Said and Gilroy to Derridean deconstruction, see Critchley (1995).

2   In my discussions of this chapter of *Speculum*, entitled 'L'incontournable volume' in the original French, I use the David Macey translation in Margaret Whitford's *The Irigaray Reader* (1991a) rather than the section entitled 'Volume-Fluidity' in Gillian Gill's 1985 English translation.

3   See, for example, Elizabeth Spelman (1990), for the way Woman and Black are constructed as mutually exclusive categories, and Tina Chanter (1995), for a critique of de Beauvoir's reading of the master–slave dialectic.

4   See Spivak (1987, 1989, 1991, 1993), Bhabha (1990), Niranjana (1994b) and Gates (1986), among many others.

5   For example, one contribution to a debate on the pertinence of feminist theory to India in the pages of *Economic and Political Weekly* discusses

a number of American and Australian feminists in some detail, but limits its references to Irigaray to the now familiar version of her work that predominated in early Anglo-American responses: that she equates woman with nature, that woman is defined essentially by her body, etc. (Thapan 1995: 1400).
6 On this point, see Battersby (1998: esp. 56 and Chapters 5 and 6).
7 See Grosz (1989: 31–7, 101–4) and Whitford (1991b: 130–5) for discussions of how Irigaray contests Derrida, and Chanter (1995: 225–54) for a reading which focuses more on their convergences.

5 'All that counts is the going': Rosi Braidotti's nomadic subject

1 In addition to those already discussed in Chapter 1, such as Chakravarti (1990), Mani (1990) and Sangari and Vaid (1990), see Bhabha (1990), Chakrabarty (1992), Loomba (1991) and Sangari (1987).
2 There is a growing body of literature within Black feminisms, and increasingly within postcolonial feminisms, on the question of race and psychoanalytic models. See, for example, Abel, Christian et al. (1997), Seshadri-Crooks (1994) and Spillers (1987, 1996).

Bibliography

Abel, Elizabeth, B. Christian *et al.* (eds) (1997) *Female Subjects in Black and White: Race, Psychoanalysis, Feminism*, Berkeley: University of California Press.

Adam, Ian and H. Tiffin (eds) (1991) *Past the Last Post*, Hemel Hempstead: Harvester Wheatsheaf.

Agnes, Flavia (1995) 'Redefining the Agenda of the Women's Movement within a Secular Framework', in T. Sarkar and U. Butalia (eds) *Women and the Hindu Right: A Collection of Essays*, Delhi: Kali for Women, pp. 136–57.

Alaimo, Stacy (1994) 'Cyborg and Ecofeminist Interventions: Challenges for an Environmental Feminism', *Feminist Studies* 20(1): 133–52.

Alarcon, Norma (1994) 'Traddutora, Traditora: A Paradigmatic Figure of Chicana Feminism', in I. Grewal and C. Kaplan (eds) *Scattered Hegemonies*, Minneapolis and London: University of Minnesota Press, pp. 110–36.

Alexander, Meena (1989) 'Outcaste Power: Ritual Displacement and Virile Maternity in Indian Women Writers', *Economic and Political Weekly* 18 February: 367–72.

Anderson, Benedict (1991) *Imagined Communities*, London: Verso.

Anthias, Floya and Nira Yuval-Davis (eds) (1989) *Woman-Nation-State*, London: Macmillan.

—— (1992) *Racialized Boundaries*, London and New York: Routledge.

Anzaldua, Gloria (1987) *Borderlands/La Frontera*, San Francisco: Aunt Lute.

Ashcroft, Bill, G. Griffiths and H. Tiffin (1989) *The Empire Writes Back*, London: Routledge.

Bacchetta, Paola (1994a) 'Communal Property/Sexual Property: On Representations of Muslim Women in a Hindu Nationalist Discourse', in Zoya Hasan (ed.) *Forging Identities: Gender, Communities and the State*, Delhi: Kali for Women, pp. 188–225.

—— (1994b) ' "All our Goddesses are Armed": Religion, Resistance and Revenge in the Life of a Militant Hindu Nationalist Woman', in K.

Bhasin, R. Menon and N. Said Khan (eds) *Against All Odds: Essays on Women, Religion and Development from India and Pakistan*, Delhi: Kali for Women, pp. 133–56.

Bagchi, Jasodhara (1990) 'Representing Nationalism: Ideology of Motherhood in Colonial Bengal', *Economic and Political Weekly* 20–7 October: WS65–71.

Bannerjee, Sikata (1995) 'Hindu Nationalism and the Construction of Woman', in Tanika Sarkar and Urvashi Butalia (eds) *Women and the Hindu Right: A Collection of Essays*, Delhi: Kali for Women, pp. 216–32.

Bartky, Sandra (1990) *Femininity and Domination*, New York and London: Routledge.

Basu, Amrita (1995) 'Feminism Inverted: The Gendered Imagery and Real Women of Hindu Nationalism', in Tanika Sarkar and Urvashi Butalia (eds) *Women and the Hindu Right: A Collection of Essays*, Delhi: Kali for Women, pp. 158–80.

Battersby, Christine (1989) *Gender and Genius: Towards a Feminist Aesthetics*, London: Women's Press.

—— (1995) 'Her Blood and His Mirror: Mary Coleridge, Luce Irigaray, and the Female Self', in R. Eldridge (ed.) *Beyond Representation: Philosophy and Poetic Imagination*, Cambridge: Cambridge University Press, pp. 249–72.

—— (1998) *The Phenomenal Woman*, Cambridge: Polity.

Beauvoir, Simone de (1949) *The Second Sex*, trans. and ed. by H.M. Pashley, London: Picador (1988).

Benhabib, Seyla (1992) *Situating the Self: Gender, Community and Postmodernism in Contemporary Ethics*, Cambridge: Polity.

Bernal, Martin (1987) *Black Athena: Volume 1, The Fabrication of Ancient Greece, 1785–1985*, London: Free Association Books.

Bhabha, Homi (1990) *Nation and Narration*, New York and London: Routledge.

Bhattacharji, Sukumari (1990) 'Motherhood in Ancient India', *Economic and Political Weekly* 20–7 October: WS50–7.

Bordo, Susan (1989) 'The Body and the Reproduction of Femininity: A Feminist Appropriation of Foucault', in A. Jaggar and S. Bordo (eds) *Gender/Body/Knowledge*, New Brunswick and London: Rutgers University Press, pp. 13–33.

Brah, Avtar (1996) *Cartographies of Diaspora: Contesting Identities*, London and New York: Routledge.

Braidotti, Rosi (1991) *Patterns of Dissonance*, Cambridge: Polity.

—— (1994a) *Nomadic Subjects: Embodiment and Sexual Difference in Contemporary Feminist Theory*, New York: Columbia University Press.

—— (1994b) 'Towards a New Nomadism: Feminist Deleuzian Tracks: or, Metaphysics and Metabolism', in C.V. Boundas and D. Olkowski (eds)

Gilles Deleuze and the Theatre of Philosophy, New York and London: Routledge, pp. 157–86.

Butalia, Urvashi (1993) 'Community, State and Gender: On Women's Agency during Partition', *Economic and Political Weekly* 24 April: WS12–24.

—— (1995) 'Muslims and Hindus, Men and Women: Communal Stereotypes and the Partition of India', in Tanika Sarkar and Urvashi Butalia (eds) *Women and the Hindu Right: A Collection of Essays*, Delhi: Kali for Women, pp. 58–81.

Butler, Judith (1990) *Gender Trouble: Feminism and the Subversion of Identity*, New York and London: Routledge.

—— (1992) 'Contingent Foundations: Feminism and the Question of "Postmodernism" ', in J. Butler and J. Scott (eds) *Feminists Theorize the Political*, New York and London: Routledge, pp. 3–21.

—— (1993a) *Bodies that Matter: On the Discursive Limits of 'Sex'*, New York and London: Routledge.

—— (1993b) 'The Body Politics of Julia Kristeva', in K. Oliver (ed.) *Ethics, Politics and Difference in Julia Kristeva's Writing*, New York and London: Routledge, pp. 164–78.

—— (1994) 'Gender as Performance: An Interview with Judith Butler', *Radical Philosophy* 67: 32–9.

Carby, Hazel (1982) 'White Woman Listen! Black Feminism and the Boundaries of Sisterhood', in CCCS, *The Empire Strikes Back*, London: Hutchinson.

—— (1987) *Reconstructing Womanhood*, Oxford: Oxford University Press.

Chakrabarty, Dipesh (1992) 'Postcoloniality and the Artifice of History: Who Speaks for "Indian" Pasts?', *Representations* 37(Winter): 1–26.

Chakravarti, Uma (1983) 'The Development of the Sita Myth: A Case Study of Women in Myth and Literature', *Samya Shakti* 1(1): 68–75.

—— (1989) 'The World of the Bhaktin in South Indian Traditions – The Body and Beyond', *Manushi* 50–2(Jan.–June): 18–29.

—— (1990) 'Whatever Happened to the Vedic *Dasi*?', in Kumkum Sangari and Sudesh Vaid (eds) *Recasting Women: Essays in Indian Cultural History*, Delhi: Kali for Women, pp. 27–87.

Chanter, Tina (1995) *Ethic of Eros: Irigaray's Rewriting of the Philosophers*, New York and London: Routledge.

Chhachhi, Amrita (1991) 'Forced Identities: The State, Communalism, Fundamentalism and Women in India', in D. Kandiyoti (ed.) *Women, Islam and the State*, London: Macmillan, pp. 144–75.

—— (1994) 'Identity Politics, Secularism and Women: A South Asian Perspective', in Zoya Hasan (ed.) *Forging Identities: Gender, Communities and the State*, Delhi: Kali for Women, pp. 59–73.

Clément, Catherine (1994) *Syncope: The Philosophy of Rapture*, Minneapolis and London: University of Minnesota Press.

Coole, Diana (1996) 'Is Class a Difference that Makes a Difference?', *Radical Philosophy* 77(May–June): 17–25.

Critchley, Simon (1995) 'Black Socrates?', *Radical Philosophy* 69: 17–26.

Crosby, Christina (1989) 'Allies and Enemies', in E. Weed (ed.) *Coming to Terms*, London and New York: Routledge, pp. 205–8.

Deleuze, Gilles and F. Guattari (1988) *A Thousand Plateaus*, London: Athlone.

Dietrich, Gabriele (1994) 'Women and Religious Identities in India after Ayodhya', in K. Bhasin, R. Menon and N. Said Khan (eds) *Against All Odds: Essays on Women, Religion and Development from India and Pakistan*, Delhi: Kali for Women, pp. 35–49.

Doane, Mary Ann (1989) 'Cyborgs, Origins and Subjectivity', in E. Weed (ed.) *Coming to Terms*, London and New York: Routledge, pp. 209–14.

Douglas, Mary (1966) *Purity and Danger*, London and New York: Routledge.

Dube, Leela (1986) 'Seed and Earth: The Symbolism of Biological Reproduction and Sexual Relations of Production', in L. Dube, E. Leacock and S. Ardener (eds) *Visibility and Power: Essays on Women in Society and Development*, Delhi: Oxford University Press, pp. 22–53.

Dyer, Richard (1993) 'White', in *The Matter of Images*, New York and London: Routledge, pp. 141–63.

—— (1997) *White*, New York and London: Routledge.

Foucault, Michel (1976) 'Two Lectures', in M. Foucault, *Power/Knowledge*, ed. C. Gordon, London: Harvester Wheatsheaf (1980), pp. 78–108.

—— (1977a) 'Truth and Power', in M. Foucault, *Power/Knowledge*, ed. C. Gordon, London: Harvester Wheatsheaf (1980), pp. 109–33.

—— (1977b) 'Power and Strategies', in M. Foucault, *Power/Knowledge*, ed. C. Gordon, London: Harvester Wheatsheaf (1980), pp. 134–45.

—— (1977c) 'The Confession of the Flesh', in M. Foucault, *Power/Knowledge*, ed. C. Gordon, London: Harvester Wheatsheaf (1980), pp. 194–228.

—— (1977d) *Discipline and Punish: The Birth of the Prison*, New York: Vintage (1979).

—— (1978) *The History of Sexuality, Volume I: An Introduction*, London: Penguin.

—— (1981) 'Practicing Criticism', in L.D. Kritzman (ed.) *Politics, Philosophy, Culture*, New York and London: Routledge (1988), pp. 152–6.

—— (1982) 'The Subject and Power', Afterword in H. Dreyfus and P. Rabinow, *Michel Foucault: Beyond Structuralism and Hermeneutics*, London: Harvester Wheatsheaf, pp. 208–26.

—— (1983) 'On the Genealogy of Ethics: An Overview of Work in Progress', in P. Rabinow (ed.) *The Foucault Reader*, London: Penguin (1984), pp. 340–72.

—— (1984) 'Polemics, Politics and Problematizations: An Interview with Michel Foucault', in P. Rabinow (ed.) *The Foucault Reader*, London: Penguin (1984), pp. 381–90.

Frankenberg, Ruth (1993) *White Women, Race Matters: The Social Construction of Whiteness*, New York and London: Routledge.

Frankenberg, Ruth and Lata Mani (1993) 'Crosscurrents, Crosstalk: Race, "Postcoloniality" and the Politics of Location', *Cultural Studies* 7(2): 292–310.

Fraser, Nancy (1989) *Unruly Practices: Power, Discourse and Gender in Contemporary Social Theory*, London: Polity.

—— (1995) 'From Redistribution to Recognition? Dilemmas of Justice in a "Post-Socialist" Age', *New Left Review* 212(July/August): 68–93.

Fuss, Diana (1989) *Essentially Speaking: Feminism, Nature, Difference*, New York and London: Routledge.

Ganesh, Kamala (1990) 'Mother Who is Not a Mother: In Search of the Great Indian Goddess', *Economic and Political Weekly* 20–6 October: WS58–64.

Gatens, Moira (1996) *Imaginary Bodies: Ethics, Power and Corporeality*, New York and London: Routledge.

Gates, Henry Louis (1986) *The Signifying Monkey*, Oxford: Oxford University Press.

Gedalof, Irene (1996) 'Syncopating India: Catherine Clément's *Syncope*', *Women's Philosophy Review* 15(June): 31–5.

Geetha, V. and T.V. Jayanthi (1995) 'Women, Hindutva and the Politics of Caste in Tamil Nadu', in Tanika Sarkar and Urvashi Butalia (eds) *Women and the Hindu Right: A Collection of Essays*, Delhi: Kali for Women, pp. 245–69.

Gilroy, Paul (1993) *The Black Atlantic: Modernity and Double Consciousness*, London: Verso.

Griffiths, Morwenna (1995) *Feminisms and the Self: The Web of Identity*, New York and London: Routledge.

Grossberg, Lawrence (1988) 'Wandering Audiences, Nomadic Critics', *Cultural Studies* 2(3): 388–9.

Grosz, Elizabeth (1989) *Sexual Subversions: Three French Feminists*, Sydney: Allen and Unwin.

Halberstam, Judith (1991) 'Automating Gender: Postmodern Feminism in the Age of the Intelligent Machine', *Feminist Studies* 17(3): 439–60.

Hall, Stuart (1996) 'Introduction: Who Needs Identity?', in S. Hall and P. du Gay (eds) *Questions of Cultural Identity*, London: Sage, pp. 1–17.

Haraway, Donna (1991) *Simians, Cyborgs and Women: The Reinvention of Nature*, London: Free Association Books.

—— (1992a) *Primate Visions: Gender, Race and Nature in the World of Modern Science*, London: Verso.

—— (1992b) 'The Promises of Monsters', in L. Grossberg *et al.* (eds) *Cultural Studies*, New York and London: Routledge, pp. 295–337.

—— (1992c) 'Ecce Homo, Ain't (Ar'n't) I a Woman, and Inappropriate/d Others: The Human in a Post-Humanist Landscape', in J. Butler and J. Scott (eds) *Feminists Theorize the Political*, New York and London: Routledge, pp. 86–100.

Hartsock, Nancy (1990) 'Foucault on Power: A Theory for Women?', in L. Nicholson (ed.) *Feminism/Postmodernism*, New York and London: Routledge.

Hasan, Zoya (ed.) (1994a) *Forging Identities: Gender, Communities and the State*, Delhi: Kali for Women.

—— (1994b) 'Minority Identity, State Policy and Political Process', in Z. Hasan (ed.) *Forging Identities: Gender, Communities and the State*, Delhi: Kali for Women, pp. 59–73.

Hayles, N. Katherine (1990) *Chaos Bound: Orderly Disorder in Contemporary Literature and Science*, Ithaca, NY and London: Cornell University Press.

Hill Collins, Patricia (1990) *Black Feminist Thought*, London: Unwin Hyman.

Hirsch, Elizabeth and G. Olson (1995) ' "Je – Luce Irigaray": A Meeting with Luce Irigaray', *Hypatia* 10(2): 93–114.

Hodge, Joanna (1994) 'Irigaray Reading Heidegger', in C. Burke, N. Schor and M. Whitford (eds) *Engaging with Irigaray*, New York: Columbia University Press, pp. 191–210.

hooks, bell (1982) *Ain't I a Woman? Black Women and Feminism*, London: Pluto.

—— (1984) *Feminist Theory: From Margins to Centre*, Boston, MA: South End Press.

—— (1991) *Yearning: Race, Gender and Cultural Politics*, London: Turnaround.

—— (1992a) 'Representing Whiteness in the Black Imagination', in L. Grossberg *et al.* (eds) *Cultural Studies*, New York and London: Routledge, pp. 338–46.

—— (1992b) *Black Looks: Race and Representation*, Boston: South End Press.

Irigaray, Luce (1974) *Speculum of the Other Woman*, trans. Gillian C. Gill, Ithaca, NY: Cornell University Press (1985).

—— (1977) *This Sex Which is Not One*, trans. Catherine Porter, Ithaca, NY: Cornell University Press (1985).

—— (1984) *An Ethics of Sexual Difference*, trans. Carolyn Burke, London: Athlone (1993).

—— (1989) *Thinking the Difference*, trans. Karin Montin, London: Athlone (1994).

—— (1990) *Je, Tu, Nous: Towards a Culture of Difference*, trans. Alison Martin, London and New York: Routledge (1993).

Jardine, Alice (1985) *Gynesis: Configurations of Woman and Modernity*, Ithaca, NY and London: Cornell University Press.

John, Mary E. (1996) *Discrepant Dislocations: Feminism, Theory and Postcolonial Histories*, Berkeley: University of California Press.

Kamuf, Peggy (ed.) (1991) *The Derrida Reader: Between the Blinds*, New York: Columbia University Press.

Kandiyoti, Deniz (1993) 'Identity and its Discontents', in L. Chrisman and P. Williams (eds) *Colonial Discourse and Post-Colonial Theory*, London: Harvester Wheatsheaf, pp. 376–92.

Kannabiran, V. and K. Kannabiran (1995) 'The Frying Pan or the Fire? Endangered Identities, Gendered Institutions and Women's Survival', in Tanika Sarkar and Urvashi Butalia (eds) *Women and the Hindu Right: A Collection of Essays*, Delhi: Kali for Women, pp. 121–35.

Kaplan, Caren (1987) 'Deterritorializations: The Rewriting of Home and Exile in Western Feminist Discourse', *Cultural Critique* 6(Spring): 187–98.

Kapur, Ratna and B. Cossman (1995) 'Communalising Gender, Engendering Community: Women, Legal Discourse and the Saffron Agenda', in Tanika Sarkar and Urvashi Butalia (eds) *Women and the Hindu Right: A Collection of Essays*, Delhi: Kali for Women, pp. 82–120.

Kishwar, Madhu (1989) 'Introduction – Women Bhakti Poets', *Manushi* 50–2(Jan.–June): 3–8.

Lakshmi, C.S. (1990) 'Mother, Mother-Community and Mother-Politics in Tamil Nadu', *Economic and Political Weekly* 20–7 October: WS72–83.

de Lauretis, Teresa (1990) 'Eccentric Subjects', *Feminist Studies* 16(1): 115–50.

Loomba, Ania (1991) 'Overworlding the Third World', *Oxford Literary Review* 3(1–2): 164–91.

—— (1993) 'Dead Women Tell No Tales', *History Workshop Journal* 36: 209–27.

Lugones, Maria (1990) 'Playfulness, "World"-Travelling and Loving Perception', in G. Anzaldua (ed.) *Making Face, Making Soul*, San Francisco: Aunt Lute, pp. 390–402.

McClintock, Anne (1993) 'The Angel of Progress: Pitfalls of the Term "Post-colonialism" ', in P. Williams and L. Chrisman (eds) *Colonial Discourse and Post-Colonial Theory: A Reader*, London: Harvester Wheatsheaf, pp. 291–304.

McNay, Lois (1992) *Foucault and Feminism*, Cambridge: Polity.

Mani, Lata (1990) 'Contentious Traditions: The Debate on *Sati* in Colonial India', in Kumkum Sangari and Sudesh Vaid (eds) *Recasting Women: Essays in Indian Colonial History*, Delhi: Kali for Women, pp. 88–123.

—— (1992) 'Cultural Theory, Colonial Texts', in L. Grossberg *et al.* (eds) *Cultural Studies*, London and New York: Routledge, pp. 392–405.

Marsden, Jill (1996) 'Virtual Sexes and Feminist Futures: The Philosophy of "Cyberfeminism" ', *Radical Philosophy* 78(July–August): 6–16.

Martin, Biddy (1991) *Woman and Modernity: The (Life)Styles of Lou Andreas-Salomé*, Ithaca, NY: Cornell University Press.

Mishra, Vijay and Bob Hodge (1993) 'What is Post(-) Colonialism?', in P. Williams and L. Chrisman (eds) *Colonial Discourse and Post-Colonial Theory: A Reader*, London: Harvester Wheatsheaf, pp. 276–91.

Mohanty, Chandra (1991) 'Under Western Eyes: Feminist Scholarship and Colonial Discourses', in C. Mohanty, A. Russo and L. Torres (eds) *Third World Women and the Politics of Feminism*, Bloomington and Indianapolis: Indiana University Press, pp. 51–80.

Moi, Toril (1985) *Sexual/Textual Politics: Feminist Literary Theory*, London and New York: Routledge.

Moraga, Cherrie (1986) 'From a Long Line of Vendidas: Chicanas and Feminism', in T. de Lauretis (ed.) *Feminist Studies/Critical Studies*, Basingstoke: Macmillan, pp. 173–90.

Mukta, Parita (1994) *Upholding the Common Life: The Community of Mirabai*, Oxford: Oxford University Press.

Natarajan, Nalini (1994) 'Woman, Nation and Narration in *Midnight's Children*', in I. Grewal and C. Kaplan (eds) *Scattered Hegemonies*, Minneapolis: University of Minnesota Press, pp. 76–89.

Niranjana, Seemanthini (1994a) 'Femininity, Space and the Female Body: Reconsiderations', paper delivered to the Workshop on Femininity, the Female Body and Sexuality in Contemporary Society, Nehru Memorial Museum and Library, New Delhi, November 1994.

—— (1994b) 'On Gender and Difference: Towards a Rearticulation', *Social Scientist* 22(7–8): 28–41.

Parry, Benita (1997) 'The Postcolonial: Conceptual Category or Chimera?', *The Yearbook of English Studies* 27: 3–21.

Pathak, Zakia and Saswati Sengupta (1995) 'Resisting Women', in Tanika Sarkar and Urvashi Butalia (eds) *Women and the Hindu Right: A Collection of Essays*, Delhi: Kali for Women, pp. 270–98.

Phoenix, Ann (1987) 'Theories of Gender and Black Families', in G. Weiner and M. Arnot (eds) *Gender under Scrutiny*, London: Unwin Hyman.

Porter, Eleanor (1995) 'Mother Earth and the Wandering Hero', paper presented to the Women/Time/Space Conference, Lancaster University, 25 March 1995, unpublished.

Ramazanoglu, Caroline (ed.) (1993) *Up Against Foucault: Explorations of Some Tensions Between Foucault and Feminism*, London and New York: Routledge.

Rao, Vidya (1990) '*Thumri* as Feminine Voice', *Economic and Political Weekly* 28 April: WS31–9.

Rich, Adrienne (1986) 'Notes Towards a Politics of Location', in *Blood, Bread, Poetry*, New York: W.W. Norton, pp. 210–31.

Roy, Kumkum (1995) 'Where Women are Worshipped, There the Gods Rejoice', in Tanika Sarkar and Urvashi Butalia (eds) *Women and the Hindu Right: A Collection of Essays*, Delhi: Kali for Women, pp. 10–28.

Said, Edward (1978) *Orientalism*, New York: Vintage.

Sangari, Kumkum (1987) 'The Politics of the Possible', *Cultural Critique* 7(Fall): 157–86.

—— (1990) 'Mirabai and the Spiritual Economy of the Bhakti', *Economic and Political Weekly* July: 1464–75, 1537–52.

—— (1993) 'Consent, Agency and Rhetorics of Incitement', *Economic and Political Weekly* 1 May: 867–82.

Sangari, Kumkum and Sudesh Vaid (eds) (1990) *Recasting Women: Essays in Indian Colonial History*, Delhi: Kali for Women.

Sarkar, Tanika (1987) 'Nationalist Iconography', *Economic and Political Weekly* 21 November: 2011–15.

—— (1991) 'The Woman as Communal Subject', *Economic and Political Weekly* 31 August: 2057–62.

—— (1995) 'Heroic Women, Mother Goddesses: Family and Organisation in Hindutva Politics', in Tanika Sarkar and Urvashi Butalia (eds) *Women and the Hindu Right: A Collection of Essays*, Delhi: Kali for Women, pp. 181–215.

Sarkar, Tanika and Urvashi Butalia (eds) (1995) *Women and the Hindu Right: A Collection of Essays*, Delhi: Kali for Women.

Sawicki, Jana (1991) *Disciplining Foucault: Feminism, Power and the Body*, New York and London: Routledge.

Sen, Samita (1993) 'Motherhood and Mothercraft: Gender and Nationalism in Bengal', *Gender and History* 5(2): 231–43.

Seshadri-Crooks, Kalpana (1994) 'The Primitive as Analyst: Postcolonial Feminism's Access to Psychoanalysis', *Cultural Critique* 28 (Fall): 175–219.

Singer, Linda (1989) 'True Confessions: Cixous and Foucault on Sexuality and Power', in J. Allen and I.M. Young (eds) *The Thinking Muse: Feminism and Modern French Philosophy*, Bloomington: Indiana University Press, pp. 136–55.

Sinha, Mrinalini (1987) 'Gender and Imperialism', in M. Kimmel (ed.) *Changing Men*, London: Sage, pp. 217–38.

—— (1995) 'Nationalism and Respectable Sexuality in India', *Genders* 21: 30–57.

Smart, Carol (1989) *Feminism and the Power of the Law*, New York and London: Routledge.

Spelman, Elizabeth (1990) *Inessential Woman*, London: Women's Press.

Spillers, Hortense J. (1987) 'Mama's Baby, Papa's Maybe: An American Grammar Book', *Diacritics* 17: 65–81.

—— (1996) 'All the Things You Could Be by Now if Sigmund Freud's Wife was Your Mother: Psychoanalysis and Race', *Critical Inquiry* 22: 710–34.

Spivak, Gayatri Chakravorty (1987) *In Other Worlds*, London: Methuen.

—— (1989) 'Feminism and Deconstruction, Again: Negotiating with Unacknowledged Masculinism', in T. Brennan (ed.) *Between Feminism and Psychoanalysis*, London and New York: Routledge, pp. 206–23.

—— (1990) 'Reading *The Satanic Verses*', *Third Text* 11 (Summer): 41–60.

—— (1991) *The Post-Colonial Critic*, ed. S. Harasym, London and New York: Routledge.

—— (1993) 'Can the Subaltern Speak?', in P. Williams and L. Chrisman (eds) *Colonial Discourse and Post-Colonial Theory: A Reader*, London: Harvester Wheatsheaf, pp. 66–111.

Stoler, Ann Laura (1996) *Race and the Education of Desire: Foucault's History of Sexuality and the Colonial Order of Things*, Durham, NC and London: Duke University Press.

Sunder Rajan, Rajeswari (1993) *Real and Imagined Women: Gender, Culture and Postcolonialism*, New York and London: Routledge.

Sunder Rajan, Rajeswari and Z. Pathak (1992) 'Shahbano', in J. Butler and J. Scott (eds) *Feminists Theorize the Political*, New York and London: Routledge, pp. 257–79.

Thapan, Meenakshi (1995) 'Partial Truths: Privileging a "Male" Viewpoint', *Economic and Political Weekly* 10 June: 1399–400.

Tharu, Susie and Tejaswini Niranjana (1994) 'Problems for a Contemporary Theory of Gender', *Social Scientist* 22(3–4): 93–117.

Trinh T. Minh-ha (1989) *Woman, Native, Other*, Bloomington: Indiana University Press.

Whitford, Margaret (ed.) (1991a) *The Irigaray Reader*, Oxford: Blackwell.

—— (1991b) *Luce Irigaray: Philosophy in the Feminine*, New York and London: Routledge.

Williams, Patricia J. (1991) *The Alchemy of Race and Rights*, Cambridge, MA: Harvard University Press.

Williams, Patrick and L. Chrisman (eds) (1993) *Colonial Discourse and Post-Colonial Theory: A Reader*, London: Harvester Wheatsheaf.

Woolf, Janet (1995) *Resident Alien: Feminist Cultural Criticism*, Cambridge: Polity Press.

Young, Iris Marion (1994) 'Gender as Seriality: Thinking about Women as a Social Collective', *Signs* 19(3): 713–38.

Personal interviews cited

Butalia, Urvashi, Kali for Women Press, Delhi, India, 14 September 1995.

Chakravarti, Uma, History Department, Delhi University, Delhi, India, 15 September 1995.

Menon, Ritu, Kali for Women Press, Delhi, India, 14 September 1995.

Sangari, Kumkum, Research Fellow, Centre for Contemporary Studies, Nehru Memorial Museum and Library, Delhi, India, 21 September 1995.

Sarkar, Tanika, History Department, St Stephen's College, Delhi University, Delhi, India, 18 September 1995.

Index